Sacred Places

JOHN R. LITTLE

SACRED PLACES

A FICTION IN GRAY

PUBLISHED BY

AKA SCOSHI

229 State Route 115
Ocean Shores, WA 98569

Printed in the United States of America

ISBN (paperback) 0-9667881-1-7

Table of Contents

Acknowledgments

I wish to thank Donna B. Rosen, Ph.D., my wife, my companion and friend, who gave me her love and the strength to complete this novel.

Synopsis

Just prior to the massacre of the 7th Cavalry and General George Armstrong Custer by the Indian Nations of the Plains, the Indian Spiritual Leader, Sitting Bull, gave a grave message to his people. This was nothing less than the prediction of their pending and long-lasting anguish at the hands of the White man. Since then, lots of water has flowed and grasses have grown as it was written in the treaty, but, as he predicted, nothing has become better.

Now, some hundred and twenty years have passed since that battle, as our pretty, sandy blonde, thirty-something heroine, Renee, starts her path of self-examination and re-education toward a new life. Renee seeks the solitude of the Mojave Desert to contemplate her failing relationship with her boyfriend, Mike, while working on an assigned project in Early American Studies for her unscrupulous college instructor, Mr. Palmoroy.

During a fitful sleep in Saline Valley, Renee is awakened by a stranger, Jack Barlow, who falls across the front of her tent suffering from hypothermia. She learns that the man is a deputy sheriff and saves him from succumbing to the cold. She also learns he is a half-breed from the Ogalla Sioux Reservation. A turbulent relationship entwines itself around the search for wagons containing the artifacts of the Battle of Big Horn; the rogue Indian cop, Nick Whitewater, who enjoys hurting others just for the rush; Mike, the opportunistic boyfriend who takes a severe beating from everyone until his untimely murder; Mr. Palmory, the instructor who set Renee up for his own personal gain and glory by having her find the personal property of the long dead General; the reincarnation of Renee in the person of Elizabeth "Libby" Custer at the stranger of times; the cat, Man-Thing, who defends Jack's mother until the tip of his tail is shot away; the peoples of the past and the present who unwittingly fulfill the request Libby Custer had made to a friend; and Renee, who through tears and laughter, love and hate, makes her way to the last naked man and frees him to his loving wife.

A Happy Time

Before the coming of the white man, it was a happy place. A happy time. My earliest memories go back before the battle. Things were different. Indian life was better.

The blood in my veins is Sioux. I am Lakota. My father is Lakota. He is a proud warrior and has fought well against his enemies. We were once in victory of the white soldier. But now we are enslaved by them, these white men who wanted to push us from our land.

We fought our enemies with honor. It was truly a good day to die. Now I fear our hearts will be broken in our victory. Our spirits will not have the happy times as they once were. But one day it will again be a happy place. A happy time. I am Sioux.

PROLOGUE

Following the letting of his blood and the start of the performance of the Sun Gazing Dance, Tatanka Iyotake rose from his place against the sacred tree trunk. Bleeding from the wounds inflicted upon his arms and body by the ceremony attendants, he faced the sun and danced for a day before he staggered and fell to his death. When he resurrected himself, he told all the Chiefs of all the Clans of all the Nations that had come to the Greasy Grass River, "These soldiers are gifts from Wakan Tanka. He gives us these soldiers, for they have no ears and do not hear our words. Kill them, but do not take their guns or horses. If you set your heart upon the goods of the White Man, it will prove a curse to the Nations of the Plains."

"Out of the mists, I have heard disembodied voices and seen human form taking shape. They wandered against the blackness in their delirium. These are the soldiers of the White Man's Army entering the great Sioux encampment. These soldiers fall from the sky like so many grasshoppers in the fields. But surely, they are not coming as conquerors. These are surely men in defeat; their heads are bent; campaign hats are falling. They will stay on Mother Earth until they are released from these Sacred Places by the Watching Buffalo."

Sitting Bull
Spiritual Leader of the Sioux Nations

1

"A Safe Haven"

Renee Mitchell had always been afraid of the night, and especially of those little annoying sounds that weren't easily explained through logic or an educated guess. She had intentionally placed herself in probably one of the most inhospitable places in the whole of the United States—in Saline Valley, California, in the upper regions of the Mojave Desert. Many times since her arrival to the valley, and especially now that evening was rapidly turning to night, she had asked herself, *Why am I doing this to myself?* Then suddenly some scraping noise just off to the right would be caught by her ear once again.

That has to be a Kangaroo Rat! Renee promised herself as she stirred the little red-hot coals of her fire with a long stick. Her eyes darting from one place to another, she searched the bushes for some pesky little rodent.

Remembering back just a couple of days, she reaffirmed her justification for being here in mid-winter; since the day-time temperatures were a much more tolerable 80 degrees.

"Professor Palmoroy and the old trunk from the warehouse; that was it." She spoke loudly to break up the gray area between the silence and the infrequent desert noises.

She thought back to her apartment in San Francisco and the first time she had opened the cumbersome lid and saw the label affixed to the underside: The Spokane Steamer Trunk Company, January 15, 1915. She knew then her first solo adventure as an amateur archaeologist was at hand. Even her professor had stayed long enough when it was delivered to help her sort out the various letters and books to find the hand written diary. Not quite a journal, but more like haphazard entries of a semi-literate field hand or farmer. And especially that last entry on May 14th, 1877, when they abandoned their wagons not far from her remote little camp. All those wonderful entries which the professor suggested would make for a great paper for his class in American Studies, and then there was his suggestion of finding and photographing the wagons which could bring her a top grade.

Ever since she had entered his series of classes, he seemed taken by her abilities and let her know it. Over the last semester, especially during the occasional field trips, he stayed close by and directed her personally through a complete "dig" on her own. His insistence that she be alone in this endeavor would be a natural progression with the culmination of her work and study. Time and time again he instructed her that she could handle it and was destined to become a true professional in her chosen field.

Then again, she thought as her mind wandered back to late last Thursday night when she had indulged herself privately. *It was that wonderful Indigo dress that had been hidden away for so many years.* Just as clearly as if she were there now, she recalled standing in front of her antique beveled, full-length living room mirror holding the high collar under her chin. Looking down its length, she was delighted to see that she and the previous owner were nearly the same size. Very little alteration would be needed for a perfect fit.

All these things together reinforced her profound desire to become more than just a good amateur archaeologist. Possibly with nearly as much importance, she needed to show her boyfriend, Mike, that she could make it on her own. And now was truly her time; that chance to accomplish the things she had always wanted. Most of all she wanted to prove to the world she didn't need to be coddled, protected or in general kept from harm's way by anyone other than herself. Renee smiled to herself and felt more comfortable and confident in the darkness now that she had thought these things out.

Then again, following her freeze-dried dinner, she convinced herself it might have been the ruthless bite of the night air that made her slide a bit deeper into the warmth and security of her boyfriend's overly large sleeping bag. With the exception of her heartbeat in her little dome tent, there was a lack of really recognizable sounds beyond the zippered and tied door flaps. All in all, it would have been very spooky without the illumination from the backpacker's lantern. She pulled herself into a tight fetal position and tried to concentrate on the bright flame, but her senses still recoiled with the trickery of every unsuspected noise. No matter how small, the sounds left her wondering about the cause and ultimately heightened her expectation of impending disaster. Even while setting up her tent and camp she thought of what John Wayne had said in some motion picture about keeping snakes away. If only she had brought length enough of rope to uncoil around her sleeping area.

The Duke would have told me the snakes would not cross over it. On the other hand, she continued thinking. *Wasn't there a joke about the nearsighted snake that fell in love with a rope? E-Gad! My first night out and my mind is already becoming ragged with stupid thoughts.*

Why does it have to be so quiet? Besides, most snakes aren't out this time of year. Are they? She interrupted herself while her head moved from one side to the other as she strained to separate reality from her fears.

• • •

From the fog of sleep, she found herself fumbling for her bedside alarm clock to stop the "bee-waa" sounds breaking the stillness of the desert. Then suddenly Renee realized she hadn't brought it with her. She felt the blood drain from her face and her eyes snapped open as she listened intently to the now more recognizable sound.

"Someone is out there! There—There—There can't be anyone!"

Still distant, the noise was becoming louder and louder. At first, the images of many men yelling and screaming in agony slipped into her perceptions and then just as quickly fluttered away. As much as she didn't want to, she fought to convince herself that the only way to see what was going on was to pry herself up and out of her stronghold. Lighting her small and now not quite so adequate white gas lamp, she unzipped her sleeping bag and untied the security flap. Briefly looking at her wristwatch and taking note of the time, she discovered it was only three a.m. and a long way from the safety of morning light. So far, the night for Renee had been a hard one and she knew she couldn't have been asleep but a few paltry hours. As she crawled from the puny little exit of her tent, the suddenness of the cold night air hit her like she had been flung into a deep freeze. So quick was the change from the warmth of her sleeping bag to cold, her teeth immediately started an uncontrollable chatter.

A glance up revealed a billion stars and a sliver of a moon sneaking out from behind slow moving clouds. In the darkness, the tiny silver dots gave little illumination to the situation that was unfolding. Renee strained to see what seemed to be miles off along the edge of the valley floor. Squinting her eyes tightly, she could barely make out the faint dots of headlamps moving down towards the flats of the canyon floor. She thought the vehicles must be using the same poorly maintained country road she had entered the valley on the afternoon before. The siren she was hearing from the same direction couldn't be anything other than that of a patrol car chasing some lowly crook who was escaping into her habitat. She hoped and prayed the cops would catch whomever they were after. The last thing she needed in this lonely place was some vicious criminal slinking through the brush and rocks to find her unprotected and defenseless.

Before returning to the safety of her dome tent, Renee added her few remaining chunks of wood to the low fire. Hurriedly completing that task, she quickly crawled back to the still warm folds of the sleeping bag. With still trembling fingers she searched out a small flask of Johnny Walker Red in her backpack. Inhaling before she took a more than generous nip, she carefully replaced it in to the pack's pocket. With the added courage from that silver flask of confidence, she closed that extra large bag over her head. Nearly forcing herself she tried her best to think about something more pleasant than what might be going on across the valley.

In some ways, Renee wished she had brought Mike with her to share in this adventure. For any one of a number of reasons, this would have been a good time for them to work out some of the petty problems that had opened the gap between them. She thought back over the past six years she had been involved with him, how their relationship had started off with all the excitement of a grand and newly found love. In retrospect it seemed strange how over the last couple of years she had become bored with him. Her feelings had become dulled by Mike's lack of change to meet her needs. Even in bed, their lovemaking had suffered and had become little more than routine bump, grind and thanks by either side for the quickie. Often he would leave her with little challenge for imagination or the acting out of each other's fantasies. Being a healthy woman of twenty-seven years, she dearly enjoyed the acts of uninhibited lovemaking. It made no difference how or when, as long as it was enjoyable and fulfilling to both of them. If only he were there now, she would show how eager she could be to give more of herself and try to help make things right. Her only wish was not to be taken for granted any longer by him, let alone any other man. As she continued to think about these things, the minutes stretched like hours until sleep finally brushed her eyes closed and granted her the much needed rest she would require before her search for the abandoned wagons described in the diary would begin.

• • •

Startled, Renee bolted upright from what was really a very shallow sleep. New sounds of footsteps were just outside the thin fabric of her hiding place. The heavy thump of boots against the ground was shortly followed by a very disturbing crash somewhere near the rear of her tent. Through the still of the night air she started to shake with the crumbling of little bushes and an unexpected gasping for breath. In seconds the sounds changed to that of her uninvited guest rolling back and forth in the dirt. Then came the unmistakable noises of someone dragging themselves across the small pebbles and dirt along the side of her tent. Her breathing almost ceased as she followed those sounds toward her smoldering fire and her door. She wasn't really sure which came first, the gurgling sound from the uninvited stranger in the pale light just outside, or the gasp which erupted beyond her control from her own lips. Some way she had to break out from what had been a place of security but which now had slammed closed tightly around her; a place which unexpectedly became a self imposed prison filling her with a lot of very real fears.

As quietly as possible, Renee once again slipped from her sleeping bag; she did not bother to unzip the closure but pushed herself stealthily out the small opening. Fumbling in the dark, her fingers pulled savagely at the ties to the tent flap. The knots she had so carefully tied only a short time before would not release! Against Renee's will, her panic thrust itself upon her and overcame any semblance of sense or order. Frantically she pulled and tore at the door until the threads finally gave way and the fabric ripped, tearing loose two of the lower ties on the same side.

Scrambling on all fours from the smaller than normal opening to freedom, she jumped to her feet and started to run as fast as she could. In her haste to leave what was left of her domain, she knew she would not have time to locate her shoes or grab her pants and other clothes, clothes that she knew would have protected her legs and body from the many small sharp pebbles and prickly bushes surrounding her tent. She had hardly made a few lunging steps in her desperate attempt to flee her intruder when she stumbled over a large mass and crashed to the ground. Rolling over onto her back and sitting up as fast as possible, she tried to stand. Her legs refused to lift her weight and felt like noodles whose strength had been soaked away. With all the concentration she possessed, she pushed hard with her feet into the loose dirt and stones. In her tremendous effort, she separated herself by only a few more inches from the dark form lying prone not far from her tent door. In that very dim light of the pale sky, Renee was able to make out that the form was that of a man, a man not moving. Holding her breath, she stopped what she was doing and stared intently at him.

Maybe he's dead! She thought fearfully.

Ignoring, or at least not feeling the pain to her knees and legs, she managed to crawl and drag herself back and forth in a half circle around him. Keenly, she looked for any sign of movement or life. Anything to let her know she was no longer in danger and that he was not playing possum in order to do her in. At some point in what seemed like an eternity, Renee found she had maneuvered herself closer to the fire pit. Without averting her eyes from the man, she slowly pulled a partially burned stick from the ashes to use as a weapon. Now armed, she found enough strength in her shaking legs to scoot closer to her unexpected adversary. She was not sure why she felt the need for the weapon since he seemed to be unconscious; all she knew was it was the most prudent thing to do at this time in her life.

Trying to remain on the safe side, Renee stopped short of touching him with her legs and sat back on her feet and knees. Her trembling stick was partially raised in preparation to strike down against the head of this marauder. Taking the briefest of seconds to look at her club, she suddenly realized that some kitchen spoons were larger and more ominous than the one she held. Gradually she lowered her arm and pointed her weapon at the man's side and brutally jabbed him with the wicked smoldering point. He did nothing more than gasp and flinch against the impact and singeing heat.

God, that has to hurt! She thought as she pushed the stick just a little harder. The man's arms pushed down against the ground and he lifted himself just a fraction before he dropped back again.

Quickly looking about her, she could see nothing that could be deemed a more formidable club. The rocks ringing the pit were too hot to touch, so those were definitely out of the question. Now she wished she had not burned all the larger chunks of wood the evening before. She prayed for anything more deadly than what she held in the tight grip of her clammy and white-knuckled fingers.

For at least five minutes Renee sat and watched with lessening fear while the slow transition of night turned to dawn. As the light brought forth the identifying features of the form lying almost deathly quiet before her, she was able to see with clearer detail the figure of a dark-haired man in tattered and torn clothes lying face down. His light-colored shirt was shredded and his dark pants were torn from the knee to the hem, exposing a muscular calf. A thick belt surrounded his waist.

"A thick gun belt? You're wearing a gun? You're armed?" she asked him in complete surprise at her discovery.

Renee leaned closer and reached across the man and felt the telltale texture of a large revolver's checkered grip. With the tips of her thumb and forefinger she pulled on the handle to slide the pistol from its resting-place. It wouldn't budge. Feeling around the hammer of the weapon, she located the safety strap that locked the gun to its holster. Ripping the snap from itself, she finally freed the weapon to her hand. As she was doing these things, her forearm repeatedly brushed the cold skin of the stranger's back through one of the long rips in his shirt.

He seemed to be shaking, but unconscious. Moving her head closer to his, she was able to hear his shallow but labored breathing. Renee set his pistol aside and took hold of what felt like an extremely muscular arm and shoulder, and pulled him onto his back with all the strength she could muster. His body had not stopped rolling when she again seized his revolver and pointed it toward his head with both hands. He still did not move on his own. Although she was still much more frightened than she ever had been in her life, Renee's nerves were starting to calm. She was beginning to think more rationally about the situation she had encountered.

"You are so cold!" she told the man even though she knew he could not hear her. "I'm so cold!" she uttered almost silently to herself in trying to rationalize her own shaking.

Until that moment, and in all the excitement, Renee had not realized she had been shaking violently. Her legs and arms started to feel numb and cold as ice. As quickly as possible, and while trying to keep as much distance from the stranger as she could, she circled around him. Untying the remaining knots of the flap, Renee rushed into her tent and quickly donned her clothing. After much scrambling and fumbling into some clothes, she pushed his gun into the waistband of her pants. In what seemed like only seconds she had returned to sit beside the obviously injured man. The morning light being bright enough now allowed her to see most of the details of his face. Looking closer at the injuries to his head, she identified the many small cuts and minor lacerations on his cheek, throat and forehead; some of which looked jagged and really horrible as they were caked with dried blood. A thick red fluid mixed with dirt, sand and small pieces of twigs and debris had eventually dribbled down and stained the collar of his shirt. Above his torn left shirt pocket was the unmistakable shine of a cop's badge; a golden star. While using extra caution so as not to bring him into consciousness, she unhooked the clasp that held its pin through the light material.

Renee removed the badge, she held it closer to her eyes and read the words, "County Sheriff's Department—Deputy." "You must have been the one driving the police car I heard this morning," she told him before she realized that was a stupid thing to say.

Based on his breathing alone Renee knew without further question that time was of the essence. She had to help this man right now or he surely would die needlessly from exposure. As quickly as possible she began to feel and touch every inch of his body. If there were any broken bones, bleeding, or other life threatening problems, she would have to deal with them first. Only superficial wounds, nothing life threatening as she had imagined prior to her touching him.

"Then why is he unconscious? Can it be a concussion? No, no, it must be the cold," she reassured herself. "It must be the freezing night air. Oh God! You're freezing to death!" she said.

Touching his stomach Renee discovered his abdomen was excessively cold. His temperature had fallen too far below normal, below what even a strong person could sustain for long. Renee knew she had to use all her strength and abilities to warm him as quickly as possible.

She quickly surveyed her surroundings and determined the best place would be in her tent where she could utilize the heat from her lantern and pump some hot fluids into him. But misfortune was still with her; the harder she tried to pull him toward the door, the quicker she discovered that his weight and bulk were much more than she could handle. Pushing herself around him and back to the door of her tent, she dragged her sleeping bag out and unzipped it to its full length. Although she had never had the opportunity to use the techniques she had learned from the E.M.T. classes she had taken at City College, she was astounded at her own ability to remember what to do.

"First strip the hypothermia victim, then undress yourself and lay with him to transfer you body heat," Renee remembered. "Massage him to regain circulation in the extremities." she repeated the words out loud to herself while trying to recall if she had left anything out.

Stripping the victim is a lot harder than it sounds! She thought as she ripped his shirt even more while trying to pull it off his shoulder. Giving up on saving what was left of the material, she then intentionally ripped and tore away what she could. Her task was difficult as she struggled to remove his remaining clothes and western boots. Then rolling him onto the fully opened sleeping bag, she pulled the heavy layers of material over him and rezipped the bag almost completely closed. Returning to the fire pit, Renee struck a match and proceeded to rekindle the flames with a small piece of paper and several broken twigs. Her fingers started to sting at the tips from the cold that caused her to fumble with the package of dehydrated soup. Half spilling the cooking container, she managed to set the concoction near the growing flames.

Renee stripped herself of her warmed clothing and slid in alongside him. With an insufficient amount of her compared to all of him, she tried to cover as much as possible of the man with her warmer body. However, in the now tight confines of a bag that was really meant to sleep two moderately small people, she found any movement was extremely difficult for her. Whatever the situation, she had to massage his arms, legs and his whole body to bring him back to consciousness. Renee prayed she had it in her to bring up his body temperature to as close as normal as possible in a relatively short period of time. Vigorously she assaulted his arms, hands and chest. Her own legs and feet moved up and down on his, creating a warming friction.

During a brief rest, she looked closer at the Deputy lying so near her. From what she could see of his face, he appeared to be very rugged looking with handsome and slightly graying salt and pepper hair.

Maybe forty years old or maybe a little younger, Renee thought. He had strong facial features with darkened leathery skin. Obviously the years of working under the desert sun had taken its toll. He was tall, perhaps six foot one or even possibly two with very little fat hanging off anything. Feeling somewhat stronger again, Renee raked herself briskly over his arms and stomach in another series of tiring maneuvers. She tried to reach lower to his calves, but found that her position and length of reach prevented her from feeling them.

Very muscular, very well kept. Not at all like Mike. She thought comparing this man to her boyfriend, who by his own admission did not like muscular bodies.

As she drew her hand back, she shivered as the soft skin of her hand brushed delicately against his penis and testicles. She hesitated momentarily and involuntarily looked around as if trying to see if anyone was watching. Although he was soft, she discovered he was unquestionably well endowed, and they hung heavy in her palm. Just as quickly as she had found his manhood she released him to continue her attempt to bring him back to her world.

For what seemed like forever, Renee agonizingly rubbed and moved over every inch of his body within her reach while allowing him to keep his remaining dignity. Her hands and arms grew heavier and ached miserably from her constant massaging. Occasionally she would alternate with her feet and legs to rub his lower extremities. She so wanted her efforts to be helping. Although his eyes had not opened, she took note that his breathing was becoming regular and less labored. She was delighted that his color was returning to his once almost pale face. While Renee watched for a change of the expression, his eyes began to flutter then slowly opened. She knew she could not stop her efforts now since she was well aware she had only won a small battle and not the war. She told herself she had saved him from a fate of freezing to death and the early meeting of the grim reaper.

Such a stupid time to become melodramatic, Renee admonished herself.

Renee suddenly remembered the soup in the fire pit. She crept out from the bag and discovered that a good portion of the water had boiled away. Quickly adding a tad more water, her actions did the trick of making the temperature more tolerable and easier to swallow. Stirring the soup briefly she crawled back into the bag alongside her unnamed patient. Resting herself on one elbow, she held his head up with one hand and slowly poured a sip of the soup between his slightly parted lips. When a dribble ran down the side of his cheek, she removed the cup. Even though some dribbled from his mouth she was sure enough made its way down his throat as she saw a small swallow. With each consecutive sip, he seemed to allow more to flow down his parched throat.

The deputy turned his head from side to side as if he were trying to relieve a pulled tendon. He looked into the cloudless sky for several seconds before rotating his head slightly enough to face her.

His eyes fully opened and he uttered in raspy words, "Thanks. Just who in the hell are you?"

"Renee. Renee Mitchell. Please don't talk now. Just rest."

His eyes slowly closed again and he quickly succumbed to sleep. Lying beside him as the warmth continued to return to his body, Renee started to feel the security of his presence. She herself was exhausted from the night's seemingly endless interruptions and tension. A few moments later sleep came upon her as well.

• • •

Renee figured it must have been an hour or more before she was awakened with a strange sensation again. Opening her eyes, she saw the stranger's features for the first time in the full light of morning. She found the handsomely rugged face and piercing deep blue eyes staring into hers. Pulling her head back an inch or two, what she saw of the man lying beside her was exciting for her to say the least. She didn't recall a single time in her life that she had been so enraptured by anyone. And now she found herself deeply moved by the enticing presence of such tremendous looks. *My boyfriend isn't bad looking, but he wouldn't make a reflection in your presence,* she said silently to the Deputy.

Renee felt the onslaught of a genuine romantic interlude itching deep inside her groin. *Frozen or not, you are definitely a turn on.*

Neither spoke as they spent several seconds staring into each other's eyes. Trying to break the spell, she muttered in an attempt to be a little more medical, "Do you remember my name?"

"Of course," he said matter-of-factly in a raspy but forceful voice, "It's Renee."

"Now that you know my name, I'm kind of at a disadvantage. What are you called?"

"Deputy."

"Deputy what?"

"Oh I don't know, around this country I come with many names, none of which is any more important than the other. Let's just say Deputy for now," he added with a small grin.

"Don't do that," Renee admonished him. "Who are you?"

He lifted the cover and looked into the bag. "It seems you know me well enough to call me Jack!" he replied with a small and twisted grin.

"Are you feeling any better? Is anything broken?"

"I've felt worse from time to time, but at the present I really can't complain. I am very sore on the side you're lying on. If you would, roll to the other side of me. I'm sure we will both be a lot more comfortable."

His strong arms helped Renee to raise her petite frame above him in the still very tight sleeping bag. For the first time she felt the real impact of his broad chest as she scraped her naked breasts against his taut skin. Almost lost in the moment and his intoxicating smell, Renee found it most difficult to restrain her breathing through that kind of passion. As much as she would have hated to admit it to herself, there are some fires not made to be extinguished. Not even the small cuts and dried blood on his face made a difference at this moment in time; Renee felt she just couldn't get enough of the feel of Jack's massive body.

Not wanting to go all the way over to his opposite side, she hesitated directly over him. With an imposing look of sincerity, she remained poised with her legs straddling his well-proportioned sides. Her swollen lips were but a suggestion away from his while she looked deeply into his questioning eyes. She shivered. Just as suddenly as she had started, she tried to break her own spell and slow down her aggressiveness.

"Do you know what a Bachelor Button is?" she asked with a small look of concern over such a stupid thing to ask at a time like this.

"Is this a mental test or something, lady?"

"No. I was curious if you knew."

Jack started to help her from her position over him when she pushed up against the sleeping bag to brace herself.

"Is there something else?" he asked sounding a little confused.

"No. No. I want to be sure you're warm enough."

"Well, I am."

Renee again prevented herself from being moved for several seconds to continue feeling his massive frame under her. Surprising even herself, she pushed herself down his narrow waist just a few inches very slowly and deliberately. Her nipples tingled as they scraped against his chest as she started her slide toward the bottom of the sleeping bag. Renee had almost reached the limits of her move when she expectantly was effectively stopped by a very large, erect and titillating obstruction. Shivers of anticipation vibrated deeply in her soul as she gasped her submission through an involuntary mini-orgasm. Her mind reeled briefly with the thought she would never have allowed herself to be taken by such a man under any other circumstances. The heat being generated between the two of them in such a short period of time had become a singeing fire of desire.

She found herself transfixed even more by the tenderness of this wonderful moment when she felt Jack tenderly lower his hands down her back. Ever so gently his callused grip cupped her baby soft cheeks as his fingers squeezed lightly into the firm flesh of her succulent buns. Renee tried to help him as best she could and applied pressure by thrusting her pelvis forward and down against his abdomen.

"Now! Now!" she hissed in anticipation of the better things to come with the strength of his grip and the pulsation of his manhood against her swollen lips. And now he did— Jack gripped his fingers tighter and lifted Renee out the top of the sleeping bag with a firm but gentle push.

"Now is not the time!" he whispered when her head passed his. "What are you? Some sort of crazy, or something? Look, Lady, there are more important things to do than to satisfy your animalistic needs right now. Not that I don't appreciate the thought, though." he added, grinning.

Dumbfounded, Renee sat on the ground not far from his head, completely confused by what had just happened. Absolutely beside herself, she didn't know whether to laugh or cry. *What man in his right mind would ignore what I have done for him!* She demanded to herself in quite muffled words. Even after several moments of fuming she couldn't decide whether to really get mad, laugh or pretend none of this had ever happened.

While Jack struggled himself free of the sleeping bag, she had no choice but to take delight in what she saw. His passing of her unspoken offer really had to reflect great personal fortitude. Before her eyes, the sight of his enormous erection made it seem very apparent that he was truly ready for her.

He immediately turned away in an attempt to prevent her from continuing to stare at his upturned appendage. She smiled with the knowledge he had to be one of the best specimens of manhood she ever had the pleasure to witness. Even from his backside his strength abounded. From the tight small buns, to the rippling muscles of his broad shoulders and back, he was truly beautiful. His thighs and calves were those of a mighty gladiator; a real warrior of strength and stamina. *A beast to be reckoned with at my leisure.*

"Wow!" Renee exclaimed in excited delight. "You're gorgeous!"

Jack ignored her and tried his best to keep her from seeing his blush. Quietly and quickly he gathered his clothes while hiding the red of his face from her unlady-like comments. He dressed with as much precision as possible considering the rags of clothes with which he had to contend. Placing his gun belt over his shoulder, he retrieved the revolver from beside her clothes and started to walk away from the small camp.

He looked back over his shoulder to her. Almost as a command, he ordered, "Stay here. I'll be back."

Not twice in one day are you going to do this to me, she thought. "Hey!" Renee yelled, "Where are you going?"

"To bathe!"

I guess the cold really got to him—his mind's gone. I suppose I could let him go alone. She nudged herself with very little effort. But she couldn't bring herself to letting him just walk away in his weakened condition. Somehow she felt really responsible for his safety and continued well being.

Hurriedly, Renee gathered her clothes and shoes. Without stopping, she rushed off trying to dress and catch up at the same time. Once she had caught him, she made her best effort to divert his strange ideas and steer him back towards the campsite. Persistently he pushed on, ignoring her futile requests to return to the warmth and security of the fireside.

They were some two hundred yards from her camp when they came upon a natural hot spring surrounded by thick desert flora.

"Who would have known this place even existed?" she said out loud. Not on the map and hidden here among the boulders and brush was a pool with a slight fog lingering just above the surface. "It's amazing to find such a beautiful spot in such a rugged place. Not many people must know how to find this."

Jack didn't respond to her words. Stepping closer to his side, Renee saw the water was crystal clear and deep as could be imagined. As they stood near the edge, she knelt and dipped her fingers into the water. She was surprised to find it so very warm and inviting.

"One hundred six," Jack said.

"Your age?" Renee replied with a giggle and trying to make light of the still very strange situation.

Nothing more came from him; just a funny look as if she were from another planet. Quietly Jack removed his clothes. He took utmost care to keep his back towards her to prevent her from acting like a pervert and staring as she had not too many moments before.

"Are you really that modest? Hell! We just spent the better part of this morning naked together."

Again he did not answer. As he peeled away each rag, becoming more undressed with each passing second, she did take note that his skin was dark all over; more than just a handsome tan.

Very slowly and deliberately Jack lowered himself backwards into the water as if every inch of his body had been damaged. He let out an ever so soft moan, if not from the pleasure of the water, then from his bruises and minor injuries the heat soothed. He took a small metal mirror from what remained of his shirt pocket and turned to face her. His gun lay at the ready near the edge of the spring close to him. He looked into the reflection of himself and then at her, boasting quite a strange expression.

All she could think to say was, "It's superficial. The blood and all."

Wetting her hanky that she had taken from her back pants pocket, Renee came around the boulders surrounding the pool and closer to him.

"Please let me help," she said as she knelt down on the edge of the pool beside and just behind him.

Reaching alongside of his massive shoulders she dipped the hanky then wrung out the excess water. Just when she was about to reach around him to wipe his face, Jack leaned forward. He dunked his head and face completely under the water. Renee remained still and watched as he scrubbed his face with his open hands while his whole head was just under the surface. When he resurfaced, his face was clean of debris and glistened with the morning light striking the beads of water. She looked down upon an even more exciting and vibrantly handsome man than just a moment before.

"The blood was from those tiny scratches, nothing significant," Renee added.

Jack pushed his wet hair back over his head with both hands. To Renee, the water made it seem darker and glitter in the morning rays of the sun. When she looked at his face, she noted the marvelous feature of his high cheekbones. Furthermore he had wonderful eyes accented by small spider web lines leading away from the corners. Not in need of a shave, he bore a slight resemblance to an Indian.

Then again—blue eyes? Nonetheless, such a very handsome man.

2

"Broken Bronco"

Are you better now?" Renee asked as she took note of the expression of pleasure that continued to warm over his face. The whole episode since he lowered himself into the hot spring pool was like watching the birth of a new man. He did not reply straightaway and acted like he expected Renee to repeat her question. He did nothing more than lie back into the crystal water staring up at her, his big hands purposely covered his genitals, removing her from any temptations to further view him. He just sat calmly as if there had never been a problem of any consequence in his life. Occasionally he would look away and then back toward her like she wasn't really there. Then at other times he would look deeply into her eyes as if he were searching for the answer to her question.

All of a sudden he crushed his left eye closed, wrinkled his nose and pushed his lips to the left side, paused and released the strange expression and said, "I haven't heard that expression since I was in boarding school."

"What expression?" she asked in total confusion.

"Bachelor Button. In the sack you said I smelled like a Bachelor Button. You don't remember things very well, do you? And to answer your question, Yes, I am."

"Yes, you are what?"

"See what I mean? That's not telling me what a Bachelor Button is."

"Do you want the official translation or do you—"

"The official one will do fine," he said, making his interruption annoying and very obvious.

Renee looked him squarely in the eye. "Why are you being an asshole? You got some sort of problem or something?"

"I apologize for that. It's just that I don't understand you. First you help me, then you try to rape me. It's just confusing."

"It's a little muslin bag of sweet smelling herbs the young men carried when they went courting." Renee smiled and puffed herself up along with her pride of putting him in his place.

"You don't look like a country girl. So how would you know that?"

"Well, if it's really that important, I read about it in Volume One of the *Century Dictionary and Cyclopedia*. Printed in 1897 in New York City, I might add."

Jack leaned back against the side of the natural granite stones of the pool and shut his eyes against her smart aleck wisdom.

"I'm really sorry for what happened earlier. I meant well, just got carried away a little," she said, hoping for any kind of a more civil reply.

Again he did not answer. It seemed to her it was as if he were extremely uncomfortable and not sure what to say to a woman. Renee sat above him refusing to play his game any further.

"Carried away a lot, I would say," he said following a long, long couple of minutes of silence. "But maybe I owe you an apology as well."

"I would think so."

"I didn't mean to be so abrupt in separating us back at the camp."

She decided not to interrupt his unexpected questioning of her motives and apology for a bad attitude.

"It just seemed a real inopportune time for that sort of thing. Besides, you never know. I may not be that kind of guy."

"What kind of guy is that?" she asked somewhat softly to check her building anger.

"I really want you to respect me in the morning." He started to laugh while he spoke. "So please be gentle from now on."

Having said that, a larger smile emerged on his face. His words and expressions suddenly surprised her. Renee tried her best to giggle and play along with him in his strange jest.

A few moments later, he again went quiet and was looking off into the distance as if searching the surrounding area for someone.

In a lowered and slightly muted tone he told her. "You'd feel much better from this brisk air if you got into the water. It's really very therapeutic," he added a little louder with a touch of encouragement even though he still appeared embarrassed.

Realizing her imagination had not been playing tricks on her, she began to see he was more than just a very modest person. Subconsciously or not on her part, Renee turned around to undress as quickly as possible while doing her best to be coy. Fighting her curiosity and not turning to look, she wondered if he had averted his eyes from her backside as she suspected he would. Deliberately she backed into the pool to hide her breasts and other parts of private concern from him. Thinking back over the last several years, she couldn't remember a better attempt to shield her nakedness from anyone since before meeting Mike. She hadn't had many lovers in her life, but enough to know how to direct and channel herself so it would seem she was doing what was expected of her.

"After all," she confirmed to herself, "My body is nothing to be ashamed of."

She wouldn't admit it to anyone that this did seem somehow very erotic to her. She sighed out a small breath of pleasure as the warm water swirled and caressed around her ankles, legs and then her bottom as she sank deeper. Renee suddenly experienced she was truly in "Hot Tub Heaven." With lessening speed she continued lowering herself. The cold left her breasts and shoulders when they too were hidden from the cool air in the crystal waters. Turning around to face Jack, she settled herself onto the same outcropping of submerged rocks he was resting on.

"Stay here on the ledge," he instructed her in a sterner voice than he had used since their arrival at the pool. Possibly out of curiosity or more than a touch of rebellion, Renee leaned forward slightly while reaching out with her foot in an attempt to touch the bottom of the pool.

"It will burn you down there!" he admonished her more firmly.

Jack simultaneously straightened out his massive arm across the front of her to keep her from moving any further forward. Brushing across her breasts, her nipples scraped his arm. Realizing what his well-intentioned actions had done, he quickly retracted his arm again with almost frightening speed.

"The water is deep there and much hotter. It's near boiling just a few feet further down."

In an attempt to show her gratitude for his concerns, she placed her hand on his arm in a most gentle manner. She then thoughtfully applied a firm appreciative and seductive squeeze before dragging her fingers from him. This one gesture seemed to be the trick that broke the tension he had shown around her.

The rippling of the water had slowly subsided from the lack of movements in the small pool. It seemed as if she were looking through an old piece of leaded window glass; clear, yet slightly rippled. Staring into the water, Renee suddenly realized someone would have to move the water around or Jack's modesty would surely go to the wind. She looked up into his face from having been enthralled momentarily by his submerged body. It was then that she caught his eyes looking deep into the water at her. He was obviously taking in her presence as well before his eyes suddenly lifted to meet hers.

Jack looked directly at her with his first real expression of compassion. He managed to say in a calmer voice than he had used before, that he did not recall knowing such a beautiful and caring woman since met his wife.

This time it was Renee's turn to remain silent and somewhat awestruck. Jack seemed to take note of her uneasiness. Without her saying anything else he started to explain that several years before and during another time in his life, his wife and child had died during the birth.

"Another time?" Renee asked not knowing exactly what to say to such a statement. "Please tell me, why another time?"

"I'm part Indian," Jack stated with some pride.

Looking a foot or so below the surface of the water and then back into his eyes, she couldn't help herself as a naughty little smile curled across her lips. "What part?" Renee smiled a great deal more and continued as she laughed. "I'm sorry! That just seemed like a good thing to ask."

Jack's grin seemed a sincere one for the first time since they'd met. But still, his answer did not satisfy her question, and she was sure he knew that as well.

Fascinated with this systematic cleansing of himself, Renee watched him as he rubbed the length of his arms methodically with what appeared to be an imaginary bar of soap. As if well edited in his thoughts, he began to speak of the other time as that of his life on the Pine Ridge Indian Reservation in South Dakota. He told her of the hard times and modern day uprisings for better conditions by the people who were forced to live there. He described his home at Cuny Table in a somewhat modern government house that seemed to him to be a shortsighted attempt to help the Indian.

This was the place where his mother and his obnoxious yellow ringed Tabby Cat—inappropriately named "Man Thing"—lived. Renee held her laugh in check and listened quietly for only a moment.

"Man Thing? That's an Indian name isn't it?"

Jack gave her a very serious look through somewhat squinted eyes and then continued.

Fascinated by his dialogue, she paid explicit attention to the description of his long-time residence that turned out to be only a few hours from Wounded Knee.

"And that's another place where battles have taken place with Federal agencies over the conditions on the reservation." Jack went on to relate his feelings of the modern reservation and the many shortcomings brought on by the White man for the Indian. Thoughtfully, he explained how he and his wife had overcome many of the difficulties through shared love and devotion to one another, and that their combined beliefs in the old ways and traditions of the family and the Indian Nation made for a wonderful marriage.

Renee thought Jack's sorrows seemed to be as deep as could be imagined. For not only his wife and family, but that of the others who have had to endure the life style the poverty stricken reservation offered.

"Were you the one I saw this morning coming down the hill with your siren on?" she asked changing the subject since he seemed to be becoming somewhat melancholy again.

"Yeah!" Jack surprised her by saying. "Boy, was that a trip! I rolled the company car over when I tried to take a short cut."

"Then you didn't catch the guy you were after?" Renee started to become a little nervous again.

"Catch him?" Jack grinned out the words. "Hell, I was running from him!"

Slowly Renee started to slide away from Jack, finding the rocks on the ledge a little rougher than she had been expecting and scraped her bottom.

Just who am I dealing with here? She asked herself. "Aren't you a cop? A Deputy? You know, the person that's supposed to be chasing the other guy?"

"Yeah, normally. That's why I tried to take a short cut."

Renee believed it now dawned on him that she was becoming even more uneasy with what he was telling her.

"I really am the good guy in this. It just looks a little weird. Let me give you an idea what happened. If you try real hard, maybe then you will understand better. And then, if you do, you can explain it to me, because I don't."

"I don't like being patronized," she said crisply.

Again Jack ignored her and continued to talk. Calming herself, she reached behind him to his gun belt. Hanging on a narrow leather strap with a silver fastener was a pair of chrome plated handcuffs.

"May I look at these?" Renee asked interrupting him in his now seemingly edited explanation of events leading to his entrance into the valley.

"Try not to lock them on yourself. Don't have a key," he advised her in the use of caution.

What kind of cop carries handcuffs without a key? she wondered to herself.

In his attempt to be helpful, Jack explained the way they're applied was to hit the single edge of the handcuff against the wrist. From the force it would swing over and around to lock into position. Before he could stop her. Renee did just that.

"Didn't I tell you I don't have a key?" he muttered with more than a little disgust.

"But you said to do that," Renee snapped back.

"Crud," he answered back. The word was as much to himself than to her.

"You hate me, don't you?" she sneered at him.

Jack reached into his pants that were folded under his shirt. From his pocket he took out a folding church key. He slipped the pointed end under the double steel bars of the cuff that was around her wrist. He carefully pushed the point between the steel and her wrist and up against the ratchet. The handcuff swung open.

"I'll be damned!" Renee said in surprise.

Once the cuffs were fully off her wrist, Jack showed her where he had pushed with the opener.

"You can only do that with the old-style handcuffs," he related. "And then only when they're not double locked."

Jack ignored her when she asked why he didn't have better ones and handed them back to her.

"I don't hate you. But you are starting to make me believe in an old white man's saying."

"And what, pray tell, would that be?"

"You sure you want to—"

"Tell me."

"If you must know. It goes like this; A woman, a dog and a walnut tree. The more you beat them, the better they be."

"What in hell is that supposed to mean?" she said in mild anger.

"I don't know. It just seemed to fit somehow."

It became difficult for him to tell his story as he found it annoying when she started to twirl the cuffs around the index finger of her right hand. In near horror he saw her fumble and nearly drop them into the pool.

He tried to relate to her that he had come to Saline Valley to look into an official matter involving some lost property. It was shortly after he had turned onto Saline Valley Road and started the climb to the mountain pass that another vehicle seemed to appear out of nowhere. A car or a truck, it really didn't matter. Even so, he wasn't really sure which had gotten behind him.

"I don't understand. It just came out of nowhere. I think they were on one of the old abandoned mine roads off the main road. Maybe the old—" Jack stopped in mid-sentence and thought for a second. "I really don't know. I wasn't paying close enough attention to where I was at the time. You know, the night was too dark and I was too deep in thought."

Renee started to feel a little confused over his lack of attention. He seemed to be making excuses for being lost in the place he works.

"They raced right up and onto my bumper and stayed there. If I were to speed up, so would they. That must have been when you heard me using my siren to try to clear the road in front of me. You know, wild animals, oncoming cars, whatever."

Renee decided to remain silent and continued to listen to his poor excuse of a story.

"When I slowed down, they did as well. That leaves little to my imagination, other than I was being followed, maybe even pressed."

"I guess," she sighed with a detectable lack of enthusiasm.

"Really, since I didn't know who I was confronting I decided to take a short cut down another old mine road. That's a different route to the bottom of the valley which I thought they wouldn't take."

"Obviously," Renee grunted.

"Whoever was chasing me tried to follow, but they must not have gotten very far. I felt sure they didn't have a four-wheel drive to follow me with." Jack broke off what he was saying as if really thinking for nearly a minute. "When I was near the bottom of the grade, about a mile over that way." he pointed toward the southeast. "The old road turned real rough and passed by a deep ravine. I believe I could have made it had it not been for the edge of the road giving way. The Bronco rolled over into the gully." Stopping for several seconds in his description, he then continued while squinting his eyes, "I must have hit my head or something. Things get a little fuzzy from there on."

"Yeah, I can imagine," Renee injected with lessening belief.

"I remember leaving the Bronco and walking toward a dim light. It was too dark to really see anything." Smiling a little he continued, "The way my clothes and face look it must not have been too easy a trip. The last I remember is drinking some really horrible soup and seeing your face next to mine. You know, of course, you probably saved my life. Are you a nurse or something?" Jack asked as he was feeling uncomfortable by her curious stare.

"Not really," Renee replied as she kind of looked over the end of her nose at him. "I have had a little emergency training. How did you know about this hot spring?"

Jack related to her that he had come to the valley many times in his work and for weekend getaways.

"Why would you come to this spot?" she questioned him. "To be in this hot tub?"

"Didn't," Jack replied. "Found it when I was looking for something a while back. As a matter of fact, there are other more developed hot springs in the valley. They're over that way." He pointed off to the north. "Other than myself, I believe you're the only one that knows about this one. I've tried to keep it a secret."

"Looking for what?"

He seemed to ignore her question and asked whether or not she had any coffee in her camp. When Renee replied "Yes," he turned away from her as he stood and tried to hide himself from her.

"Let's have coffee," he said while he dressed and then placed his gun belt over his shoulder. "We've been here too long. The sun is well over the Panamints."

"The what?"

"The Panamint Mountains," he answered while pointing off to the east.

"Oh! I knew that."

Renee quickly followed Jack's lead in putting on her clothes and followed him closely toward her dome tent.

"Why didn't you call for help?"

"Hell!" he said, "Don't you know where you are?" he continued before she could again speak. "Any help for me is several hours away. Even if I asked for some, they would be too late getting here anyway."

"I guess that's reasonable. Then why didn't you call in when you turned your car over?" she nudged him a little further for a better explanation.

"Radio's broke."

"Damn it!"

On reaching the camp, Jack gathered some small bushes and sticks and proceeded to ignite a new fire in the shallow pit. Renee rummaged around in her tent until she located her cook pot and instant coffee. "I hope you don't use cream or sugar. Don't use it myself." she said in a loud voice from within her tent.

"No problem," he yelled back. "Just as long as it's not decaf or instant."

"Damn!" she blurted a little too loudly.

"What did you say?"

"Nothing, nothing at all. Just clearing my throat."

At a low crouch, Renee duck walked from the little tent door. Somewhat embarrassed, she showed Jack the small bottle of decaf instant coffee.

"There's no doubt you're from the city. Only people from the city drink that crap, you know."

It was a strong willingness to show her independence and contempt that caused her to reach deeper into her backpack. Making sure he could see, she flagrantly produced her camper's white gas cook stove. Pouring water into the small pot, she proceeded to heat the water directly in front of him and along side the fire pit.

Jack returned with his now familiar squiggled look. "This fire will warm you!"

What is this? She asked herself without looking up. *This guy doesn't care about anything!* At about the same time she figured he may well have been thinking she might be a few sandwiches short of a picnic.

Probably isn't sure what fire is for! Jack told himself.

She slowly stirred the water round and round only to find that with each turn of the spoon her patience drew shorter and shorter. *If he only understands it's because of the altitude it's taking this fricken thing so long to boil. Naah! It's his attitude.* She delightedly affirmed to herself with silent vengeance.

Controlling herself, Renee purposely added an extra amount of the dark coffee crystals hoping the strength would make the taste closer to real thing. Offering the cup to Jack, she watched as he pressed the smooth edge of the cup to his lips and sipped.

His forehead wrinkled as his eyes pushed together in a cringe that must have been closely followed by the hair on his neck raising. A terribly sour look seemed to devour his face while the corners of his mouth shot downward. Before he replaced the cup for another try at the monster she had brought him, he dragged his open palm across his mouth and squeezed his fingers tightly together over his lips. It actually seemed to Renee that he was attempting to wring out his lips.

He sipped again, then looked her squarely in the eyes with his still screwed-up look. "Is this because I didn't make love to you this morning or do you do this to everyone you save?"

"Sorry!" she replied hoping she hadn't turned anything important to cardboard. "I just wanted it to be like real coffee." *That's interesting*, Renee thought. *He didn't throw it out.*

Even though his eyes were glassy and appeared to be watering, he continued to drink until nothing was left but the bottom of the cup.

"Tell me," he said and heaved a cough to clear his throat. "Why are you out here?"

Taking note he wasn't asking for more, she replied, "Well, I'm a archaeologist. Almost one anyway. I'm searching for some wagons that had been abandoned near here in the late 1870s."

"Really! Do you know where they are?"

"Not exactly," Renee replied, "but I am sure we are very near to them. As a matter of fact, in some papers and diaries I've read, I located the most probable location as being just over that way." Renee pointed away from her camp.

"Don't think so," Jack interrupted. "Unless they're different wagons than I have been looking for. I've already looked all through that area."

"You're looking for wagons, too?"

Jack let her question float on past him.

Trying not to be pushy, since everything else had seemed to go wrong this morning, Renee decided to show Jack some of her notes and the Xerox copy of the handwritten diary page to see how he would respond. She made sure the page that told of the exact position of the wagons wouldn't be seen.

Producing her notebook from her backpack, she stuck the papers out proudly toward him. He read quietly for several minutes with an emotionless look on his face. Suddenly he stood, and took a couple steps toward her and reached for the remaining pages of the notebook she was holding on her lap. As he pulled it from her unwilling grasp, he asked if she knew where the wagons had come from.

"That's not in my notes. But I do know."

Following a quick glance at the book marked, he handed it back to her and asked, "What state?"

"The Dakota Territories!" she emphasized with the pride that she had done her homework.

Sitting down beside her, Jack unfolded her topographical map and pointed out that she was in the wrong part of the valley.

"It's south of here. Over that way and back toward my broken Bronco. Why don't I help you find those wagons?" Jack suggested with more enthusiasm than he had shown all morning.

"Shouldn't you be more concerned with letting your department know what has happened to you?" For the first time she expected him to agree with her.

"Easier said than done. I don't think I can do much in letting them know until I find out what damage is done to the company car, now can I?"

"I suppose not," she responded almost reluctantly.

"Since my vehicle is in the same direction we can stop there on the way to the wagons."

"I don't think so."

"Huh?"

"I've played your silly game long enough. I'm not telling you squat until you become a lot more truthful with me."

"You've got a lot of grease there, lady."

Using his hands as a scoop, Jack started to throw dirt over the fire to extinguish the low flames and glowing embers. She stood, watched him and waited with the patience of a cat for his answer. Until he did, he couldn't use her folding shovel. Renee broke down the tent and refolded her equipment, placing it neatly in and on her backpack. While she was finishing up, Jack walked off some distance.

Probably going to shake the dew off his lily. Crud, Renee thought with a smile on her face, *Must be some kind of a meta-morphosis. I'm starting to sound like Mike.*

Once Jack had returned her camp area to as much of its original condition as possible, he asked if she was ready.

"No." She rocked off her squatting position and onto her butt. Looking up to him, she crossed her legs and said, "You have a story to tell, so let's make it the truth or all I'm going to do is go home."

"Like I said, you got grit. What makes you think I wouldn't use my strength or gun to take what I want or have my way with you?"

"There was a time here this morning you wouldn't have needed a gun. But now I'm not so sure. For the other part of your question, I'm a people person and not so stupid as you want to believe. You didn't become a Deputy by being a crook."

"There are crooked cops."

"I don't believe you're one of them."

"I really like that. Ya shoulda been a freaken detective." Jack extended his hand and grabbed hers firmly to pull her to her feet. "I'll tell you as we walk."

Renee pulled her pack over her right shoulder as they started their trek to the rolled vehicle.

Renee found herself really impressed with Jack's ability as he retraced his own footsteps back in the direction he had come. Pausing every now and then, he would take note of the rocks he had tripped over or the bushes he had fallen into and sigh with displeasure.

"Where do you want me to start?"

"At the beginning."

"You mean the part about my mother making love to my father?"

Renee shoved him from behind. "You know what I mean. Now get serious. Let's start with a little about you."

"Well. On the reservation in South Dakota I was known as Little Man Who Falls on Face a Lot."

"I said to get serious."

"My name is Jack Barlow. As you already figured out, I'm a Deputy and I used to be a Tribal Policeman on the Pine Ridge Reservation in South Dakota. I'm a Breed. But you probably have that figured out too. You know, kind of an accident of nature."

"So? There are a lot of people like that," she interrupted.

Without looking back, he continued. "My mother is Bright Moon of the Lakota Sioux Nation. As a matter of fact, she is a granddaughter and direct descendant of Gall, a warrior Chief back in the 1870s. He kind of had some notoriety stemming from a famous battle in Montana."

"That's all very interesting, but you're still not telling me what I want to hear."

"I'll tell you, but I don't think you're going to believe it either. The whole story is kind of strange."

"Let me be the judge of that," Renee snapped once again, showing her impatience.

Jack jumped over a relatively deep crevasse and then assisted her in making the vault over it.

"I live in Olancha. That little hamlet that's just a blink of the eye south of Lone Pine on Highway 395."

"Yeah. Go on."

"This part of the year I don't spend a lot of road time due to the lack of traffic. So I was sitting at home listening to the company radio when I heard a knock on my back door. Just as I reached for the knob to open it, a big ugly cop I worked with on the Dakota Reservation kicked the door, frame and all, in on me. There wasn't much I could do since he seemed to be controlling he situation with the buggered end of a shotgun.

"What's this got to do with the wagons?"

"I'm getting to that. The Indian, his name is Nick Whitewater, said he was going to kill me if I didn't get out here and find them. As a matter of fact, he only gave me three days to accomplish what could take a lifetime to do."

"So why are you here now? He isn't around. If he was, wouldn't you arrest him?"

Jack stopped talking while he concentrated on picking up his tracks again. They had followed the somewhat meandering trail for maybe a mile when they came upon a deep ravine. Neither Renee nor Jack would have been able to see his vehicle due to the deep gouges in the earth created by the endless seasons of flash floods. From the bank of the arroyo they could see the Bronco sitting upright on all four wheels and pretty much the worse for wear. The police light bar had been partially torn away from the roof on impact with the rocky ground. The windshield was cracked and broken with several large dents in the top, hood and fenders as a good measure of damage.

"Guess I'll be looking for another job now," Jack muttered loudly enough for Renee to hear as he sat down on the edge of the bank. When Jack pushed himself over the edge, Renee followed close behind in the dust he kicked up.

"Pretty bad!" Renee exclaimed as she walked closer to the pitiful site.

It seemed like all he could say was "Yup." Jack got behind the wheel and turned the key he had left in the ignition.

He must have been knocked silly to have forgotten his keys like that, she thought, trying to justify his explanation of what had happened.

Slowly the engine turned, seemingly building speed the longer he held the key on. It fired once, quit, then fired again. The engine finally grabbed a deep breath of fuel and air and a puff of gray black smoke jetted from the half-squished tail pipe. The Ford motor sprang to life.

While Renee looked inside the open door watching him, Jack picked the radio mike up from the floor. Turning and twisting some knobs and pushing some other things on a little gray box hanging from the dash, he finally depressed the mike button and watched a red light on the console turn on.

Jack got a distasteful look on his face, "The red light means it's broken." He shrugged it off as if he expected it.

It wasn't until some time later Renee learned the red light meant the mike was open and he could have transmitted to his office.

Jack told her to throw her pack and belt into the rear compartment and to climb on in. He pulled his safety belt across his lap and snapped the metal pieces together with a click. Holding up a loose belt end he pushed it toward her indicating she should do likewise since the ride might get a little rough. He muttered something about bouncing around a lot. Slowly he drove forward to a place some distance down the wash. At this point, Jack located a narrow stretch on the bank where he said he could drive out and onto the desert floor.

"You've got to be kidding." Leaning forward, she looked almost straight up a steep slope.

They were almost near the top when the tires gave way to the loose dirt and the Bronco made no further headway. Quickly mashing the gears into reverse, Jack backed down and then some distance further where he returned the shift lever to lowest forward gear. He gunned the engine and raced toward the bank as fast as the vehicle would go in such a short distance. All Renee could think was that they would crash again, as the vehicle seemed to bounce from rock to rock. She let out a rather loud scream when the dust and rocks went flying past her open window with more than a few stinging her elbow and lower arm. All four tires were spinning wildly when they reached the top of the embankment. The little four-wheel drive fought itself up and over the edge of the steep bank.

"I'm glad you quit screaming."

Now, if only my heart would beat again! she thought.

As soon as they hit flatter ground, Jack stopped the vehicle, turned to Renee and asked for her map. Silently he pored over it, then pointed off into the desert on the opposite side of the wash.

"The wagons are over there somewhere. We'll find a crossing somewhere up that way."

"What happened after that guy Whitewater threatened you?"

"Well, he just got into his car and left. Now here is the peculiar part. One of the reasons I took the job here was to give me a chance to look for some wagons that belonged to a party of thieves. The elders of the reservation had passed down a story over the decades of grave robbers who had stolen some significant things from the Sacred Places in the Black Hills."

"What were they?"

"No one has ever said. But whatever they were, there are some people who think I know and who want them at any cost."

He jammed the shift lever into gear from neutral, and the Bronco lurched forward. Eventually he did find a reasonable place to cross the wash and continue on to their destination. It took some thirty grueling minutes of plowing through bushes and over small rocks or around larger ones before Jack stopped and turned off the engine.

Not seeing any wagons sticking out of the brush, Jack said, "We both must be wrong!"

Opening the door, Renee slid off the seat and started wandering outward from her side of the Bronco. Soon Jack got the same idea and started his search on the opposite side. About a hundred yards from where she had started, Renee found many boards and pieces of metal trappings strewn about the ground. She was sure she had found the decayed wagons described in the diary from so long ago.

3

"A Time Long Lost"

Yelling to Jack, Renee told him in no uncertain terms she had located the remnants of a wagon. Suffering from a solid case of excitement, she found herself hopping for happiness and doing some weird sort of aboriginal dance. Maybe even somewhat like a jig that one of the long dead miners might have done after finding sought-after gold in a glory hole.

Having suspicions she was running amuk for the right reasons this time, Jack moved toward her at a relatively fast pace until he was about ten feet away.

With an ear-to-ear smile, Renee pointed out her first discovery, a long narrow piece of hardwood with a rusty old metal ring on one end and a bent round bolt on the opposite end indicating possibly an axial fitting. Taking Jack by the hand, Renee found she had more strength now than she had earlier when she had tried to move him. With a tug harder then was needed, she dragged him a few yards further away to another place, no more than a few feet away. Hardly able to control herself, she pointed out various chunks of sculptured wood and other parts that were probably the sideboards and support slats.

Protruding from the side of one large sagebrush was a portion of a metal rimmed wagon wheel. Even though many of the spokes had been broken and weathered away, there was little doubt it was significant to her search.

Never before in the history of archaeology had such a find taken place, she fantasized! Just as quickly as she had taken his hand, she released her grip on him. She went merrily off pointing and shouting and pointing again at still more of the lost items of history that had revealed themselves to her eager eyes.

A brief moment of sanity overcame her as she realized Jack may well have started wondering whether or not she was in heat or suffering a not quite so usual bout with PMS. Whatever her imagined strike on her attitude, he must have decided to remain calmer in the face of such a wonderful discovery on her part.

Renee's breath stopped in mid intake along with her heart when Jack bent down and began pulling a large group of boards from their partially buried resting-place. Quickly she raced over to him with all the speed and energy she could muster. She thrust out her arms just before impact and ran directly into his chest in her best attempt to push him away from her find.

Not moving very far from where she contacted him, he looked at her with sheer amazement and surprise. And even worse, before he could utter a single word, she proceeded to berate him with foul names and even longer "Latin" words. Some of the things she said quite possibly would have made a whore blush. Words, which she couldn't remember the correct pronunciation for at that particular moment, she would simply make it up as she went along. Then there were those other even stranger noises of some felines' throaty growl of contempt.

"Don't touch my wagon!" she screamed and brought to a close her really one-sided conversation.

Jack, totally taken aback by her actions and foul mouth, just stood quietly in disbelief. But his rest was short-lived.

"You just don't care!" she screamed into his face following a long pause, as she wanted an excuse to verbally waste him on the spot.

Jack waited patiently until he figured she had about run out of steam. "Remember what J. P. Morgan said. 'Emotion has no part in archaeological research'."

His asinine statement convinced her his mind had been damaged the night before. Still, she felt obligated to give him what for. She started again with her best and most artful use of the English language and selected four-letter words to again convince him of her sincerity.

"For crying out loud, lady," Jack finally interrupted in desperation. "Calm down. It's only a wagon!"

"And you call yourself a cop. You don't know anything about protecting evidence," Renee admonished him while hoping she had hit a blow against his cop's ego. *One good one for archaeology kind.* She mused to herself with a wicked little smile. All the while she took pleasure in knowing he couldn't respond to her other deadly silent statements under her breath.

"Then what exactly do you plan to do if it's not to pull up the damn boards to see what's below them?" Jack demanded while restraining himself from a frenzy of ripping all the boards out of the dirt.

With a smart-ass tone in her voice she tried to set him straight as to the accepted procedures of something so important. "Photograph them, make a map, number and identify them. What else do you think a fricken archaeologist would do with the goddamned things?"

"How about producing your County Excavation Permit for starters?" Jack replied with a slightly angered but very authoritarian voice. His command stopped Renee in her tracks and she flashed a leering stare right into him.

Jack took advantage of her unexpected quietness. "While your getting that, bring me your Environmental Impact Statement and Federal Papers of Authority for a dig on B.L.M. Land."

As if hit by a bolt of lightning, Renee dropped straight down onto her butt. Tears involuntarily started to boil out of her eyes and she sat whimpering with her head between her drawn-up knees.

"Look," Jack said, as he walked over next to her and squatted down, "Maybe we can work something out. After all, I am the Law in these parts."

"You prick," she whispered not quite loudly enough for him to hear.

"Don't you remember? We're supposed to be working together on this," he reminded her.

Seizing the opportunity to use her more womanly ways, Renee lightly played her fingers over his chest and slipped her arms around his neck.

Using all the puppy eyes she could imitate she sobbed out a weak and whimpering plea. "Could we?"

He pressed a little closer and spoke in a calmer tone. "I thought we had agreed on our working together. Don't you remember?"

Making his strong shoulders her lifting bar, she pulled herself up his well-defined chest and placed a very heartfelt kiss on the side of his cheek. Renee felt for certain that little maneuver would surely convince him of her sincerity. Looking closely into his expression to see if she had struck a nerve, she observed he seemed moved by her emotions, real or otherwise. He bent his head forward and looked deeply into her eyes before he kissed her on the end of her nose in what seemed to her to be a peculiar gesture.

"Look, Jack," Renee implored, playing to his sense of understanding and fair play. "We can work together. Please, just be patient with me. I want you to know this is the biggest thing I've done in my short career in amateur archaeology. It's very important to my classes at school that I do this right." Making sure he didn't have time to answer and stop her pleading, she continued, "It's very important to me that I am successful. And even without the reasons you have, I still would want you to be a very large part of it."

Not feeling as hostile now as he had been, he agreed. "Then first things first," he said as he started walking back in the direction of the Bronco. "I'll bring the vehicle over and start setting the camp together while you do your photography work."

Renee stood and walked beside him with a renewed little smile of victory plastered across her face. Almost to the point of giggles, she practically skipped along behind him as they made their way back to the vehicle. As Jack navigated his way through the bushes, she noticed he too had a wonderful smile for her.

• • •

Driving carefully, Jack took a more roundabout route from where he had parked to where the remnants of the wagon lay partially buried.

In the meantime, Renee carried her pack to the wagon in a more direct path and beat him back by at least five minutes.

Finding a somewhat clearer location, free of large rocks and thick desert brush from what Renee's camp had been, he immediately started setting up on a low rise of the ground not far from the site of the wagon.

Renee removed her Cannon camera, tripod, flash, notebook and various other markers and string from her pack. Since it was the largest piece, she decided to start her work with the wagon tongue. When that task had been completed, she worked outwardly toward the partially hidden wheel and other scattered bits and pieces of history.

Occasionally glancing in his direction, she noticed that Jack had laid his gear out first. He then carried several large rocks to a location where a larger boulder was sticking out of the ground. She kept an eye in his direction as he enthusiastically built an elaborate fire ring using the larger rock as a backstop. Using that as a starting point, he placed the smaller stones out in a small circle. Every now and then she would stand up and lift herself onto her toes to see what else he was up to. Within a relatively short period of time he would finish one project and rapidly engage himself with another. She noticed him gathering dried roots and sticks from the surrounding area and stacking them neatly beside the fire pit for easy reach later in the evening. She was gratified to note he had not gathered wagon parts for their fire.

Her perception of time started to fade with the laying out of her first grid of string covering a fifty-by-fifty-foot square area with the wagon tongue at its center. As quickly as possible she set up her tripod and started photographing several of the pieces that were visible. She used her trusty black marker pen and drew little identifying numbers and letter codes on the pieces before she recorded the item on her graph paper.

Jack stopped what he was doing and walked to her from where he had been fervently working. He lay his large hand on her shoulder and squeezed gently before he asked if he could take her gear to the shelter. Her eyes scanned their way up from his crotch to his face from her kneeling position. Happy that she was to be protected by such a good-looking man, she nodded her head that whatever he wanted just tickled her plumb to death. Seizing the opportunity, Renee didn't hesitate in telling Jack with great pride what she had done up to that point. She found herself asking him what he thought of the work she had already accomplished.

Much to her surprise, Jack chuckled out his sentiments. "Just like a detective—always wanting praise."

Taking only a moment to look over her progress, he picked up her backpack and returned to the camp without even uttering another single kind word of encouragement. While he was walking away, Renee noticed he had changed his pants to Levi's and his shirt to a clean and less ragged looking one. She guessed she had been too engrossed in her work to have seen him change his clothes or spruce himself up.

Renee figured it was maybe some six minutes later when she heard him calling out her name and waving for her to return to the camp. Her first thought was he wanted her approval for a job well done.

"Fat chance," she cried out loudly enough to show her defiance. *But then again, maybe I should at least try to please the prick a little,* she thought.

Renee covered her camera with her handkerchief in an attempt to keep dust off the expensive lens. Taking her time, she made her way to the camp and prepared to give him a well deserved "what for?" to his interruption of her meticulous work. With every step she took toward him, the strong odor of frying bacon permeated the air and burrowed deeply into her olfactory sensors.

Being downwind at times can make all the difference. Walking faster with less thought of her discovery and work, Renee's stomach sent a message to her brain that brought forth an over abundance of saliva. Copious drops of spittle started to build and began forcing out of the corner of her mouth. *Food— I haven't eaten since last night and I'm famished.*

A quick check of her watch revealed it was almost one thirty and much later than she had thought it should have been. With her already raised shirtsleeve, she took advantage of the material to sop up the tiny droplets of saliva from the edge of her lips.

Somewhat hidden from view by the large desert brush, her first observation other than the Bronco, was the top of her little dome tent. Next was the well-combed hair on top of Jack's head as he knelt by a little column of whirling gray-white smoke. When she was about twenty feet from him, he held up a large and deep cast-iron skillet. At about the same time he lifted the fry pan he was sticking a spatula into its depths and lifted a mouth-watering bunch of semi-crisp bacon strips.

With her mouth salivating more fiercely than just a few moments earlier, she tried to spit out her gratitude. "Wonderful!" she exclaimed with much more appreciation for his now extraordinary efforts to make her feel at home in his desert. He was obviously trying to make amends for his obstinate behavior earlier at the wagon. She took curious note of a small cast-iron Dutch oven that was sitting in the coals alongside a much appreciated coffeepot.

"Fabulous," she told him with a somewhat snide tone. "I had no idea you were such a considerate person."

Showing his pride, Jack had a great smile smeared all over his face. He was almost bubbling all over himself as he removed the heavy lid off the great pot and revealed a thick layer of golden brown biscuits. Picking up a plate and a ladle, he scooped up a larger-than-she-could-ever-eat portion of hot biscuits and stew. Next he crossed the side of the plate with several strips of the now crispy and mouth-watering pork strips. Handing her the plate, he proceeded to pour an almost carbon-black cup of coffee and asked if she took it that way.

Renee took a hard look at Jack and decided he wasn't all that bad and actually looked really distinctive in his fresh change of clothes and new attitude.

"Even without the bacon you look good enough to eat," she said in a more than semi-serious voice before she realized that was not what she had meant to convey.

She wasn't really surprised when he didn't utter a single word. Instead he just used the spatula to point toward the Bronco and told her to go over next to it and eat. To her even greater surprise, she saw a dark green canvas had been attached to the side of the truck with aluminum poles holding up the outer edges. Under the canopy he had set up a lawn chair and small folding table for her. Never would she have expected such luxury based on what she had brought from San Francisco. Jack prepared his plate and then his coffee with cream and sugar. Balancing the whole thing in one hand, he casually strolled over to join her under the awning.

With Renee waiting for him and her first bite, he sat down on a large metal trunk and said, "I'll bet this is much better than that soup you eat on your camping trips."

Renee's eyes narrowed momentarily. Trying to be nice to her benefactor didn't come as easy as she expected, "It couldn't be any other way. Where did you learn to cook like this?" she smiled showing a mouth full of pearl-white teeth before allowing her lips to close more naturally.

As she was tasting the wonderful flavor of his stew, Jack looked back to her. "Reservation. One of the good things you White Folks gave the Indians—canned stew."

Not wishing to hurt his feelings, she continued gorging herself on every tasty morsel that was on the tin plate. This was the kind of meal Renee wouldn't have considered eating at any other time. There was no doubt it was spilling over with salts and animal fats. The kind of crap that overloaded the system and came from a can liberally spiced with preservatives.

Renee spoke very little while eating. She hoped Jack would start the conversation and give her the opportunity to question him with a little more detail about his past and why he was there. But he didn't say a single word and remained silent as a field mouse as he looked off to the distant mountains. Renee sighed and sat back in her chair to enjoy the coffee and to watch Jack watch the mountains.

"You're not an easy person to understand," she said breaking her own tension and hoping to start him talking.

"Not really," he answered her statement and immediately went silent again, to her disbelief.

Without much thinking about his apparent wishes to maintain his secrecy, she prodded her way to the next question. "Have you been truthful as to why you're out here? Maybe there's a lot more than you've told me about wagons?"

Renee started searching through her shirt pockets for a cigarette. As with the many other times she had reached for one, she momentarily forgot she was trying to quit the habit and tugged unhappily at her pocket. Even so, the psychological need was almost overwhelming after so many things happening in one day. She picked up a small stick, slipped it between her lips and sucked in its bitter flavor.

"I've told you everything I know," he replied while watching her again squeeze the pockets over her breasts and gnaw on the twig sticking out the side of her face with pursed lips.

"You're sure?"

"Yup," he answered, still watching her fingers race around from pocket to pocket and back again.

Again she persisted in digging for an answer. Pointedly she questioned him more directly, trying to determine if he had come to the valley to find something of greater importance, either now or in the past.

"Like you. To find these old wagons."

"You're not an archaeologist on the side are you?"

Jack said nothing. He stood, gathered the plates and cups and stacked them neatly along side where he had been sitting.

"Show me what to do to help."

Taking Renee by the hand, he gently pulled her to her feet and started toward the wagons.

Expecting to be released from his grasp, Renee was dumbfounded by his inconsistent actions. He had not let go of her hand as she thought he would and squeezed his grip tighter when she tried to pull her fingers free of his. Walking with her just slightly behind him because of the narrowness of the trail, he seemed to select the longest route through the bush. She found his grip on her hand was very pleasant, really very warm and comforting. When they approached the grid of string she had laid out over the wagon, she gave Jack's hand a small squeeze and tugged her fingers away. She thought she felt a shudder rush through him when her nails scratched a labored trail across his palm as their hands slipped one from the another.

Stepping high over the border of strings toward the wagon tongue, she told Jack he could carefully remove it. He lifted the rickety old piece from the ringed end and gingerly guided it through the maze. While Jack carried the piece out of the grid some distance to a clearing somewhat free of brush and large rocks, Renee set herself to work. She started brushing off a board that was slightly protruding from the gravel.

By the time Jack had returned, only a few more inches had come to her view. As he lifted the board when she requested, she set herself to scraping dirt off that board and several others attached to and adjacent to it. Jack lifted the wood a few inches higher. She was delighted to see he was now holding up most of an intact wagon bed. The remaining dirt and small rocks tumbled down its length finally bringing it into full light of day and Jack lowered it back down. With Jack backing away, she photographed this find and marked the boards for identification in her plan book.

"From the looks of it, you hit pay dirt," he told her with a wink and a smile.

The two of them again lifted the wood from the front end after moving the string grid out of the way. Although the boards were old and extremely dry, they did not splinter and break as she had thought they would. Together, they managed to lift the discovery about a foot before the unmistakable sounds of cracking wood erupted. Renee instantly stopped the upward strain she was placing on it. Acting on his own, Jack pulled with even greater force until he reached a point the bed seemed to become heavier. The dirt started to turn up and the burden tore away from whatever the obstruction was that held it. Half of a broken wooden wheel became visible on his side with a hundred years of desert dirt dropping away.

Resuming her assistance, they swung the end of the wagon bed toward Jack's side for only a few feet before Renee dropped her corner and jumped back in horror. The sudden change of weight to Jack threw him off balance. He fell sideways and mostly backwards to the ground with the majority of the weight of the wagon bed's remains landing firmly on top of his left leg and foot.

Jack looked up with a painfully questioning expression before he saw the scene the wagon had covered. Renee was frozen in time with her eyes wide, mouth open, and all the blood in her face had drained. Unexpectedly, the ghastly remains of a long dead human being was revealed to them. Jack, not completely alarmed at the grisly discovery, asked her to help move the boards from his leg. Transfixed, she could not shake away from this image of death. As if she was held by ancient forces, Jack's words did not pass the poor

man partially embedded in the ground and into her ears. To
Jack's amazement she was awe struck and immobilized by
terror, at least until she felt the sting of something striking
her left side. Jumping with the impact of a small stone, she
looked at Jack in disbelief as he was about to hurtle another
and larger stone at her.

"Please!" he pleaded, "That guy's long gone and I'm not.
Why don't you help me instead of standing around acting
silly?"

As quickly as she could Renee hurried to him but didn't
reply to his stupid comment. With all her might she heaved
and lifted the heavy wood a few inches as Jack pulled himself
from beneath the wagon bed. Standing with a hop onto his best
leg, he commenced walking back and forth in small circles
favoring what Renee thought could be a severe injury. She
rushed around with him to give some kind of comfort. He
finally stopped long enough for her to kneel before him. She
lifted his pant leg and found a large bump and a tender red
scrape.

"You're OK! The skin's not broken." she said as she ran
her fingers up and down his shin. "No blood!"

"Wanna bet?" he replied as he pushed her hand aside and
replaced hers with his. He ran his fingers over his shin, feeling
the bruise to his bone. Jack let out a small yelp when he
pressed against the most tender spot.

Renee felt that as a big kid he should have recovered
from his smarting leg and began to nudge and push him over to
the bones and decayed clothes of the dead man. Each was lost
in their own thoughts to this sudden change in discovery and
the reality of the past.

"My first dead person," Renee exclaimed following a
hard swallow. "Why didn't they bury him?"

Jack, taking in the way the skeleton was lying, replied
with a much more analytical approach, "Whoever killed him,
did—they covered him up with the wagon. Maybe they collapsed the wheels on him to keep animals away. Maybe to kill
him better. Who knows? Look!" he said as he pointed over to

the wheel with a chunk of axle still attached to it, "Look at the ax marks where it finally broke."

"How'd you see that?"

"Trained investigator," he replied without breaking his expression and still looking at the bones.

Returning her gaze to the skeleton following a brief look at Jack, Renee asked with a renewed feeling of irritation, "Why do you think he was murdered?"

Jack knelt down closer to the skull and pointed to the shattered cranial cap specifically where the back of the head should have been.

To her astonishment he lifted the skull slightly and commented, "Just as I suspected." He pointed to a large round hole between the eyes.

Renee watched in disgust he stuck his little finger into the hole and wiggled the first knuckle back and forth.

"That's sick! Put it back." She demanded he return the head to its prior resting place and told him they shouldn't go any further with their search. "Maybe we should find an anthropologist—an authority on old bones?"

"No," Jack replied while pushing his fingers through the soft dirt where the man's nose had once rested. "All they'll do is box him up and look at him later. Besides, this is your project. You really should continue."

Renee remained silent and argued with herself over the possibilities. Reveling in the idea of doing all the preliminary investigative work herself, she suddenly heard herself agreeing with him. Taking her camera from its tripod, she photographed the body from head to toe. When she had completed her task, Jack instructed Renee to fetch her notebook. He said he would tell her what to write while he uncovered the remains one piece at a time.

Putting the camera down with her other stuff, she returned to Jack as he requested. Renee sat close along side him and the remains to watch and learn his evidence-gathering techniques. Tablet in hand, she readied herself to make the appropriate notes he would dictate.

"Did you say something?" Renee asked as she was making herself more comfortable by pulling a stone from under her leg.

"No," Jack replied as he brushed some dirt away from the lower end of the skeleton.

"It sounded like you did."

"No. It wasn't me," he again advised her. "Maybe this guy said something," he said with a strange combination of joking and seriousness.

Renee looked at the bones and shook her head from side to side. "That's weird. I could have sworn you—never mind."

Jack gently lifted one of the crumbling pant legs. Examining it closely, he showed her a portion of the fabric. A lighter material had been hand sewn down the outer seam of the leg.

"The pants of a soldier," Jack said, releasing the material and unintentionally letting the leg drop to the dirt.

Further down the leg he lifted a weathered and brittle piece of twisted leather nearer the bottom of the cuff. Many small bones fell out as he turned the moccasin upside down.

"A moccasin?"

"An Indian," he said with as much surprise as Renee, "Maybe even an Indian scout."

"Maybe a soldier in moccasins?" she injected, trying to be helpful.

Reaching back to the area around the skull, Jack searched around, sifting the dirt through his fingers until he found a few remaining threads of hair. Very long hair.

"No," Jack affirmed to himself as much as to her. "He was Indian."

"How can you be certain? In those days a lot of men wore their hair long."

As she was talking he continued to probe into the dusty material near the pelvic area. From the darker colored dirt he removed a small chunk of lighter colored cotton linen. Holding the cloth higher, he looked closer at the weave of the material.

Matter-of-factly he stated, "A loincloth!"

Where Jack had scraped the ground while looking for the strands of hair he uncovered a strange-looking piece of curved metal. After her brushed away more earth with his fingers, the breech of a very old rifle came to view. Persistently he scraped away more dirt along its length and discovered a half dozen spent brass cartridges.

Picking one up he said, "Military issue. The caliber is 44-70." Pointing to the hammer, Jack added, "Its an old Sharps rifle. He must have been killed just after he fired his last shot."

Turning the skull closer to the original position, he lowered his head nearer to the right eye socket and looked down the rusted barrel of the old rifle. "Whoever he was shooting at was somewhere over there."

He pointed off to a large boulder some hundred feet or less away.

Jack rose, dusted himself off and directed her to follow him. Quickly they made their way in the general direction Jack had indicated.

"Why are you singing that song?" she asked, wondering why he was in such a good mood amid such gruesome work.

"I'm not singing anything," Jack insisted as he glanced back over his shoulder at her.

"Oh!" Renee replied more than a little confused as to why he wanted to play games with her.

When they reached the large boulder and looked around to the opposite side, several bone fragments were lying bleached and cracked in the noon day sun. Renee didn't see anything so ominous as a skull or hand bones or whatever, only scattered pieces of vertebra, ribs and a long bone of possibly a forearm. A few of the bone chips were lying under the sagebrush immediately surrounding the area.

"Whoever this was, he wasn't alone," Jack said as he stood and looked over the scene then back in the direction of the original discovery.

"And how do you know that?" Renee asked with amazement as to how he had drawn his conclusion so easily.

"It's elementary, my dear Watson," Jack replied with some smugness. "If this guy killed the Indian and the Indian killed him, then someone must have been around to chop the wagon down on the Indian—see?"

"Why would they kill one another?"

"Who knows? I would guess the Indian must have really been fighting for his life when he caught this one."

"Yeah, a losing fight. So tell me, why didn't they bury him too?"

"Don't know! Your guess is as good as mine." Jack started to walk back to the wagon. "Whatever the reason why the fight took place, I believe the answer will be found somewhere over there."

Jack went directly to the Bronco and took a dark blue nylon bag from the rear compartment.

Looking at how clean his things were she murmured to herself, *Probably the bag once held his sleeping bag or some camping equipment.* They returned to the long sleeping Indian scout, and Jack performed what seemed to be a ceremony of some sort. He slowly and deliberately removed the bones of the man one at a time, placing each one gently in the bag in the same cautious manner as it had been lifted from its resting-place. Bits and pieces of what once was clothing were added to the bag in the most deliberate manner. He seemed to pause for the briefest of seconds with each deposit. Jack's grisly work took an extraordinarily long time for him to complete. Once he had made sure there was nothing of the man left in the ground, he zipped closed what now served as the Indian's new resting place and then stood. Renee followed him to the Bronco and watched as he gently lowered the container inside. Wanting to be more helpful, she asked Jack for a container that would hold the remains of the fellow they had found behind the boulder.

"No!" he exclaimed with a touch of "how come" in his voice. "Let him be—he's not worth our effort."

Not knowing just what to say, she watched Jack gather her camera and some other stuff and carry them off to the Bronco. Once he had deposited her equipment and the dirty dishes in the vehicle, he proceeded to untie his lean-to from the side of the Bronco. Jack opened the passenger door and, in an almost demanding voice, told Renee to get in. She knew now was not the time to give cause for an argument with him and slid meekly into the seat as he requested. She felt certain his attitude would shortly change to the better as he thought about what had happened.

As he was starting the vehicle, Renee's curiosity got the better of her. "Where are we going now?"

"To wash," he said in a somewhat pained voice. "To wash the dishes." And he started to drive off.

While they were bouncing across the desert floor, Jack related to her that he wanted to keep the bones and take them to the reservation for a proper burial.

Failing to see any ease of identification without elaborate scientific tests, Renee questioned him as to how he knew what reservation, let alone what tribe the Indian would have come from.

"I don't. But some of the old folks there might be able to guess from the designs on the moccasins and stuff. One of the marks is similar to some I saw several years ago. The Clan of Little Snake."

"Are these the wagons you were looking for?"

"I'm not sure of that, either. I won't really know unless I can find whatever it is I'm supposed to be looking for. In all honesty, I'm not exactly sure what that is. God! I hope I'll know when I see it."

Figuring Jack's continued depressed mood was brought on by the finding of the bones of his ancestors, she decided not to press for any more about the Indian or anything else. At least, that is, not until he'd had an attitude adjustment.

They bounced and swerved over the desert bushes, trying to miss the numerous rocks and boulders that blocked their path every time and again. Jack, in his attempt to avoid the subjects of the wagon or the Indian, began pointing out the various areas he thought would be of interest to Renee.

Occasionally, during their somewhat laborious trip, Renee would start to unconsciously hum a tune softly to herself.

"What's that you're singing?" Jack asked not really being able to hear her clearly over the clank and clatter of the Bronco.

"The march melody General Custer adopted for the Seventh Calvary when he took command."

"You learned that in school, I'd wager?"

"I'm not really sure how I learned it," Renee answered while questioning her own newly acquired abilities. "I just did!"

Jack gave her a silent and strange look before he continued giving her his two-bit tour of the valley.

Interested or not, she felt this was a good time to start any kind of small talk to take his mind from the dead man that seemed to bother him so much.

Taking a different route to the hot spring than the one they had taken before caused the trip to take the better part of an hour. Once they had arrived, Jack parked the Bronco a few yards from the inviting waters and shut off the motor. Not making any movement to get out of the vehicle, Jack just sat looking out through the windshield.

"Is something wrong?" Renee questioned him without making a move to get out herself.

"Kind of," Jack replied without looking in her direction. "As I said this morning, you remind me of my wife. Because of that and the closeness we have already shared here this morning and in your sleeping bag, I'm very mixed about being alone with you. Dumb, huh?"

My God! Renee thought, *What a tender, gentle and caring thought!*

"Listen. We're here for a cause. You for your own reasons, me for mine."

"I know, but—"

"Since we have been placed here through our own needs, let's look upon our meeting as some sort of divine purpose."

"But, I don't feel it necessary to embarrass you, let alone my own self. Hell, we don't even know one another."

"Jack," Renee tried to say in her most coy, but assertive voice. "We've already passed the formal introduction stage, don't you think? So let's just enjoy the water and figure out what's next."

Whether she had talked him into it or he had just given up on his own uneasiness, she wasn't sure. Jack shoved open his door and slipped effortlessly out of the Bronco and made his way to stand by the edge of the pool and blankly look in. For a short person, slipping out of a four-wheel drive is considerably less graceful. With a plop, plop, her feet landed on the hard dirt, and she walked around to the side of the submerged ledge.

With as much fortitude as Jack could conjure up he proceeded to undress. Folding each garment neatly as he removed it, he stacked his clothes on a large and somewhat flat rock near the pool, followed by his boots, socks and shirt. He started to unbutton his jeans but stopped on about the third button from the top. Looking up to Renee, his face reddened and sank as if he was forced to again lower his eyes. He asked in a slight mumble if she was going to let him make a spectacle of himself alone.

"Not at all," Renee replied. Then for a reason she couldn't explain, she found herself apologizing. "I'm very sorry, I was just taking in a very honest and profound man." Looking him straight in the eyes she started to disrobe with the same care as he had.

Renee tried her best to act as she thought he probably wished her to. In her own mind, no matter how hard she tried to undress, she thought herself as being too sexy in such a simple endeavor. She knew this had to be the hardest time in her life to do such a simple act of getting naked.

Renee was surprised that Jack made no attempt to cover himself after he slipped his trousers off his legs. He just stood before her holding his pants in one hand and the other hand hanging motionless to his side. Not saying anything, she continued to undress until she was completely nude before him.

Now that wasn't so bad, was it? Renee consoled herself as she stepped onto the sunken ledge and slowly lowered herself into the warm water. So caught up in this somehow erotic scene she hissed out a moan of pleasure as the water almost overwhelmed her senses. She could see that any grown woman would immediately recognize that he had become involuntarily excited by her beauty. She almost found herself wishing aloud that he would not be ashamed of something so natural.

Somewhat carefully, she positioned herself on a reasonably smooth boulder, Jack finally spoke while he walked around the pool's edge and started to step in not far from her.

"We can't stay long, night's coming."

"It's OK. I understand." Renee smiled.

Once he had completely slipped into the warm waters, he took in a very long and deep breath before he expelled his air in words that took her by complete surprise. "You cut a fine figure of a woman—if it were not for the situation, at another time..." he stopped as if editing what he was really wanted to say. He waited a moment to continue. "I wish I could let you know how beautiful you really are."

Renee found there was nothing to do but blush. She didn't know if it was the place, Jack or the things that had happened through the day and night before that had hit her so hard. His oh so simple and broken comment engulfed her with more passion than she had ever encountered.

Renee's head moved up and down slowly as she spoke to herself. *Never in my life, has anyone I've known made me feel so—so—so womanly. If I say anything, no matter what, I'm sure I will destroy this moment.*

While they looked deeply into one another's eyes over that short distance between them, many pleasant thoughts filled her mind. Nothing could describe the sensation that had devoured her very being.

Beneath the water, Jack's right hand moved across the back of her left hand and gently encircled her soft flesh. He closed his hand ever so naturally around hers and squeezed. Involuntarily, a passion-filled moan escaped her lips. They sat silently with fingers entwined and caressing without the slightest of movement. With the coming of the cooler air of twilight they languished in the pool's warmth. Desperately, Renee wished this moment would never find its end.

How? She demanded of herself, *How can so much be said with so few words?*

Renee leaned closer to Jack and closed her eyes. She was pleased he did not turn or try to move away. It seemed as if only minutes had dwindled past, when in reality, almost an hour had spent itself, and he said it was time to leave. With a single step he was out of the tub. He tugged on his tall black cowboy boots and walked to the rear of the Bronco. Returning with an old but clean beach towel, he wrapped it warmly around her as she stood. Renee was in the process of patting herself dry while he fetched the dirty dishes along with a sponge and soap. Jack started vigorously scrubbing the congealed delights from the surfaces and set them aside building a clean stack.

I just can't be that emotional a person. Renee scolded herself as she realized her feeling would be given away as her tear ducts spasmed out small droplets of fluid. Her eyes sparkled with a fulfilling luster of her happiness.

This absurd sight of a naked man on his knees with only boots on washing dishes was more than she could take. Biting her lip, she cried the tiniest of tears from its reservoir in celebration of her new friendship.

4

"Intruder"

Although it had turned from dusk to dark of night by the time they had reached camp, Renee thought all was perfect for a more than pleasant stay in this secluded wilderness.

Jack pulled the Bronco to a stop near the same location where it had been previously parked. Then suddenly and without warning he grabbed her by the neck and shoved her face toward the floorboard. Whispering, he admonished her to stay low and remain quiet. He withdrew his revolver from the holster where it was lying on the seat between them. Tripping the release, he watched the spindle fall to the side. He double-checked the cylinders for a full complement and then closed it silently. He dropped out of the driver's side into the darkness with the sleekness of a hunting cat.

Holding her breath, Renee was barely able hear his footsteps in the gravel as he started a slow walk around in the camp. From those muffled sounds she could only imagine him walking silently checking for the tell-tale signs of some unknown intruder. In her mind's eye she could see him every now and then stop to look out into the darkness or listen for a faint sound foreign to what should be.

Renee was baffled by what was taking place. She wished she had a clue as to why things were happening as they were. Then again, she wasn't even sure she would do the right thing if she did know. Whatever the motivation, it was enough for her personal Deputy to use more caution than she thought she would have in similar circumstances.

Within a few moments he returned to the Bronco and told her it was all right to get out and look.

"Someone trashed the camp!" he said to her while pointing to overturned boxes and scattered equipment when she raised her head over the ledge of the Bronco's door.

He seemed to want her to see her tent. Although still erect, it had been viciously slashed many times from top to bottom. The contents in her backpack had been emptied out into the fire pit as if in some sort of frenzied attempt to hurt her. Fortunately, the coals of the fire from lunch had burned themselves out and there was no real damage to her stuff. Most of her belongings were just a little blackened and soiled from the ashes.

"Why would anyone want to do this?" Renee demanded of Jack as she drew closer to him and near the opposite side of the Bronco.

"Don't know. We should probably find out who did this first. Maybe then finding out why would be a much easier problem to solve."

Jack moved to the rear of the Bronco and returned with a large flashlight. He toured through the camp pointing the brilliant white beam of light in several different directions while Renee watched from where she was.

She looked closely as Jack stopped momentarily, took note of the ground and then moved on. He did this same maneuver many times before he worked his way back to where she was now squatting.

Without giving her a chance to ask, Jack in an attempt to calm her nerves, said matter-of-factly, "Only one person was here."

"How do you know?" she questioned him, hoping she wasn't showing as much fear as she felt.

"Footprints," was the one-word reply that didn't seem to calm her expectations of someone else's misdirected violence.

Stooping down just a few feet from her, he directed his flashlight and her attention to one of several shoeprints in the dust. Jack aimed the flashlight to cast a shadow across the print obliquely. Using a long narrow stick, he pointed out the various characteristics of the design of the intruder's sole.

"Just like yours. A Vibrum sole walking boot."

Jack wrapped his hand around her ankle and lifted her foot to look at the bottom of the boot, Renee was surprised to see an almost identical tread design as the one in the dust. Moving the stick back and forth from the ground to her foot, he pointed out the unbelievable similarities in the design but not size.

"Much larger than yours," he added as he used the length of the stick to measure the print on the ground against the bottom of Renee's boot. "Maybe five foot eleven, maybe ten," he added.

Jack told Renee to gather her things together and arrange them nearer the lean-to.

Taking the flashlight from him, she immediately started with her backpack.

Jack returned to the Bronco and drove closer to the exact location where it had been before they had left for the hot springs.

"There," he said after he had re-established the lean-to and pulled all the ropes snug one more time.

They both worked posthaste to restore the camp to a functional and secure area.

"What about my tent?" Renee asked.

It seemed the only useful parts that were left were its poles and stakes.

"Leave it up for now—Yeah, just leave it where it is. It will still give you at least some protection from the cold night air."

Looking at him in disbelief, Renee responded quickly and harshly, "Are you nuts? Not on your life am I going to sleep by myself tonight!" she quickly moved her sleeping bag to the shelter Jack had re-erected.

"Where are you sleeping?" she demanded.

Jack pointed almost straight down briefly and then motioned to another place under the lean-to.

Renee figured this probably seemed a cozy little spot to him as he pointed a short distance away and said, "Put yours over there."

Renee promptly walked up to where he first pointed and deposited her bag next to his.

"There." She pointed. "Right there. If I'm going to get any sleep at all, you won't deny me this."

"OK, OK!" Jack repeated in a halfhearted attempt to reassure her. "There isn't anyone out here now that is going to bother you. Believe me."

"I suppose your Indian training or whatever will guarantee that!"

Instantly, Renee regretted what she had said. She realized it was just too racist spoken to the wrong person. There seemed nothing else to do but cowl and cringe with a smile.

Jack gave her one of those looks that's not easily interpreted. He picked up the flashlight and gave her a book of matches. "Go build a fire." Before he walked off into the darkness, he lit a double mantled lantern and hung it under the lean-to.

Without saying a word, Renee watched the beam from his flashlight bounce back and forth around the outlying perimeter of the campsite and into the bushes beyond that. As she tried to convince herself she was in really good hands, she did her best to light the fire and watch Jack at the same time. She didn't wish to make matters worse than they already were and fought off nagging questions about "why?" rather than "who?". Renee guessed it would probably be better to know their camp was torn apart by someone they could identify. With all this becoming more complicated with what seemed like every passing hour, what else could happen on an archaeological dig?

Now all those other unanswered questions filled her head. *Why isn't Jack more upset? Why is he taking the intrusion in stride like it's an everyday occurrence? Can that son-of-a-bitch be that callused?* She wondered, not realizing that her anger was taking over from her fear. *What a change in personality since he left the hot pool.*

The farther out Jack searched the area, the more difficult it had become for her to see the faint glow of his light through the bushes. With a trembling hand she finally managed to get the pile of twigs and sticks in the fire pit to ignite. When she again looked up for Jack's tell-tale light beam she became even more worried upon discovering it was not to be seen. Feeling the fear of losing Jack to the darkness and the intruder, Renee backed up while she continued to strain her vision. She allowed her eyes to search farther and farther out from the camp as she backed herself into the Bronco. Crouching down almost involuntarily, she found herself tucked into a small ball with her arms wrapped around her knees. It seemed as if an eternity had passed with not a single sound breaking the deadly silence of this now so eerie place.

The fire she had started leaped and began to gain momentum. Its flickering light caused the shadows in the camp to dance back and forth to an unearthly rhythm. Weird sights that hadn't existed seconds ago, like a snake, crept and twisted deep into the inner recesses of her thoughts. Everything in the confines of the camp was highlighted by the purity of those rising flames. Her eyes darted back and forth with each ghostly trick her mind's eye imagined. As a radar antennae scans the sky. Renee would not allow her eyes to settle on any one location too long in fear she would miss a movement elsewhere. That is to say, not until she caught a glimpse of the human form standing just to the rear of the Bronco. Too fearful to scream, she rolled back from her squatting position and plopped heavily to the ground. Out of control and on her butt in terror, her open fingers shielded her face from a blow she knew was inevitable. As abruptly as it had appeared the dark form moved out of the shadow and toward her to the light of the lantern.

"It's me!"

Jack's words were no longer foreign to Renee; she instantly recognized his voice and then his attitude.

"Fuck," she growled.

She began to relax as he moved still closer to the lantern and spoke, "You do that a lot, don't you?"

"You're a sneaky bastard! The least you could do is make a sound or something to let a body know you're there!"

Looking down at her, he replied to her comment with a somewhat aggravated look, "Sure, and scare you even worse than you have already done to yourself?"

Renee felt she would be really hard pressed on how to answer that one.

"Did you find anyone?" she questioned him as she carefully avoided his question.

"Only the same tracks like the ones I had shown you. They returned from the direction they came. It looks to me like whoever it was has come from your old camp."

"What do we do now?" Renee asked, hoping he had a better answer than his last one.

"Fix dinner—coffee—relax—maybe even sleep," he said in broken sentences.

She thought it was kind of like he was thinking about what order to put his things in. However, what he said didn't give her the reassuring answers she was searching for.

Jack went to the rear of the Bronco and opened the tailgate to take out a great green cold chest. One of those fifty-four-quart ones she had seen in the sporting goods store not far from her apartment. He carried the box over to the fire and set it down beside her. Without saying another word, he smiled and returned to the Bronco for more stuff. It was like he was in a hurry or something as he suddenly returned with a box full of clean dishes, pots and pans and associated cooking utensils.

"Here. If you need anything else, just say so. I'll fix up our bunks and stuff."

"Jack," she girlishly whined. "I'll make dinner if I can sleep with you tonight."

Jack looked quite sternly in her direction and replied, "You don't cook, you don't eat. We'll discuss our sleeping arrangements later."

He smiled his big smile and winked.

She was pleased that the firelight on his face highlighted his very handsome features which in turn soothed and reassured some very ragged nerves. Without any more thought to the meal, she sat and fondly stared at him, taking in all his devastating looks.

"Food." He hesitated and then ordered her again. "Make food." His redundancy momentarily broke her trance.

Jack proceeded to toss rocks and sticks from under the lean-to as if nothing in the world was of any greater importance.

Renee fell back into her lustful trance and tried to watch his every movement while fulfilling his requests. She felt her heart warm as her eyes caught him laying out a tarp large enough for the both of them to be on. In an attempt to not make a big thing of this she returned to her duties and cast an occasional glance in his direction. Out of the corner of her eye she watched him spread both sleeping bags side by side on the canvas. Renee felt her sexual excitement ignite, when, by the flames of the fire and the light of the lantern, he intentionally pulled the zippered edges of the bags together over their entire length. There was no doubt that this was his unspoken invitation for her to have not only the security she needed, but also the closeness she longed for with him.

A sudden cringe enveloped her as she finally twisted the latch and opened the heavy cold box. Talking in a louder voice since Jack was a number of feet behind her, she praised, "You really know how to camp don't you!"

Turning back to what she was doing, the first thing she saw on the top was a corked bottle of chilled red wine resting on a large block of ice.

"Cabernet Sauvignon?"

Renee wrapped her fingers around the long sleek neck and raised it slightly to discover the makings for hamburgers with all the trimmings.

Kind of like a casual starlight dinner in Golden Gate Park. Then again there's no comparison at all when you get right down to it. Not to mention the company I'd be with. Fantasizing about the possibilities of that, she started the preparation of their meal.

Our very first special meal, she told everyone—yet no one.

• • •

Jack stood under the canvas of the lean-to looking out over the desert. Whether or not he was looking for anything specific, he didn't allude to it—he seemed to be just staring into the blackness.

"Can you smell it?" His unexpected questioned suddenly rattled her from some pretty neat thoughts of her own.

"Smell what?" Renee replied, wondering if he had sensed a distant fire or if some night creature had invaded the area.

"The air. The wonderful smells of the desert."

She couldn't understand how he could smell anything.

"I know I can't smell anything after being as cold as I was last night," she told him as she opened a can of ranch beans.

Renee was finding it difficult to contain the near constant sniffles of an oncoming cold.

"You know, those smells have remained the same for a million years. That's the fragrance of real freedom."

"I'm sorry? I don't understand," she told him as she half turned from the fire to face him.

Although Renee could not see the minute features of his expression, she could feel his need not to be boxed in or chained to anything that did not suit his world.

"Jack, you really do love the desert, don't you?"

"It's not just the desert. It's the mother, the center of being, the Earth herself." Jack paused for a long second before he spoke again. "Where you from?" he asked.

"San Francisco. Have you ever been there?"

"No," he replied while taking a second to look at her in return. "I've seen pictures of the bridge when I was stationed near there for a few days at Fort Ord."

"Then you were in the Army or something?"

"A long time ago, at the end of the White Man's War."

"Why in the world would you say the White Man's War? Were you sent to Vietnam?"

"Nah! I enlisted just after it ended. Went into the Military Police. I figured the training would come in handy when I was discharged."

Gathering the plates together, Renee placed a large meaty hamburger on the side of one of them. She then served up some hot ranch beans along with a slice of onion and the best and thickest slice of tomato. After pouring a steaming cup of coffee, she took the liberty to add a spoon of sugar and a dash of milk from a small cardboard carton.

"Just as you like it," she said as she stood and proceeded to carry the lot to where he was sitting cross-legged on his bedroll. When she passed the food to him she saw his eyes twinkle by the light of the fire in the most marvelous way.

Politely he thanked her and lifted his fork from the edge of the plate.

He took a small portion of the beans and drew them into his mouth and moaned.

"Wonderful! You're all the camp cook a man could ever want!"

How can you do this to me? She asked herself. *Almost everything he says or does seems to find its way into my heart. I just can't understand why I am so taken by someone I've just met! This has never happened before!* Renee tried to argue herself into believing this was something truly special.

After she had prepared her own meal, she sat down a close arm's reach from him. She ate slowly, waiting for Jack to speak and to listen to the sounds of a beautiful night. Even though she didn't understand exactly what he meant about freedom, she did agree about the smells permeating the air. Although muted, a wonderful sweet smell at last found its way into her nose. At least that small portion of the desert night she was able to smell. She wondered to herself if maybe she wasn't confusing the fragrance of something new and completely devoid of the greasy smells of the city that she had enjoyed in the past.

"Tell me more about the wagons you're looking for," Jack said in a subdued tone.

"Well," she started, "sometime back, about six months ago, I discovered a diary in a chest my professor brought to me from the university. He told me it had been stashed away in the back of the university library storeroom for many years. I don't know if I told you or not, but I'm into Early American Cultures at school in my spare time." Jack nodded "Yes" to her question even though he didn't recall anything about that.

"Anyway, I read the diary and found a half dozen pages referring to the wagon we found. The writer said the pioneers were on their way to California when they ran short of water here in this valley." In an attempt to qualify her statement, she added, "I think their guide had gotten them lost while hunting for one of the primary passes through the Sierras. The best guess I can make is they were hunting for what had become known as Donner Pass. With the party facing lack of water, the Wagon Master decided to abandon two of the wagons and try to make it over to the next valley with the third."

"What happened then?"

"According to the story, a vicious argument broke out between the teamsters over taking what extra livestock was left with them. I really expected to find only the wagons and the bones of some put down horses. Not that poor devil we found under it."

Renee purposely avoided speaking of the other dead man since Jack didn't want him gathered up for a proper burial.

Setting his plate and cup aside, Jack stood, undressed himself and slid into his bedroll.

Renee found it interesting that he felt no need for undershorts and apparently preferred to sleep in the buff.

Looking towards her, he told her she should get into the warmth of her own bag since the night air was becoming too chilly to sit out.

As usually happened when she was talking about hunting artifacts, she had not taken note of the coolness. Collecting Jack's plate, cup and utensils, she carried his and hers to the fire pit. There she scraped the remaining food scraps off the plates into the fire and stacked them neatly to the side. In the few short moments it took her to accomplish this task and shut down the lantern, she discovered he had already closed his eyes and had fallen to sleep. Quietly, Renee undressed and slipped into a clean T-shirt.

As silently as possible so as not to disturb him, she slid into her own bedroll and scooted closer to him. Although Renee could see only the outline of his face from the flickering light of the fire, she lay very still watching him intently. She couldn't help but wonder when the adventure with this man would find its end. Even more weighed heavily on her mind when she tried to guess whether or not she would see him again when all this was over.

"You must be exhausted," she spoke to him in little more than a whisper.

Pushing herself slightly out of her bag and leaning forward, her lips tenderly pressed against his cheek and withdrew. Through the unzipped side of his sleeping bag she pushed her hand in and allowed it to rest high on his firm leg. More by accident than intention, she found the slightest touch of her finger to his penis sent a rippling shock throughout her body. She raised her hand a fraction of an inch and dared not move again as his silky flesh lightly throbbed against her.

Jack snorted his disapproval and pushed her hand aside and off his leg all together.

Laying her head back on to her pillow she also faded into sleep feeling more than a little hurt.

• • •

Jack sensed urgency and danger on waking in the minutes before the morning sun broke over the ridges of the Eastern Mountains. Lying still in his bedroll, he listened intently while he tried to reduce the sounds of his breathing. Holding his breath he strained to hear beyond that of the beat of his own heart. Several minutes elapsed until he started to settle down again. He rubbed his hands over his face in trying to recapture the feeling that had awakened him. Was it from a dream or possibly some obscure noise outside the camp? He just wasn't sure. Still, his feelings of an intruder seemed very real and alarming.

Dismissing the matter as being presently unexplainable, Jack looked over to his unexpected sleeping partner in his quest for the unknown. Not able to visualize, and completely without a clue with regards to the items he was seeking, his mind aimlessly reached for any kind of a logical answer. Going back through his thoughts to the afternoon two days before, he remembered the moment he was confronted by Nick Whitewater.

A bad cop. He always seemed to be taking some vengeance out on anyone who got in the way. A real prick.

For a number of minutes he stared into the canvas overhead and continued to ponder why Nick hadn't given him any idea as to what he was looking for. *Maybe he doesn't know himself. But that doesn't make much sense either. Why would the big Indian leave the reservation and drive over a thousand miles without knowing exactly what he wanted?* Bewildered over the few facts and lack of so many answers, Jack interrupted himself and contemplated the more important matter of rising to build a fire and set on a new pot of coffee.

When Jack started to get up he heard the flutter of several birds lifting from their nesting place. Catching a quick glimpse further off to the East out of the corner of his eye, he recognized the flight as Desert Chuckers. He knew these were birds that won't take to the wing unless something surprises them or has them cornered. Quietly he slipped from his bedroll and shuffled himself into his pants, shirt and coat. Stopping long enough to listen for the approach of someone and hearing nothing, Jack pulled on his socks then his boots. At a slight slouch he backed further under the lean-to and slowly reached through the driver's window of the Bronco. Just as slowly as his arm went in, he pulled out his wide brimmed black Stetson hat. With this particular ritual, as with no other for him, he pushed his hair back with one hand while snugly fitting the hat on his head with the other. The Stetson produced a very ominous sight with the creases and rolls of the Bull Rider style. As if he needed it to begin with, you could almost visualize the added confidence it produced in him. Reaching again into the window, Jack drew his 30-30 Winchester from a scabbard behind the seat.

He took a moment to survey the terrain for the 190 or so degrees he could see around the Bronco from his position. Pulling his .357 Colt Python revolver from the belt lying beside his bedroll he carefully placed it near Renee's head. Jack hoped to himself that she had the wherewithal to use the piece if need be. He hesitated for a very brief second while making up his mind whether to unduly awaken her for what might not be anything at all.

He crept around the front of the Bronco and headed toward lower ground on the opposite side and out of view. In an attempt to circle around to the rear where the Chuckers were spooked, Jack hunched down close to the ground. He moved slowly, with great deliberation in each step and movement. Every few yards he would stop, raise himself for better observation, then lower himself to proceed a few yards more. Quietly he continued doing this time after time closing the gap to his suspected destination. With every step he was working his way further out and around to his pray in order to come in from the back. So quiet were his movements that at one point he looked down to see a quail sitting on her nest in the Bitter Brush beside him. For more than thirty minutes he continued his efforts this way to find his intruder.

Jack knew he was close to his objective when he heard the muffled sound of someone sniffling. This was closely followed by the quite peculiar noise of nylon scraping against itself.

Jesus, he thought. *How close am I?*

With the blink of an eye, from the sounds of a twig cracking, he knew he was no more than a yard away. Behind a particularly thick bunch of bushes and brush, he saw a quick and erratic movement. Slowly, Jack rose to a full stand. Looking down upon the squatting figure Jack saw the man was peering over the bushes toward Renee and the encampment. Only seeing a pair of field glasses by this person and no weapons, he felt now was as good a time as any to make his presence known.

Without realizing it, Jack said in his most heavy and authoritative voice, "What is it I can do for you?"

Startled and surprised, the man jumped to his feet. He spun around to face Jack directly. Without warning or words the man lunged forward and more directly toward him. With a clenched fist he struck out at Jack's face while his right hand was pulling a sheathed hunting knife from his belt. Whether it was his training or experience from the many fights Jack had been in didn't matter; what did was his lightning response by deflecting the punch of his attacker with the barrel of his Winchester. With clockwork-like precision that parry was closely followed by a smashing blow with the flat wooden side of the butt of the rifle to the man's face. It was a well placed smack against the cheek and mouth of the assailant. No moans, words or sounds erupted from this person's mouth. Only a splattering of blood with white pearl-shaped objects flying to the side. The body twisted violently and then fell heavily into the Bitter Brush. He was now very still and even more silent.

Jack looked at the figure lying face down on the ground amidst the broken pieces of brush and sticks.

"You're just a wimp, partner." Jack cocked his head to the side and tried to figure the man out. "Ya must have had a glass jaw or something!"

Jack didn't really believe he had hit the man all that hard. He stepped to the side of the unconscious body sprawled before him and took note that the individual had apparently spent the night where he had found him. On the ground near him was his sleeping bag rolled out. It looked to be a really good quality mountain bag, meant for sub zero temperatures. Beside that was a white gas stove with a small pan of water just beginning to boil. A cup on the ground with a tea bag and spoon was waiting for the water to be deposited into it. Jack thought this must be the reason he was able to sneak up to the man without being seen. He next took note of a forest green nylon rucksack pushed up against the bushes. It was half opened with its tie strings pulled to their knots. The person himself was clad in a heavy down jacket and wool green plaid shirt. Not only that, Jack was not surprised to see he was wearing hiking boots with the same sole design as had been found in the camp the night before. Jack believed the fellow himself to be maybe five foot nine and weighed around one hundred forty five pounds—maybe fifty pounds. At least he could now give Renee the "who"—and with a little prompting, "the why."

Jack attempted to bring the intruder around to consciousness by shaking him at first and followed with several light slaps across the face. But no such luck. His efforts proved to be useless and in complete vain.

Hell, I hope I haven't killed him. But he is for sure out like a light. Jack worried to himself.

Grasping the lapels of the man's jacket just under his bloody chin, he almost casually lifted the dangling lump of human being to his feet. With an almost annoyed little grunt, he swung him over his shoulder with a single swift movement. Slightly bending to his side, Jack picked up his rifle with his left hand while balancing the body with the other. Thusly, he started his burdened walk back to camp and Renee.

• • •

It didn't take Jack near as long to return the seventy-five or so yards back to the lean-to. While he walked, his assailant's head and dangling arms swung from side to side with each step. Unknown to him, the man's head was swinging into the various tall brush and desert weeds on each side of his chosen path. Jack didn't really wish to make a big deal out of his discovery and walked directly up to the Bronco and under the lean-to. Now all he had to do was lean slightly forward and let the limp body fall. With a thud, the man smashed onto the ground.

The noise from the thump of the limp person hitting the earth woke Renee from her sound sleep. She looked back over her shoulder to Jack then down to the somewhat mangled body lying at his feet. Cocking her head sideways to analyze the person lying there, she suddenly discovered that it was none other than Mike.

"Ah, shit!" she exclaimed in complete surprise. "You killed him!"

Jack leaned his rifle against the side of the vehicle.

"Didn't mean to," he told her as he unscrewed the lid off a large water container he picked off the ground not far from where he had deposited the intruder. He let a small stream pour over the man's face.

"What the hell did you do to him?" Renee yelled into Mike's face. "That's my boyfriend!"

Now it was Jack's turn to say "Ah, shit!" without really having meant to say the "S" word. Especially since he didn't want to say things like that in front of Renee. or any other woman for that matter. He thought about his reply for a moment before he added. "You call that a boyfriend? Hell, he's only a little bitty thing. Ain't he? Besides, I think he's the one who trashed the camp and cut up your tent last night." Jack produced Mike's sheath knife from his waistband and dropped it next to her foot. In the same swift movement. Jack retrieved his revolver from where he had left it. Trying to hide his hostility, he walked to the fire pit and proceeded to build a fire for coffee.

Renee pushed herself free of her sleeping bag and followed directly behind him. Clad only in her T-shirt she made quite an embarrassing sight to anyone who would have seen it. Jack knelt down beside the fire pit just as Renee exploded in one of her tirades about him not using his professional training in subduing a suspect—at least in not killing him. Without looking at her, Jack reminded her that it was her boyfriend lying over there under the lean-to. Quite possibly she should go say good morning or do something womanly to help him.

Stopping in mid-sentence, an exasperated Renee was interrupted by Mike's voice saying, "Yeah, damn it! That would be kind of nice!"

Looking back at Mike she saw a miserably pathetic sight.

Mike had pushed himself up and braced on one elbow. His head and chest was wet from the water poured on him and with one hand he rubbed the thinned blood from his face.

In fascination Renee watched him stick his tongue through the hole where two teeth had been a little while earlier that morning.

"God. You look awful," she said aloud.

On the way from berating Jack to the location where Mike was sitting, Renee stopped at her pack. She knew enough of Mike to know she had to fetch her flask of Scotch whiskey to give to him. She was positive Mike would want something stronger than just Jack's coffee. Popping the lid off, she handed the container to him. He took a long swig and then completely emptied the small bottle before removing it from his lips. Mike replaced the cap and shoved the empty back into her out stretched hand.

"Thanks, that helps," he said, even though the liquid had stung his broken teeth, torn gums and cut lip.

Renee reopened the bottle and turned it upside down. "That's all I brought with me!"

"Doesn't matter. We're leaving anyway. Go pack your stuff," he ordered. Raising his middle finger in an obscene gesture, he pointed towards Jack's back and added, "This is no place for you."

Jack could feel the air growing heavy with the exchange of their words. *Perhaps coffee should wait. This is only a stupid lover's quarrel anyway.*

Watching Renee wipe the blood from Mike's face, Jack couldn't help but wonder what this fellow had to offer her. *Can't weigh more than a hundred forty or fifty pounds.* He thought. *He's got a receding hairline. What he has left is set in tight curls.*

Jack chuckled to himself thinking there was a strong resemblance between Mike and Bozo the Clown, just not as colorful.

Jack stood and spoke to Renee, saying that he was going for a walk and asked if she would be OK. He felt he at least owed her that since he had put her boyfriend's lights out. Neither Mike nor Renee responded to what he had said. They continued to speak without acknowledging him in any manner whatsoever. Directing an ear towards them, Jack was unable to make out any of the whispers in their conversation. But judging by both their expressions, it wouldn't have been anything pleasant to listen to anyway. Jack walked off through the brush toward the wagons to scavenge for clues and the unknown.

● ● ●

Once back at the wagons, Jack thought now was no longer the time to concern himself with searching the way Renee wanted him to. Using a broken board as a shovel, he dug and scraped away in the area where the Indian scout had lain. He found nothing more than the few small remaining pieces of fabric, old nails and dirt, nothing meaningful. Maybe, he thought, the White men had taken it with them—whatever it was.

Looking to the large rock where the other bones were, Jack thought that possibly something else could be found there. Standing and brushing himself off, he walked to the large rock. Lifting himself up onto the boulder, he balanced himself well enough to look over the area. Nothing. Not anything that might give him an indication as to what might be hidden or what could be found. Tired of the useless searches he had made in the past as well as now, Jack decided to give up the quest at the lost wagon. He would just have to deal with Whitewater the old-fashioned way. However, he couldn't stop wondering about the strange events that had happened on this trip.

No, He admonished himself. *I've decided to give it up.*

He stepped off the rock onto the bones of whomever had been killed there so long ago by the Indian scout. The ground gave way with the impact of his foot and sank slightly, taking him off balance. For a big man, Jack easily shifted his weight with little effort to prevent his falling.

Looking down into the place the weight of his foot had crashed, he saw small rocks and grains of sand rolled into a small elliptical hole that had been created. Dropping to his knees, Jack swept away the sand and dirt that time had placed over whatever he had accidentally found. Just inches below the surface his efforts revealed an old wooden and tin trunk lid. It couldn't have been more than two feet wide and three feet long. Pulling some broken pieces of the wood and ripping the remaining rusty tin from the top, Jack considered what looked like canvas. Clearing away more sand, boards and metal, he was able to tear away the complete top of the box exposing the top of its contents.

Using as much care as possible, he reached in with both hands along the inside of the trunk. Gently he lifted a heavy bundle above the earth and lowered it to the ground beside the now gaping hole. Still not giving much care to being articulate for Renee's sake, he unfolded the edge of the canvas cover back only to find another layer folded the opposite way. Pulling this layer back revealed something he never would have expected. His eyes widened in pure astonishment and at the same time he took in a voluminous breath of air. Hands shaking, he painstakingly replaced the old canvas along the original folds. Taking off his coat he folded it over the bundle and sat back on his haunches to think.

Jack knew he could do nothing further until he cleansed himself of any sins which had come to him over the years. He needed time to speak to the ancient ones and not offend the "Ways of the Wolf or the Eagle." Although not absolutely sure, he believed this to be something so special that maybe he should not attempt it alone. Jack pulled the package tightly into his abdomen and made his way back to the opposite side of the Bronco. Without fanfare, he deposited his strange discovery on the rear seat through the open window.

5

"A Letter From Libbie"

Renee carefully completed her cautious cleaning of Mike's lower lip and cheek before she asked him what had happened between him and Jack.

"Quiet, he can still hear us," Mike said in little more than a raspy whisper. "That guy is absolutely crazy! He didn't even give me any kind of a chance to defend myself. Look! See, I was just waiting for you to wake and he hit me with that gun over there." With even more anger he added, "I should have killed that son-of-a-bitch when I had the chance!"

"Take it easy. Slow down, Mike. Tell me why you're out here." Renee pressed her hanky to Mike's lip again and dabbed a small droplet of blood that was forming on the outside edge of his lower lip.

"Don't you think you should tell me why you're sleeping with that ape?" Mike said as he pointed toward Jack. "Maybe we should talk about what you're doing in your T-shirt and nothing else." Before she could answer that one with some sort of intelligence, he spat at her again. "How about the real question of whether or not you're being faithful to me? You know, it did seem a little strange to me that you wanted to come here alone."

"Is that why you're here?" Renee asked with recognizable irritation. "To spy on me?"

"Not at all. I have something more important in mind." He responded to her accusation with his recently acquired childish attitude.

"Look," Renee argued. "I told you why I was coming here. Besides, if it wasn't for you I wouldn't have been sleeping beside the guy."

"Bull shit! Why do you have to lie so badly when you've been caught?" he said even louder.

"This could be completely your fault too. Now answer the damn question—Why are you here?" she demanded.

"I can assure you," Mike growled back at her, "it wasn't to spy on you. Even if it were, I do have the right to see what in hell you're up to. Just keep in mind, we've been together for too long a time to have secrets."

Renee tried to repeat her question, but was cut short by a wave of Mike's hand in front of her face as he silenced her.

"A couple of days ago, it was the day you left. I went to your apartment to pick up my gray suit. That's when I discovered you had left the settlers' diary sitting on your night stand. So I decided to read it and see what all this was about. Why didn't you tell me what was in it?"

"I told you most of it," Renee replied as she tugged lightly at Mike's lower lip to see his broken teeth a little better.

Bending his lip forward she exposed the still bleeding gums and fragments of enamel where teeth should have been. Mike jerked his head back from her grasp which inadvertently caused his lip to pull still farther out than she had intended.

"Ouch, damn it!" Mike spat out as the already swelled piece of his flesh slapped against his upper lip and mustache. Using the tips of his fingers he tried to push his lip back into place and mumbled something about her purposely trying to rip it off. "You bitch! You've started it bleeding again!" he admonished her.

Mike snatched the hanky from her hand and touched it to the side of his mouth. Following a couple of pressure dabs he removed the cloth and closely inspected it for the fresh traces of his precious bodily fluid. Happy with the indications the flow was nearly stopped, he continued. "I followed your route from the map you had marked. Don't you remember, the one you left on the table beside the diary. You don't remember much, do you?"

Renee pushed him on, "You found my car then?"

"That's dumb! If I found your map, then certainly I found your car. It was easy finding your car. Anyway, after that, it nearly took a day following the directions from the diary."

"Then how did you get here?" Renee asked as she again probed Mike's face with her fingers.

"Stop that!" Mike said brushing her hand aside. "I don't need your help anymore. But, it's pretty apparent you need mine though."

"What do you mean by that?" Renee snapped.

"If you don't need help then why aren't you with the wagons instead of with that idiot?" he said pointing toward the place they last had seen Jack. Feeling disappointed that his purposefully indignant gesture was for naught, Mike continued, "You know, that ass-hole you slept with last night." He moved his out stretched finger toward her face when he emphasized "You." "Who the hell is that person?"

"Believe me, he's no one you would know. And don't be such a—" Renee cut herself off to edit what she was saying. "Is there a reason not to trust me?"

"Most of the time I do. That still doesn't tell me why you're not with those oh-so-important wagons?"

"How stupid can you be?" Renee hissed. "They're right over there!" she pointed into the direction that Jack had gone without their knowing it.

"Who do you think you're kidding?" Mike said as he tried to stand to look where she was pointing. "I found them yesterday, back that way!" Mike motioned with his battered chin in the direction of her old camp.

A confused look came across Renee's face. "We looked all around there. We only found some old boards that possibly came from a nearby mine. Nothing was there that could be possibly construed as part of a wagon!"

Regretting he had not searched more thoroughly than the two boards he found near her first camp, all Mike could do was change the subject by trying his best to expose her. "Then I suppose you slept with whoever that is the night before as well."

That statement, along with all the rest of Mike's jealous innuendoes, infuriated Renee and completely taxed her patience.

"As a matter of fact, I did! I even slept naked with him! And how do you like that?" she added, even though she felt like a teen-ager for saying it. "Is that why you cut up my tent and trashed the camp?"

Again trying to stand, Mike struggled out a "Damn straight I did!" Still slightly dizzy, he thought he had received a concussion from Jack's blow to his head.

"Listen!" Mike continued while he walked around the camp, "I love you and you know it."

"I'm not sure anymore," She responded with casual arrogance.

"I know I went off the deep end last night. I had a hard time when I found you were cheating on me."

"I didn't cheat on you!" Renee spat out the words.

"That's beside the point now. When I leave, you'll leave with me or you can forget the whole thing we have!" Mike commanded.

With their relationship already on shaky ground, Mike's demands didn't help his case in the slightest. Reorganizing her perceptions, Renee thought better of continuing the argument since he wasn't all that eager to believe her anyway. She was much more bitter at him now than she had ever been in the past. As she spoke, she had a hard time believing the words that were emanating from her mouth, things she felt she should have said a long time ago.

"I'm sorry, too," she said almost quietly and then added, "This has nothing to do with Jack, the guy who hit you."

"Malarkey!" Mike replied to what he actually believed was her absurdity and another way out of the difficult situation in which she found herself.

"I know you can't understand, but it's the way things have gone between us. All the little arguments. The lack of understanding. All of it."

Mike turned himself to face her directly and was taken aback by her attitude. "I don't believe it," he said as he rotated his head from side to side. "I still think there's more here than what you're telling me about. Besides, I don't believe you would have it in yourself to do this all on your own. After all, you know that I know you far better than anyone else. And furthermore, you know you can't turn me away. Ever. I'm even sure there's no doubt in your head that I love you. I can even prove it here and right now."

Renee watched him go from an uncertain shuffle in his walk to a strut with his chest pushed out proudly, as if he had beaten his foe with logic—not brute force.

"How can you prove it?" Renee demanded of him.

"Here." Mike slipped his fingers into his shirt pocket and withdrew a folded white envelope. "Open it. Read it," he ordered and simultaneously pushed the letter onto her chest.

Stepping back slightly, Renee unfolded the envelope and opened the unsealed flap before Mike spoke.

"That paper was pushed into the binding of the diary. I found it quite by accident when I was inspecting the old leather cover."

The letter had been folded tightly and was disintegrating with age. No matter how gentle she was, the sharp folds cracked and split as she slowly pulled it open. She didn't pay much attention to what Mike was saying, or for that matter, to what he was doing, other than bits and pieces. Her thoughts and energy were focused on the paper until it was completely unfolded. Renee held the beautiful script of a woman's hand close to her eyes and began to read. She felt a wonderful sensitivity to the writer as the words crept over her with strange feelings of personal involvement in the past.

1876, October 12th

My Dear Mr. Boyer,

I have sent this dispatch to you knowing the love and devotion you have given my husband throughout the years. Since our first meeting before the war, you often offered your services to me should I find myself in a time of need.

That time has now arrived. I believe you are aware of the massacre at the Battle of Little Big Horn and the loss of my beloved Autie. The Cheyenne Dog soldier who has brought you this note will assist you in finding some things that have been hidden away. By his spoken word the Sioux had hidden Autie's personal belongings in their Sacred Places not far from the Black Hills. The Indian has been well paid by my friend Captain Godfrey and there is no need to concern yourself for the safety of the party or yourself from the likes of him.

Crazy Horse, you know him as "Curly", has taken Autie's personnel Pennant, deerskin tunic and his favorite Ivory handled revolver. He intends to use them as his honor and as big medicine in the defeat of the White man and The Army of the West.

If you can retrieve them, I will have Captain Godfrey meet with you in the Port of San Francisco upon your word. I know you will accomplish this deed with all safety and speed.

Forever in your debt,

Elizabeth Custer

P.S. God speed and protect Libbie

Renee stared at the loving wife's personal letter with its passionate cry of the help of a friend. Staring through the writing, Renee completely disregarded Mike or anything he had been saying. All of her thoughts went to Jack and what he had said. "When you know who—you will find out why." Without a doubt the letter she held in her hands was priceless in and of itself. But now she knew she had found the Cheyenne Dog soldier under the wagon and possibly the scattered sun-bleached remains of Mr. Boyer. If the bones were not his, then surely the items Elizabeth Custer wanted would have been delivered.

What she had found in this arid desert valley would have to be one of the most valuable archaeological finds of the century inside the United States. She pondered not only on their value to the country, but to that of any living relatives of Custer himself. Looking off toward the wagons, a sudden rush lifted the tiny little hairs on the back of her neck and she cringed with the thought she would be the discoverer. Goose bumps raised on her arms as she thought of all the possibilities such a find would bring her. She did not feel the almost womanly softness of Mike's hand as it slid over her shoulder and onto her breast. Her mind reeled back to reality when she felt the tip of her nipple being rolled between his thumb and forefinger and heard out of a fog the words he was speaking.

"I love you Renee, and you love me. That's why you're going to prove your love to me right now."

"Are you nuts? This is neither the time or the place for such things."

Releasing her breast from his suddenly not quite so tender grasp, Mike returned, "You're a damn fool! If you don't change your attitude you'll destroy everything we have!" After a short pause, he continued as he pulled the old letter from her grasp. "Or will ever have."

"What do you mean by that?" Renee asked in a more demanding voice.

"Take this letter, for instance. I took it to that old bookstore on Sixth Street. The one you like to browse through. The appraiser there said it could be worth over a thousand dollars."

Mike bent down closer to Renee and continued in a softer voice. "If we were to find those items old lady Custer wanted, I know of a private collector who would be willing to pay as much as a million—maybe even more!"

Shoving Mike away from her threw him off balance momentarily. Renee gritted her teeth and found little difficulty in replying to such an absurd statement. "This isn't something you sell. It's for humanity. For everybody."

As much as Renee wanted the letter to show to Jack, she knew taking it away from Mike would be nearly impossible. She thought to herself how she had never seen this side of him and she did not care at all for what he had become.

"You're right, you know," Renee said as she stood up.

"About us?" Mike asked.

"No, about the wagons; they're where you said you found them. Jack and I planned to go over there this morning to dig them up. Now with this letter and what it says, this whole project is even more important."

"Wait. Can you get rid of that guy, you know? We don't need anyone else in on this. Right?"

"No. I don't think that will be all that easy. But I also have a better idea. A real plan," she said knowing she had hooked him with her discovery of his greed. She laid out her orderly plan of deception to him. "You go and gather your things and return to the wagons. That is, if you can put up with me keeping Jack here for a couple of days in some way. You should have enough time to find the stuff and we can meet later." Renee stood and looked into Mike's eyes. She could see the evil in his mind working its way into overdrive.

"Yes, yes, that's good. But how will you keep him here?" Mike stopped to think about what he had just said, then continued, "Never mind, I know how you'll keep him here. That's the woman I fell in love with. A real devious little wench just like me." Again he thought over what he has just said and wrinkled his forehead.

Reaching forward, Mike took her hand and pushed her palm against the crotch of his pants.

"Yeah! Just like you, all right."

"After we make love you could keep him busy the same way, if you know what I mean. After all he is an animal, and I know you would sacrifice yourself for the cause."

His smile would have made a grown woman want to vomit. She thought to herself and fought back a strong desire to do precisely that on his chest.

Seizing the opportunity Mike had thrust upon her, Renee fought the impulse to injure him and instead manipulated his genitals with a tender grasp as she moved closer to him. Renee dropped her head and allowed it to rest on his shoulder.

"Listen," she whispered, "If this thing is going to work you have to leave now. We must make him think you left angry and hurt. He won't have any suspicions then." As an added touch, she gave his penis a couple of long and deliberate pulls and felt it harden under the pressure she exerted.

Mike quickly agreed, kissed her with a smashing of his lips against hers and started to walk back to his hiding place to collect his belongings.

Renee heard him as he turned toward the desert from the camp saying to himself, "Good plan—excellent plan."

Before Mike had gone more than a few yards, Renee spoke louder to grab his attention.

"Mike, is it all right with you that I make love to Jack to keep him here?" she asked as seriously as she could while trying to hide her anger.

"Yes. Yes!" he snorted like the pig she now found him to be. "Use all the tricks you know. It's for us and a good cause." Mike turned from her and continued to walk away.

If there was anything worth saving in their relationship, that last comment surely shook it out of the mud and made it crystal clear.

Renee felt obligated and knew she owed Jack an explanation about Mike's intrusion. More importantly now, she wanted to recite to him the contents of Libbie Custer's letter to Boyer. Together, they could find the lost items and leave the valley long before Mike discovered her deception. Renee returned to her sleeping bag and pack to dress. Stopping long enough to look into the direction Mike had gone she saw him in the distance. He was walking away wearing his backpack and carrying his sleeping bag. In a sparkling gesture of emotion, she held up her arm, clenched her fist and extended the middle finger of her right hand. "Asshole" was her one word comment as her finger reached the peak of its reach.

• • •

Jack was walking around from the side of the van after depositing his bundle and exclaimed, "That's not lady-like, you know."

Renee recoiled. Her arm shot to her side even quicker than she had intended it. She felt like a little girl caught in some nasty act by a watchful uncle. Quickly recovering from her embarrassment, she hurriedly walked over to where Jack had stopped and smiled at him.

"We must talk," she told him with excitement nearly bubbling over in her voice. "I've got great news."

"We do have to talk," Jack said, preventing her from continuing. "There are things I must explain to you. I hope you understand, but there is an important matter I must attend to first."

"Please," she begged. "What I have to say has got to be more important."

Not wishing to hear Renee's problems with Mike and the details of their quarrel, Jack again emphasized she should wait.

She could see in his eyes that he was deeply troubled and sensed whatever it was, it was definitely wrong. Knowing what she had to say was by far more important, she reluctantly decided the best thing to do was to hear him out.

Taking Jack by his hand Renee pleaded, "Please tell me. Was it Mike being here? Our argument? Please tell me!" she repeated and found herself expecting the worse from him.

"I'm sorry about the problem with what's-his-name?—Mike, but that's not it. There is something I must do. So allow me a short while to gather myself."

"But!" Renee started.

"No!" Jack again interrupted, "Let it be. I guarantee we will talk in a while." Jack let Renee's hand slip from his own.

"Would you like your coffee now?"

"Yes, that would be nice." *Good,* Jack thought to himself, *that should keep her busy for a little while.*

Renee walked to the bushes closest to the fire pit and gathered enough wood for a small cook fire. At about the same time she was lighting the sticks and branches, Jack proceeded to take down the canvas lean-to. Once he had completed this task, he surveyed the encampment to find something to secure the canvas to for his own creation of a sweat lodge. Focusing on Renee's shredded tent, he removed the fiberglass poles. They weren't as long as he desired, but he would make them work. Laying the poles on the haphazardly gathered up canvas, he scooped the whole thing up into his arms and strode off toward the large rock where he had found the scattered bones. By this time Renee had deposited more sticks into the fire pit and she stopped long enough to watch Jack walk away towards the rock. She resumed making the coffee she had offered him as she worried about anything and everything she might have done to offend him.

When he reached the boulder, he gathered a number of large round rocks that would be placed into a shallow hole he would scoop out with his hands. He used these stones to line not only the sides but the bottom as well. Once he had finished this, he gathered several pieces of wood and a few more rocks and placed them in close proximity to his fire pit. Using Renee's tent poles, Jack fashioned a crude teepee-shaped frame utilizing the larger boulder for one side. Diligently, he wrapped the canvas over everything and created his sweat. Jack stood back and admired the large cavern he had constructed.

Not the perfect sweat hut, but it will do. He thought to himself. Crouching down, Jack dragged himself through the small opening and stacked some wood and sticks on the rocks in the shallow hole. He then struck a match and lit his sacred fire. He squatted momentarily in the makeshift hut watching the fire grow and the heavy smoke swirl upward to the apex. He was pleased he had made sufficient room which would allow him to do all that needed to be done. Confidently, he backed his way out and made sure the opening for air to enter the little room was sufficient to feed the fire. Looking over the top of the little structure, he saw the smoke swirl out the small opening toward the Father Sky.

Just as Jack was stepping inside the outermost perimeter of their camp, Renee poured his fresh cup of steaming coffee. She was in the process of adding sugar and creamer when he reached her and abruptly stopped and looked down at her. Renee tried to hand his promised offering up to him when he just as abruptly started to walk on past her.

"Can we talk now?"

He did not answer. From his expression, however low Jack's spirits were, they had become better since he had left with the canvas and poles. Jack picked up a gallon water jug from the rear end of the Bronco and told Renee as he again passed her that they would talk in just a few moments. Then he walked off and left her hand in the air holding his cup of coffee. Once back to the hut, he put still larger chunks of wood on his fire and set the water bottle inside.

Jack picked up his cup of coffee from a rock near the fire pit and walked to his bedroll. He sat down and motioned for Renee to sit across from him on her sleeping bag.

"Now we can talk." He took a large sip of coffee.

"Jack, Mike has told me of some things that may be buried here."

"What?" he asked in surprise almost as if he hadn't been listening. She related to him the content of the letter and especially of the possibility of the value of what might be found. Jack looked away from the direction of the hut he had built and deep into Renee's eyes. He thought a moment and asked her what she planned to do if they actually found what had been described.

"There is only one thing I can do. I have to take the artifacts to the museum for all the people to have." She told him that the items would be beneficial to not only the people, but to society as a whole. "It's the history everybody has a right to see and understand."

"Tell me again about the Indian in her letter."

"From what she wrote, the scout had turned against the Sioux and his own people for money," she said.

Jack interrupted her at this point saying his thoughts out loud more than directing them to her. "Indians rarely used the White man's money or his gold—it just doesn't make sense. What was his tribe again?"

"Cheyenne. A Dog Soldier. I believe the letter said that," she replied thoughtfully.

"That just doesn't make much sense." he repeated. "The Cheyenne and Sioux fought together against the soldiers along with other Indian Nations of the Planes." Abandoning his thoughts, his attention returned to Renee. "I guess there are turncoats in all of us."

While he was listening to what she was saying, he drew the picture of a hand and a paw on the dirt between his legs.

"Yes," Renee replied while she thought of Mike turning against everyone.

Out of nowhere Jack blurted out "Red Cloud or maybe Yellow Hand or even Gall."

Renee was bewildered. She didn't have any idea what he was talking about.

"Don't you think it would be more fitting to return the artifacts to the Sacred Places from where they had been taken?" he asked as he looked at her for that true inner worth that was in her soul.

"And be buried again?" she said with a puzzled look.

"I don't believe that would be any different than being put in a box in the dusty back room or basement of a museum. Even worse, if someone like Mike were to sell them on the black market…" Jack stopped and shook his head. "Those things would surely wind up on someone's mantle in Europe or who knows where."

Renee knew exactly what he was saying. So many places had been vandalized by the pot hunter because of the tremendous value that had been placed on Indian artifacts in recent times. History had proven so often that a whole criminal society, like grave robbers, destroyed many archaeological sites for profit and little else.

"What would you do?" she asked over the edge of her cup before she took another drink of her coffee.

"I'm not sure," Jack replied after thinking it out for a moment. "I do know there are things that I must do first. Please, be patient and stay here. I will return with my decision after I've had a little while to think on it."

Renee could feel Jack's innermost thoughts and emotions returning to his heritage. She didn't understand why, but felt he was surely torn between what should be and what had to be. Just exactly what it was, she couldn't put her finger on it. Reluctantly she agreed to wait and hear what he had to say. Jack stood without speaking of anything else and walked off to his sweat hut. Renee remained seated and sipped from her cup as she watched him move back and forth through the brush until he reached his destination. Across the relatively short distance to his lodge, she saw him duck his head and disappear.

The temperature had turned warmer. The sun was bright and the air smelled clean and new with promise. Although not understanding all the recent occurrences, Renee wished her own mind would come to peace with itself. Leaning back onto her bedroll she felt the heat of the sun bearing down on her. In the warming near 80-degree temperatures of mid day she felt the serenity and the quietness of the valley. Renee was glad her relationship with Mike had met its conclusion. All that remained was to find a way to tell him it was completely over between them. She knew she could leave no room for doubt so that he would really understand and not be hurt any more than necessary.

With Jack off doing whatever he thought was necessary, she seized the opportunity to relax and get a little mellow. Reaching over to the cold box she opened the lid and removed the bottle of wine Jack had brought with him. Uncorking it, she touched the neck of the bottle to her lips. So cool the liquid felt as it passed over her tongue that she shivered for a brief moment. As far as she could imagine, she had positive success at her fingertips. Renee now felt that going back to San Francisco with her prize should be highlighted by the best golden winter's tan. Using that thought as a good excuse, she stripped off her T-shirt and pants. Tilting herself back onto her elbows she permitted the sun to have its way with her and caress her entire body. She felt really wonderful lying back exposed to no one, yet to everything. A slow smile crept over her face as her eyelids closed over the glassy orbs.

So gentle to her touch, her own hands glided over her breasts and whipped upon and tantalized her erect nipples. Only seconds were spent before she lowered them down and across the flatness of her stomach. As if it were second nature she allowed her fingertips to reach lower and at first brush over her finely trimmed and shorter than normal pubic hair. Opening her eyes she looked up into the sun and felt exotic and wonderful. She dragged her fingernails through her fine curly fur and touched herself briefly as she fantasized that this was with Jack. Her eyes closed and color added to her splendid fantasy.

When it was over, she remained motionless for nearly an hour before she had realized how much time had passed. Propping herself onto her right arm, she scanned the area for Jack, as she was not sure if he was still in his makeshift tent or not.

• • •

Jack entered the sweat lodge before removing all his clothes. He knew he had to purify his soul of any evil before opening the bundle he had found. Taking note of the red and yellow coals, he placed several rocks upon them. Then opening the water bottle, he carefully poured some of the fluid onto the rocks lining the outer edge of the circle. The water sizzled and instantly turned to steam that filled the shelter with heavy humid air. Compared with the many rituals he had watched or been involved in, he knew the cleansing of the soul to be one of the most important. Sitting cross-legged opposite the door, he started his chant to his God and the ceremony that was required of him. Now and then, and without breaking the cadence of his chant, he would add small amounts of water to the rocks—and they would sizzle, hiss and steam their song to him. For an hour he sat asking for a sign from the Ancient One. His chants were low and meaningful and could not easily be heard outside the center of his real world.

• • •

Not wishing to disturb Jack, Renee stood and dressed. Placing the bottle of wine back into the box, she slowly walked off to the wagon to look for the desert's hidden treasures. When she finally approached the area the wagon was in, she immediately saw something was terribly amiss. The ground had been scrapped deeply here and there as if a wild animal was seeking some forgotten hidden meal. Her strings were broken and in disarray. The various boards had been tossed to the side or turned over and left exposed to the sun. Her first thought was that Mike had done this horrible thing. Hurrying from place to place, she found that she was unable to determine whether he could have found anything of value or not.

No, absolutely not, she decided. If he had found the artifacts he wouldn't have shown me the Elizabeth Custer letter.

At a brisk pace she headed for the little hut Jack apparently was still occupying. Not being able to look inside, she circled around the structure. Behind the boulder Renee first saw the old wooden trunk sunk into the ground and then the lid that had been torn away and scattered. It was almost completely empty except for some clothes and a worn Bible on the bottom. And now the truth struck deep and hard. Jack had found the artifacts and was keeping them for himself.

Renee felt completely beaten and bewildered at the destruction of the site. How could he have done such a despicable thing to something as important to her as this? Her dreams of discovery had now been stripped from her, along with the history of which she so wanted to be a part. In her mind, Renee compared this outrage to a feeling of having been raped and pillaged by friends. She completed her circle to the front of the hut and sat down across from the flap that hid Jack from his crimes. As she looked up into the sun, tears of hurt welled up in her eyes and flowed silently over her cheeks. Each painful tear fell off her chin only to be absorbed by the dry desert sand below her. This was such a cruel place. Unable to constrain herself any further, small blubbering moans and sighs escaped her lips. She didn't realize her sobs were audible enough for Jack to hear so she didn't try to muffle them more. She felt devastated, helpless and worse—betrayed.

• • •

Jack prepared to leave the sweat when he first heard Renee's faint crying. He knew now that she had discovered he had found the bundle. Deciding to dress in at least his Levis before reentering the outside world, he pulled on his pants and hurriedly buttoned his fly. Pushing the canvas flap aside, the cold air rushed in to smash against him. He was weak from the heat and humidity in the hut and from the ceremony he had put himself through. Jack was surprised that he had some difficulty in crawling out and into the light. Drained of energy as he exited, his eyes momentarily stung from the bright sun's rays. Shielding his eyes through his fingers, he finally saw her directly in front of him sitting on the ground. Her cheeks were wet with tears. Her head was heavily bent down into her chest. Jack had found the unexpected in her—he didn't need to be prepared for the verbal battle he knew was coming. He had not contemplated this situation at all. Regardless, he knew what he had to do.

But now, seeing her so profoundly shaken, his only recourse was to bring her fully into whatever needed to be done. One of the things he was certain of was he did not wish to hurt her any more than he already had. It wasn't just the guilt he felt for his acts, but mostly the seeds of admiration that had grown inside himself for her and her ways. Jack believed her to be a strong and sturdy woman, who through misfortune of events, had succumbed to her own fears of failure. Jack believed Renee to have resilience far past that of most women. He knew he could convince her all was not lost.

Instead of standing, Jack crawled like a snake on his stomach and hands and knees the few feet across the earth to her. Pushing himself up on both legs, he cupped each side of her face with his hands and gently lifted her head.

"Your purpose here is greater than you had imagined. I and my people desperately need your help and knowledge of the past," he implored her.

The line of tears somewhat subsided as she gave him a most curious look. Although angry, she still felt his concern for her. After all, she thought, only the excavation had been damaged beyond recognition. The importance of the find was just as meaningful as it had been.

"Do you mean together there is something we need to do? Or are you just trying to make amends and steal more from me?" Renee asked in a whimpering and shaking voice.

"Really," Jack went on as he caressed her soft skin below the peak of her cheekbones with the tip of his thumbs. Becoming this close was not a part of what he intended at all. Jack realized his actions simply had become an affectionate, unconscious reaction to a caring, beautiful and intelligent woman. "Yes," Jack assured her. "I wouldn't have it any other way."

He removed his hands from her face, and she changed her position from sitting to kneeling closer to him. As if drawn together by undefinable forces, one touched the other. Their embrace filled with the beat of their hearts and mingled one with the other. A wisp of a desert breeze brought the slightest of caresses to them as they held each other breathlessly.

6

"By Light of Day"

Jack stood and held his hands out to assist the still whimpering woman to her feet. As if drawn together for the first time, each stared deeply into the eyes of the other for a long tantalizing moment.

Jack was first to break the somehow strange, loud silence. "Thank you for having enough faith in me to hang in there."

"I believe our goal wouldn't have had it any other way. Besides, you have me over that proverbial barrel. So, just for me, please don't do anything dumb again, OK? Please."

Turning toward the Bronco she took his hand in hers and started toward the bundle that held the secrets for which so many good men had longed for. Nothing at all was said as they walked to the opposite side of the Sheriff's vehicle. Somehow entwined, they were deep in the thoughts of the closeness they shared as they contemplated what was about to come.

In unspoken terms Jack offered to have Renee assist him with the artifacts. A simple task, any other time he would not need or want any help at all. Now, more than ever he wanted her to feel his pride of their working together. He wanted her to be as much part of what he wanted as humanly possible. To show his credibility he pulled the bundle through the window, smiled at her and firmly laid it in her waiting hands.

Renee carried it to the sleeping bag and sat cross-legged staring with almost melancholy abandon into the folded fabric. Her hands were pushed deep into her lap, her eyes were riveted while not knowing what discoveries were just ahead. Now she totally focused her new energies on what was about to take place. Her fingers intertwined and clasped one another tightly to slow her trembling as she wanted so to tear into the folds to feel and marvel at those things she had been seeking.

Jack moved around from behind her to sit directly across the bundle. Both, for whatever their reasons, took in heavy breaths as they prepared to progress into that gray place between what is and what was.

With unsure hands she folded back the flap only to expose a second one. Looking to Jack for a brief reassuring moment, she reached for the second fold of canvas.

In a sudden and startling move, Jack instantly stopped her with, placing his hand on hers and giving a squeeze of some firmness.

"Wait. Your camera. Maybe pictures of this step by step."

"Good idea," she said at the same time quickly pushing herself to feet. Renee sped off to fetch her tripod, camera and a new roll of film.

Returning, she quickly photographed the bundle from three different angles after Jack had folded the first flap back into place.

"That's overkill, don't you think?"

Kneeling down again, Renee set her camera to the side and gave Jack a less than enthusiastic glance. Hands still shaking, but with somewhat less vigor, she reopened the first flap. Looking at Jack with a freshened, excited smile painted across her face, she pulled the second covering of material to the opposite side. They both gazed upon what Jack had seen earlier. It took her a moment or two to absorb what lay before her. At first with still trembling fingers and then with her whole shaking hand, she touched the magnificent covering of deer hide. She caressed her hand back and forth over the smooth surface.

Like chamois, the material was soft and pliable and silken to the touch.

Jack spoke in a raspy voice, "The paintings. See—the paintings?"

He pointed to various faded symbols that had been stained onto the hide many years before. Renee stared intently while Jack pointed with his own trembling finger to each of the symbols. The well-prepared colors appeared to be men lying on the Earth in all sorts of purposely placed haphazard positions. Many of the figures lay twisted or broken with their heads lying beside them. Dabs of red paint portrayed where blood would have spurted from the headless necks or dripping from the throats. Others had red splotches where their genitals should have been. Still more had similar splatterings on their arms and legs where they had been cut and slashed in deliberate torture.

"Do you know what this is?" Jack asked her.

"A picture," Renee replied. "Like a scene of massacre."

"Sure is," he answered not realizing a strange pride was showing through. "This is the Sioux Medicine Man's view of Custer's last battle on June twenty-fifth 1876."

He had seen only one similar to this long ago in a photograph from an old history book. Jack felt he knew exactly the significance of this when he first opened the flaps of the bundle near the rock.

"Before the Battle of Little Bighorn, Sitting Bull, the Medicine Man of the Sioux Nation, made a ceremonial painting of that future moment in time. This may well be the original from which others have been copied." Jack paused for a long time before he again said anything. "The Old Ones of the Reservation have passed the story from father to son in the most private of ceremonies. To confuse his prior prediction of the battle, he redrew a similar picture for reporters a year later."

Renee prevented her puzzled look of confusion to appear.

"Did you know that only about a hundred warriors were killed in that battle?"

"No!" Renee suddenly discovered she had completely forgotten her history of that time and place. She shook briefly as the tiny hairs on the back of her neck began to rise. "How many soldiers died there?"

"If I remember correctly, there was some two hundred and sixty five. The way I understand it, some of them were civilians."

Renee picked up her camera, adjusted and focused the lens and snapped the shutter. She took two more pictures up close to record the fine details of the painting. While she was setting the camera back down, Jack put his hands inside the covering to cradle the mural. Renee, being extremely cautious, finished removing the canvas outer shell from under the painted hide. Jack set the remaining bundle down again. Renee held the canvas up and turned it while inspecting both sides.

Jack watched the fabric turn and said, "That's probably a piece of tarp from one of the regiment's wagons."

Thinking for a moment, she replied to his suggestion, "It even could be from Boyer's stuff." Suddenly, she felt a little silly in trying to add her limited knowledge of Boyer's party.

"That's right," Jack agreed and brought a smile back across her face as she was sitting back down.

Turning the leather clad bundle over, Renee discovered it had been neatly folded on the bottom as well. On the bundle's sides were more prints of soldiers and horses. Some of the horses appeared to be lying on the ground in death. Other horses, with figures of Indians astride them, were shown racing between the fallen men. Those warriors were wielding knives and lances and clubs or shooting long guns as they rode through the fallen bodies.

Renee thought to herself, *This must be a fine reflection of the disaster and the annihilation of the 7th Cavalry,* and ignored what Jack said about it being created before the carnage.

Renee continued unfolding the skin on which the scene had been painted. It seemed, with each blink of her eyes, greater detail of the battlefield was revealed. Along a thin and ragged line of blue, which Jack told her was Rosebud Creek, stood several lodges and teepees painted in a similar fashion. Although Renee had read some published material of the battle—books like *Custer's Luck* and *The Sioux Battle of 1876*, she had not put into perspective this overwhelming field of death. All the agonies of brutality this picture revealed took her by complete surprise. She was awestruck at the story's testimony of the massacre and the true fate of the soldiers. Even the exact position of Lt. Col. Custer's body among the dead was depicted in graphic detail. Not wanting to embarrass Jack, she refrained from pointing out that Sitting Bull couldn't have known who would die where.

"Why would the Sioux bother to cut up the soldiers like that?" Renee asked, while studying the marks of red more closely.

"It is the belief that if the tendons and muscles of the legs and arms of the best fighters are cut, the spirit will be unable to rise to the heavens," Jack replied.

"Then you would think they must have really destroyed Custer's body even though the picture doesn't show it?" she wondered about the commander of the Seventh specifically and why he hadn't been dismantled and abused like the others as well. There were so many questions she felt she needed to answer.

"Custer was one of the few that had not been mutilated. He died of wounds to his side and head. The story that has been told on the reservation is the soldiers who fought the worst to their death were not allowed to enter the hereafter either. They were laid face down so that the eyes of death would not see the heavens and their souls would be forced to walk before the others in shame."

"Then his soul was freed!" Renee stated while at the same time feeling a bit relieved.

"I don't think so," Jack replied. "I would imagine he was left alone because he was such a valiant leader—or maybe such a stupid one. Either way, he surely would have remained with his troops to haunt his field of horror forever."

"Do you believe that?" Renee asked looking at Jack in disbelief.

It was as if Jack refused to answer her question while he began to unfold the skin.

The second item came to view. Easily recognizable by both herself and Jack, they sat speechless. Renee picked up her camera and photographed a black and red headband with a hundred feathers flowing back and to the sides.

"Could it be?" Jack asked himself while waiting for her to snap the shutter.

Seizing it with both hands, Jack very gently lifted the magnificent War Bonnet from the pile. The higher he lifted it, the more it unfolded back and forth until his arms were stretched well above his head. There before them was the full headdress of a chief of the Sioux Nation. Quickly Renee pointed her camera and photographed the rare and exciting piece from several angles. She placed her camera's strap over her head to free both of her hands. Carefully she helped Jack lay the headdress on the bedroll to its full length while making certain not a single feather was bent or broken.

"Absolutely beautiful," she said as she "oooooed" at the mass of eagle feathers, beads, mounted hair and furs. "There must be more than a hundred feathers."

Jack was really taken by the beauty as well as of the great importance of this find to his people. Even without the thick lump in his throat, he could not have spoken if he wanted to. While not knowing exactly what to say anyway, he remained guarded and amazed.

"Look at this!" Renee instructed him again while he was trying to position himself before the items they had been dissecting in a near religious way.

Still looking toward the headdress he found it almost impossible to pay much heed to Renee's demands. Renee was amused by Jack's inability to tear himself away long enough to look at her next discovery.

"PAY ATTENTION!" she yelled with a grin.

Jack's head snapped up sharply while his dark eyes immediately found hers. His eyes seemed to have the presence of some evil thought burned into them for the briefest of seconds. For the first time Renee felt fear flapping its wings in the pit of her stomach. Cautiously she drew his attention to another piece of fabric wrapped around something quite large. He picked up the clump with his left hand and found the contents to be heavy and solid through the fabric. From the feel of it, he immediately knew it was a handgun wrapped in the satin-like material of a flag. Removing the firearm from the tassel edged fabric that had protected it so long was a wonderful task for him. Jack held the weapon up high and let the sun reflect from its silver surface. Never had he seen such craftsmanship in a firearm. Renee knew he held a silver-plated Officers Colt 45. Finely engraved from the rounded sight at the end of the barrel to the sweeping curve of the back strap. A beautifully smooth ivory grip, which had yellowed over time, completed the ballet of its flowing lines. Jack turned the barrel toward his eyes so he could look into the black caverns of the cylinders. He saw four of the five visible chambers were empty. The fifth contained a round that had oxidized over time and had turned the tip of the large bullet green. From what she could see, it appeared like the face of a frog peeking out. It was as if it were waiting to be turned under the hammer when cocked and then hurled on some deadly mission.

"A last round to be fired by a man who could have been the last to die on that bloody field," Jack told her with grave authority in his voice.

Renee watched him fondle and touch this magnificent piece. Looking into his eyes, she saw he had calmed to the point of almost resembling a large and thankful puppy.

Renee tugged the flag from Jack's hand while he continued to drool over the revolver.

"You know who this belonged to, don't you?" he almost demanded when he finally looked over to Renee.

Her reply was that neither of them could really have any doubt. Jack set the Colt down beside his leg and seemed somehow frozen in his thoughts. Before he removed his fingers from the pistol, he ran them back and forth over its smooth lines one more time.

Renee held the flag up and off to her side with both hands, looked at the brilliant crimson and blue colors with a Golden American Eagle embroidered upon it with gold braids on three sides.

"This, no doubt, is his personal pennant that Libbie had asked to be returned," she offered in explanation.

The flag moved ever so slightly in the gentle zephyr that was blowing from the east. With one hand Renee gave Jack the camera hanging from her neck. She wanted him to photograph both sides from as close as he dared. She wanted the pictures to be completely full with the elegance.

While Renee folded the flag, Jack took several pictures of the wonderful old Colt that he had placed on his sleeping bag.

Now before them on the deerskin one last item remained. Neatly folded, as if it had been lying in a sideboard waiting for its owner, was a heavy tanned, elkhide jacket. At the tips of the long and wide collar were hand-sewn silver stars painstakingly sewn by some master clothesmaker so many years ago. Renee lifted the coat by the dark blue shoulder boards that indicated Custer's rank as being Lieutenant Colonel. The beautiful tanned color of Custer's jacket had blemished to dark reddish brown on the side of the front left panel. As she inspected the material closer she discovered a large and smoothly rounded hole near the top of the stain. Jack leaned forward to see for himself and then sat back erect. He pointed with the index finger of his left hand to his own side.

"Here," he said. "This is where he was wounded."

Although it had happened more than a century ago, Renee could not help but feel the sting of the wound Custer had sustained in his side.

"In all probability," Jack related, "the bullet didn't kill him right away. With all this blood he must have suffered a severe stomach wound. Probably was in unbelievable pain for hours," Jack added while slowly shaking his head from side to side. "I remember a long told story of the Medicine Man that Custer had been shot in the temple, but nobody would say who actually did it, ours or theirs."

"I suppose, during the heat of battle, it wouldn't be hard to be killed by friendly fire either?"

"It's still strange though. At one time there was a story that a white woman walked right up to him and shot him through the temple. I don't think much of it, as only the very oldest of the elders would speak of it among themselves."

Renee opened both front panels of the jacket and started her search for a maker's label or tag sewn into the lining. Finding none, she slipped her hand into one of the large pockets that had been hand-stitched onto the side of the coat. She froze and did not allow her hand to explore further. Renee gasped and then barely breathed before she slowly withdrew. Her fingers tugged a long silver chain from the pocket's depths on which was suspended a large round locket.

"Everything Libbie had asked for is here!" she told Jack in a surprised voice.

"No," he replied. "Too much is here. I don't believe the headdress was to be part of it." He directed his questioning eyes to the flowing feathers and then briefly to the direction where the scout had lain.

Renee grasped the locket between her fingers and manipulated the small latch to its side. As she slowly opened the tiny door a small curl of brownish auburn hair fell onto her leg. Renee wondered if it was Libbie's. Quickly, she gathered the hair before it could be blown away by the increasing desert breeze. Looking closer into the inner sides of the locket she found it contained no pictures of Libbie as she had hoped; nothing at all except the strands of hair.

"That sure looks like your hair. You couldn't have asked for a better match." Jack added his spoken thoughts.

Renee held the little clump of hair close to her own before replacing it back into the locket.

"Do you really think so?"

"Sure do!" he responded to her obvious pride.

From Renee's movement of the jacket, a corner of a yellowing piece of paper revealed itself from the opposite pocket. With the tips of his fingers Jack slid a small bundle of parchment free. "It looks like more than one letter!" he felt the paper's weight and thickness in his hands.

Renee stood and walked around all the things they had discovered. When she reached a space large enough to see over his shoulders, she knelt behind Jack. Now close to his side, she placed her right arm around his shoulder and pulled herself even closer to him. Together they would discover what had been written on that terrible day in the spring of 1876. Slowly Jack unfolded the paper taking notice that two sheets of paper had been placed together with a third in the center that had been crumpled. That particular piece of paper appeared to have been straightened out before folding the three together. This center sheet was stained with small dark brown droplets of what was probably dried blood, Jack told her. On one side of the page was the telltale pattern of a partially smudged fingerprint. As clear as the day it had been left on the parchment, every whorl, loop and bifurcation of the print meant that it could only have been left by Custer as he pushed it into his pocket. Renee tilted her head towards Jack and rested her chin on his massive shoulder. In a barely audible tone she began to read along with Jack the excited and painful scribbling.

25 June 1876

Lt. Cooke, bring forth your forces as well as
Captain Benteen's and the pack animals. If you
are not immediate, all will be lost. Take the best
route across the drainage of Rosebud from the
L—

Renee looked at Jack then back to the letter and said, "He must have been writing this when he was hit."

"Either that, or just after."

"I'm surprised he didn't have the company secretary write this for him." Renee said, not really expecting a response.

"The Sergeant-Major was probably already dead. You do know that's who generally was the secretary, don't you?"

"I knew that!"

Moving to the second dispatch, the one that had been on top of the three, they again read together.

25 June 1876

General Custer

My Crow scouts have informed me their esti-
mates of the Sioux encampment to be no less
than 4000 warriors. Please hold your position
until my troops arrive. It will be suicide to continue alone.

Major Reno

"He was warned!" Jack responded to what he read.
Jack placed the last letter on top of the other two. They
both began to read again.

25 June 1876

General Custer

I have relieved the Crow scouts to fight on their
own. I have instructed them to ride to your aid
with all speed if they are victorious. I am under
heavy attack from the encampment but can
hold my position.

Major Reno

Jack turned his head toward Renee slightly and murmured, "If it hadn't been for your work in finding the diary and
this place, all this would never have come to light."
Renee leaned closer and kissed him lightly on the cheek
near the corner of his mouth. "I love you, Jack," she whispered
into his ear. Giving him a warm squeeze, she then stood and
picked up her camera. As rapidly as possible she finished off
the last of the unexposed film.
Not wishing to look like a fool by misinterpreting her
statement, Jack felt it best not to acknowledge Renee's comments. He watched her move back and forth around all the stuff

they had discovered; taking picture after picture until all 36 exposures of a second roll had been exposed. With a deep sigh of relief Renee lowered her camera.

Jack stepped back to get a good view of everything on the bedrolls. "Put everything back as it was. There is much more we need to do."

Renee wanted to just stay to touch and look in greater detail at all these magnificent things. Her unrelieved excitement made it hard to agree with his request. Following a fierce inner fight and with much reluctance, she started to replace the artifacts as they had been found. It took her thirty minutes or better to fold everything back into the bundle.

Jack set himself upon the camp with a vengeance, taking down some things while rolling up others. In general, he returned the site to its original condition. Even the campfire ring did not escape Jack's renovation. By the time he had retrieved Renee's tent poles and his canvas cover from the rock, she had just finished with the bundle and he neatly folded the canvas lean-to.

Renee held the artifacts out proudly. Jack winked at her and gave her the praise that she earned and desired from him.

"Perfect," he said with a smile.

It looked as though she had returned everything to its last fold. No one would ever know the artifacts had even tampered with. Carrying the bundle to the open rear of the Bronco, Jack placed it on the floor. Renee rolled the remaining sleeping gear while he filled the back of the vehicle until only the sleeping bags were left. Snatching them off the ground, Renee put those on the rear seat herself.

Renee stepped into the passenger's side to wait for Jack. Fidgeting while she waited, she bent the rearview mirror around to look at herself for the first time in nearly three days. "My God! How awful!" she told the face in the mirror. Pointing a finger into her open mouth, she acted out a vomit. Suddenly she remembered Jack and hoped he hadn't seen her do such a stupid thing. *After all, he probably wouldn't have seen the levity in it,* she thought.

Satisfied with his work, Jack finished cleaning up the area by kicking the footprints out of the dirt. He walked around the Bronco to Renee's side and asked if she was ready.

"Yes," she agreed, giving him a loving look that she knew he probably didn't understand.

He just stood close looking at her. Somewhat startling her, Jack extended his arm through the window and grasped the back of her neck and began pulling her to him. She was surprised at how little pressure it took to draw her closer to the open window.

Looking deep into her eyes, he asked, "Did you mean it?"

"Yes, and I still do," she replied, somehow knowing exactly what he was asking. Without more coaxing her head moved closer to his. Tenderly their lips touched lightly. Almost against his will, Jack's hand drew her tighter to him. Her mouth opened slightly as his tongue explored her moist, full lips and the tip of her searching tongue. Renee heard a low, gutteral moan come from deep somewhere in Jack's soul. How long the kiss lasted was of little importance to either of them; regardless of the length, the impact to her seemed unbelievable. Even the release of his grip on her neck didn't encourage their lips to part. With considerable reluctance, their lips separated leaving a shiny thread of saliva stretched between them until it too finally snapped. Her eyes remained closed in ecstasy. She felt lightheaded, with her heart throbbing and a growing desire to have him here and now. The effects subsided when she leaned back into the seat and heard the sound of the driver's door being opened.

"When we arrive at my car, what happens?" she asked, hoping they would not separate, never to see one another again.

"I want you to go with me," he replied. "The way I see it we have only started this adventure." Hesitating for just a little too long to her way of thinking, he continued, "I want to be with you to the end."

The blood rushed into her face and cheeks and a warm flash engulfed her whole body in an instant. She felt that if she smiled any wider the whole top of her head would probably fall off.

Lord, he's neat, She moaned to herself. "Then you're going to San Francisco with me?" she said, making a statement out of her question.

"That's not exactly what I had in mind," he replied as the Bronco's engine fired and started to rumble.

As he put the vehicle into gear, the high rev of the engine caused it to lurch forward when he released the clutch. With that jolt they started their journey to the county road by a different and seemingly easier route. The Bronco bounced and jerked from side to side as Jack fought the wheel for control when an unseen rock occasionally got in the way. Swerving back and forth as they bounced up and down, Renee didn't seem to notice anything other than a new-found happiness. Jack, Renee and the four-wheel drive slowly made their way across the valley floor to her car.

"If it's not to my home with me then where are we going?"

Trying to avoid a very large rock that was partially hidden by a bush, Jack pulled at the steering wheel heavily while he spoke.

"Wouldn't it be better to really authenticate your find before you do something with it?"

"Naturally."

"Then let's go to the Battle Ground to see where all this happened."

"The Little Big Horn?" she asked, a little confused over his offer.

"I couldn't think of a better place."

"I can't do that. My clothes are filthy, I don't have anything really nice to change into."

Quickly Jack smoothed out the wrinkles of her indecision. "We'll buy what you need along the way—what do you say?" Before she could answer, he added, "I'll bet some of the Old Ones on the reservation would be able to help you fill in the blanks."

"Even about Boyer's raiding party and the men that stole all this stuff?" she questioned him for reassurance.

"I'll bet they can."

"I kind of feel like I'm being led down a primrose path," Renee blurted out. "It's almost like you're leading me on. Are you?" she pushed for an answer by putting her hand on his arm. "In a way, but I do have my reasons. To be honest, I have several reasons."

"What are they then?" she questioned him in a somewhat leery tone, at the same time hoping she wasn't being used again.

"Like I said before, most of the things we have uncovered are very sacred to my people. Although they are from the past, they will be very meaningful to those who stay with the ways of the past. Let me tell you something else I feel. All this will benefit you as well."

"How?"

"I would like you to present our Indian Cultural Center with the artifacts yourself. Who knows, maybe a place could be found for you there. You know, maybe our Associate Curator of the Indian Cultural Center or something."

While Jack went on talking he made it quite apparent to her that he wished her to be near him for a long time to come.

"But your job here—you'll lose it!" she said, appealing to his sense of reality. "Isn't employment poor on the reservation?"

"I probably lost it anyway when I broke this thing." Jack slapped the dashboard impressing Renee with his dissatisfaction with the dents. "I miss my home, my country and my mom. I just don't want to miss you while I'm there."

Goosebumps broke out all over Renee's bare arms. The thought of something meaningful with Jack filled her mind.

"I got to admit it. I have my reservations."

With that statement she broke into a very big smile. It took Jack a moment to catch on to her statement before he began to laugh with her.

Renee was in an exceptional mood, which made the trek to the graded county road seem short in comparison to the last few days. Nor did it seem to take long for them to reach her little car parked under the cottonwoods where she had left it. But now the only difference was the expected appearance of Mike's white Buick sitting close by.

Renee unlocked her trunk and then the doors while Jack proceeded to unload the bundle and her other things into her car's trunk. She then busied herself doing something he couldn't see on the far side of the Buick. Not quite finished with the hidden task she returned to her car. Starting the motor, as she normally did to allow it to warm up for a few minutes, she walked back over to Jack at the Bronco. She knew for certain she could trust him since he had put Custer's stuff and the War Bonnet in her car.

"Look," he said without looking at her. "I want you to drive to Furnace Creek Inn in Death Valley and wait for me there." Taking his Visa card from his wallet he handed it to her. "Check in under your own name and buy some clothes or whatever you need. I've got to get this thing back. I'll be there a couple of hours behind you."

The idea seemed reasonable to her, and with the things that already had happened she agreed without hesitation. Besides, she was looking forward to a long hot bath and the comfort of a meal at a regular table.

Looking at Jack with apprehension she felt inspired to ask, "Is it reasonably nice there or is it just a motel in the desert?"

"That depends on your outlook," he replied as he put the Bronco into gear and prepared to drive away.

A moment of silence fell between them. Passionately he touched his lips with his fingers and blew her a kiss through the short distance separating them and drove off.

It seemed to Renee that she heard him singing while he was driving away. She watched him leave until the dust trail behind the Bronco made it impossible to see. Walking back to the driver's side of Mike's car she reread the partial note she had secretly written to him. She thought what to say for a second and then finished it.

Dear Mike,

I am off with Jack to Custer's battlefield. I am
truly sorry for the deception today and the lie I
made up to send you on a wild goose chase. I
just knew your greed and attitude had finished
us forever. Please don't be angry. Just wish me
well.

Renee

Placing the note under the windshield wiper she returned
to her car and drove off. By the time she had reached the Inter-
section with State Route 190, Jack's dust had cleared from the
air. Where he had turned West toward Olancha, she swung the
front of her sedan to the East. Her thoughts thrilled with all that
had happened and what she hoped would take place when she
and Jack were once again together.

• • •

It took Jack a little less than an hour to reach his trailer
from the turnoff at Saline Valley Road. Except for his handgun
and Winchester, he left the county vehicle loaded near the rear
door of his mobile home. Racing in through the splintered
remains of his door, he turned and went into his bedroom.
Grabbing his suitcase from the less than adequate walk-in
closet, he threw it onto his bed. Going back into the closet he
selected an armload of clothes he felt would be suitable for the
mission he was about to undertake. When he turned to walk
back into the bedroom he picked his savings passbook and a
Beretta .22 caliber automatic from its hiding place on a high
shelf. Stuffing all that into the suitcase he quickly went into the
kitchen to the telephone. Picking the hand set off its resting-
place on the wall, he dialed the main office of the Sheriff's
Department. Not wishing to talk to the Watch Commander or
anyone else of higher authority, he felt it would be wiser to
leave a message with the dispatcher. Nothing more elaborate
than that an emergency had come up at his home in South

Dakota and that he would call the undersheriff when he arrived there. Jack knew this would give him ample time to formulate an explanation for the damage to the Bronco. He didn't believe anyone would be suspicious enough to check on his story unless they came to his house.

Jack pulled a six-pack of Coors from the refrigerator. After picking up his suitcase, he scurried out the door to his old broken down Ford pickup. He believed it hadn't taken him fifteen minutes to gather the stuff he wanted and to make the call. He started the engine, which was closely followed by a glance at the fuel gauge to let him know he had enough gas to reach Renee at Furnace Creek. Opening a can of beer he turned on his headlights and sped away only to retrace his path on Highway 190 to Renee and the unknown.

• • •

Stopping her vehicle in front of the Furnace Creek Ranch store, Renee felt a little disappointed that her destination wasn't the castle she had conjured up in her mind's eye. Stepping out of her car she made her way to the registration desk and hopefully a vacancy. Just to make sure of the location, she asked the clerk why the place was named Furnace Creek Ranch and not Furnace Creek Inn as she had been told.

The clerk, looking up from the paper he was reading and over the glasses he wore low on his nose, said, "That's because you have the wrong place, Miss!"

"I do?" she replied with confusion in her voice.

"Down the road further on the left." The clerk directed her more politely than she had heard in a long time. Looking up to her the clerk added, "Have a nice stay and enjoy the Valley," before he returned to his newspaper.

Thanking him, she turned and walked back to her car. Standing beside her automobile she could see in the yellowish light from the Mercury Vapor lamps and the many palm trees in front of the store.

"Clean, nice and pleasant," she said to herself. "Maybe this is where we should stay."

Not far from the door to the general store she heard laughter emanating through the double swinging saloon doors leading out to the parking lot from the bar.

A vacation resort? She thought to herself.

Now a feeling came over her that quite possibly this would be a better place to stay than a dingy old motel. Knowing she had agreed to do as Jack had asked, Renee sighed and got into her car and continued east.

Within a few minutes she reached the entry gates to the Furnace Creek Inn. Pulling her car onto the narrow paved drive, she followed the road up a slight incline. Driving slowly, Renee bent forward looking up toward the building. Brightly lit by hidden floodlights, it was a massive grand old building. *Probably built in the twenties or thirties*, she thought as she looked at the old masonry architecture. The further she drove the more excited she became until she reached the parking lot. Renee located the only remaining parking space in front of the main doors to the lodge. When she stepped out of her car she realized the parking lot overlooked many trees and palms surrounding the front of the massive building. Taking the few short steps to the front of her vehicle, she leaned against the old pipe handrail and looked down. To her delight, spread out before her, was the most sensational botanical garden she'd ever seen. Green and gorgeous, and the view was enhanced by hidden romantic lighting. Breaking off her enraptured stare with some reluctance, she remembered she had more to do before Jack's arrival. She paused only long enough at her car to pull her purse from under the seat and throw on a jacket. Cheerfulness filled her mind while she hurried up the stairs to the main level. Swinging one side of the double wood doors open she skipped inside.

Renee marveled at the many beautiful items displayed in the gift shop on the left, after making about four paces onto the richly appointed carpet. Absolutely as good, if not better than the places where she had been a guest in San Francisco. Beautiful huge paintings and portraits hung from the stucco walls.

"If this isn't a castle," she said aloud to herself, "then they certainly missed a good bet."

The formalities of checking in went without a challenge to Jack's bank card and were quickly completed. Waving off the Bell Captain, Renee decided to visit the little store for some much needed supplies before trying to find her room. Hurriedly, she searched out and purchased the essential items she wanted and a few pieces of clothing she would need to spend the night. Paying the storekeep with her own cash, she scurried off to her room. Renee knew that neither she or Jack could afford the prices at this place, but for just the one night, she couldn't resist the indulgence.

Room 210 was the number on the door she searched for. Turning the lock with her key, she pushed the door wide open and stood there feeling the coziness of the old palace.

Beautiful. Tastefully decorated with earth tones and already warm from the heater. This couldn't be more perfect.

In the center of the room was a king size bed with a wonderful satin like spread draping down the sides. Western pictures adorned the walls to help set the atmosphere.

Those may not be Charlie Russell's, she thought as she inspected one of them, but certainly as good.

"First things first," she said to herself when she toured her way into the almost sterile bathroom.

Adjusting the faucets to her liking she started to fill the deep bathtub. Renee watched the water splash into the great white cavern for the longest time thinking if she relinquished her view, the tub would disappear. Moments later she returned to the large sleeping room and removed her clothes. Renee tossed each piece she took off through the door and onto the bathroom floor. She made the promise to herself that she would wash them out in the sink before Jack arrived. Looking into the mirror over a large chest of drawers, she saw herself fully for the first time in quite a while.

"WOW!" she exclaimed while feeling a little ashamed for getting in such condition. "I certainly have a lot to fix!"

Returning to the bathroom she slowly slipped into the hot waters to her waist. Taking a deep breath of pure pleasure she slid in deeper until the water covered her entire body to her chin.

"Ahhhhh! Wonderful!" she groaned out loud.

Even though there was so much to prepare, hair to wash, legs to shave and other girlish things to do, Renee just relaxed. Forever, she decided to just stay forever. In assessing her thoughts one more time, she knew lovelier things were to come to her. Renee knew Jack would hurry himself and be there in little more than an hour. If there was anything in this world she wanted to be, it had to be beautiful, squeaky clean and ready to please him.

She had just completed her momentous task and had gotten out of the tub when she started her ritual of make up and brushed hair. She had to look her absolute devastating best for him. Nothing else in her mind seemed to matter since his second impression of her had to be considerably better than the first. Renee was applying the finishing touches of her lip liner when there was a knock on the door.

Jack? So soon?

She pulled a large bath towel from its rack and wrapped it around her vibrant body. Quickly she stuffed her make-up back into her purse, pulled the plug in the bathtub and kicked her dirty clothes behind the bathroom door. One last quick check in the mirror told her she was as ready as she could be for such a short period of time.

Upon reaching the only door leading to the hall, she wrapped her hand around the knob. At that very second, he again wrapped his knuckles against the wooden frame.

7

"A Touch of Class"

Swinging the door completely open in anticipation of Jack's wonderfully brawny body, Renee stood in the middle of the short hall leading into the room. Her heart pounded and a naughty smile was on her lips in preparation to meet the best person that had happened in her life. Her expression was suddenly stolen away to one of unhappiness and disgust when she recognized the man who had rapped on the door.

"Wh—what are you doing here?" she stammered when she tried to speak.

"I followed you. What else?" Mike said, cocking his head in a "so what?" fashion as he pushed her aside and made his way into the bedroom portion of the suite.

Taking a moment to look up and down the hallway, she cautiously pulled the door shut behind her. Renee leaned back against the cold flat surface of the door still grasping the knob behind her back. She stood motionless, contemplating for a moment what to say or do, how to rid herself of this ugly, filthy bastard she had come to resent. For just showing up, her hatred was raging, but even more for his putting her relationship with Jack in jeopardy. Renee was positive her face had reddened enough to even deepen her new tan. She took a breath slightly deeper than usual to regain control of her mental processes and then at a quick pace walked past Mike. Renee properly sat poised and erect on one of the two large armchairs beside the small table under the window.

"How did you find me?" she demanded with more than a touch of fury in her tone.

Mike took a moment to look around the room before firmly settling himself deeply into the chair opposite her before answering.

"Easy," he said, smiling.

It was the first time she had recognized how sick one of "I got ya!" smiles could be.

"When you left, I just got into my car and followed you. You see I didn't believe the cock and bull story you tried to feed me."

"You mean about the first camp site being the right one?"

"That's right," he answered and then started to fidget and act nervous. Mike stood and walked to the end of the bed. "When I followed you in here, all I had to do was ask the night clerk what room you had registered for us." Turning to face her, he bounced himself down hard on the edge of the bed's mattress. "Really nice room!" he added.

"Then you found my note?"

"Yeah," he said while his eyes continued to roam around the room as if looking for something. "Me and a couple of other guys did."

"What do you mean, you and a couple of other guys? Did you bring someone else into this?" she felt a strong urge to direct Jack to clobber him again.

"No. I saw some other men when I was leaving my hiding place. I slid about half way down the side of the hill across from where you were parked. That's when I saw a big sedan stop behind mine. Actually, it looked like a cop's car except it didn't have a light bar. Then some big Indian looking guy snatched your note off my windshield and read it before he threw it on the ground and drove away. It was kind of freaky. You know? It was almost like he knew exactly what you were saying to me. And then some other man, who had remained in the car, spent a lot of his time yelling something at the Indian."

Before Renee could ask who the Indian could be, more to herself than to Mike, her thoughts were once again interrupted by him.

"I picked it up and read it. Now I know where you're going as well."

Mike patted the bed beside him, indicating for Renee to sit close to him.

"I don't think that's such a good idea," Renee replied while shaking her head in the negative. "We both know I can't do that anymore." Renee pushed herself harder against the firm cushion of the winged chair.

"Who are you trying to kid? You know you can't get along without me. Besides, other than me, who else would want to put up with your bull shit?"

Renee felt her anger start to show through again. *Keep that up buster and I'll give you more pain than Jack has.* She thought.

Again Mike patted the bed beside him. She remained firm and was glaring at him with as much contempt as she ever felt for anyone.

"You just won't take the hint. How clear do I have to make it?"

Mike himself, began to show his anger and reacted with a harsher tone, "You found the stuff, didn't you?"

"Yes," she meekly replied in less than in a more normal voice, "but it's not here."

She was praying that Mike had not seen Jack put the artifacts in her car when he suddenly stood and walked into the bathroom. Renee remained still, listening intently for a sign of what he was doing.

The room isn't that big to be taking that long to look through, she thought, worrying about his silence.

Deciding she had best go and see what he was up to, she put her hands on the arms of the chair and pushed herself up. Suddenly the sounds of a stream of water into the toilet bowl stopped her. Obviously, it was nothing less then the uncouth sounds of Mike urinating.

"God! You don't have an ounce of class! Why don't you shut the door?"

Mike walked back into the room as he was pulling the zipper up on his pants and stood very close to her.

"You think you're a virgin again or something?" Not waiting for her answer, he demanded, "Where are the artifacts?"

All Renee could think to say was that Jack had the stuff with him.

"I can wait," Mike replied as he moved himself closer to her. Running his finger up her arm to her shoulder then down over her collarbone, he finally stopped at the edge of her towel. With an unfamiliar reaction that surprised even her, she slapped his hand causing him to snatch it away with equal surprise.

"When will he get here?" Mike demanded with a much more savage tone.

Trying not to show hesitation, Renee quickly responded, "I'm expecting him right now."

Mike turned his head toward the door to make sure it was closed and strained to see if the lock was engaged.

"You know, I can think of a number of things to do while we wait. Can't you?"

"You're being absurd, Mike. I told you we're finished." Renee told him with a lot more authority in her voice.

"Besides, when I tell your friend Jack what that stuff is worth, whatever we do now won't make a bit of difference to him."

Feeling he had laid a logical groundwork, he moved closer to her again. Only this time he didn't take the time to run his finger tenderly up her arm. He just twisted his hand down inside her towel cupping her right breast as he dug his fingers into her flesh.

"You're hurting me!" Renee snapped as she tried to turn away from him to him to break his grip on her.

Mike ignored her pleading and continued his torturous squeezing. Using both hands, she pulled at his arm with all her strength. The more she pulled, the harder he squeezed and inflicted greater pain in her ample breast.

Mike grinned widely and showed her a lot of grinding teeth. "I think we probably have time for a quickie. You know, just like you usually want it, from behind. Isn't that what you want, lover? Why don't you beg for it? Why don't you just say you can't do without my cock."

Before he was able to say more, she lowered her head and bit him viciously on the forearm through his shirt. Even knowing she had intended to bite to bite him hard, it surprised her when she felt her teeth sink deeply into his flesh.

Ripping his arm from her mouth he shouted out with a yelp of pain. Mike raised his arm before his eyes and quickly inspected the place she had bitten him. The material of his shirt started to turn red from the rich flow of his own blood staining the fabric as it oozed from the wound. The longer he watched, the larger the stain grew until it started to form small drops on the edge of the fabric.

"Bitch! You fucking bitch! You got to be rabid or something!" he snapped, while drawing his arm back over his shoulder in preparation to strike down across her face.

The phone rang. Mike froze with his arm suspended high in the air. He seemed to be certain that someone had heard him. It rang again, then again and again.

"Don't you think I should answer that?" Renee asked in a voice that not only showed her anger with him, but her fear as well. Again the phone rang.

"If I don't answer it, the hotel detective will come to see what's wrong," Renee said, hoping the resort did have one.

Mike walked to the night stand, picked up the entire phone unit, then turned and slammed it down on the table in front of her. She lifted the receiver in mid-ring while glaring back into what could have been fire red eyes.

"Room 210," she said into the mouthpiece still looking up at him. Give me a couple of minutes before you come up. I'll be ready for you."

After replacing the hand set on the cradle she spoke in a calmer voice, "I really don't think you have forgotten what Jack did to you this morning, have you? Do you really think he'll be happy with what you just did to—"

Before she could complete her sentence the door to the room flew open and Mike raced out, turned left and ran down the hall. A few seconds later, following the first door smashing open against the wall, the sound of another door slamming shut echoed in the hall. Grinning, Renee sat back in the chair as she massaged her breast to relieve the pain.

Knock, knock, knock. The familiar sound came through the door. Renee stood, adjusted her towel and pushed back her bangs. Reaching for the door, she tugged it open a few inches and looked through the crack she had just made.

A fellow in a gold Captain's style jacket announced to her, "Bar order," and then apologized for having inconvenienced her with a call about the substitution of Scotch.

It was the bottle of Jack Daniels for her new partner and a bottle of Scotch for herself that she had phoned for just after stepping out of the tub.

Happy with herself, she carried the tray of liquor, glasses and ice to the table where she had been a moment earlier. Setting the tray down she turned the tallest glass upright. Taking a small scoop of tiny ice cubes from the bucket, she added to them a liberal portion of Johnny Walker. Holding the drink before the light, she stared into the caramel colored liquid and mused to herself, "That bastard really is a wimp." In a gesture of a toast she added with a smile, "Here's to the wimps of the world, as he really is one." Renee lifted the glass and took one of those large swigs from the glass that only a woman can manage. Although she felt a slight sensation of burning when it reached her empty stomach, it was still the very best she had had in a very long time.

Following a second and somewhat smaller sip, she started to set the glass on the table when she heard a rap on the door. Different somehow, not at all like the skin-covered knuckles of a hand, but more like metal striking wood. Cautiously she walked to the door and slowly cracked it open. Pushed back by the force of the door against her hands and arms, she was thrown into the room.

Mike immediately stepped inside the little hall leading into the room. Renee's eyes quickly saw he held in his right hand a very menacing looking tire iron.

Pointing the weapon toward her face, he spoke in harsh terms, "Now, I'll give you yours, you cunt. You'll never treat anyone like that again!"

Renee backed further into the room with more fear than she ever had felt in her life. Mike just stood there. He did not move or speak or telegraph his next move. She could see that his eyes were still dark and inflamed, and an almost hypnotic look covered his face. His appearance was as if he had gone completely insane with his hatred toward her.

"You'll regret not staying gone," Renee said, trying to smile. "The fellow behind you won't like you hurting me."

"Bullshit!" Mike said with a grunt. "You dumb fuck, bitch, where do you think we are? At the movies or something?"

A voice behind Mike asked a question in words too memorable for him to have forgotten so easily.

"Is there something I can do for you?"

Mike's eyes opened briefly and then closed to little slits. His mouth hung open in disbelief as his heart skipped a beat or two. Knowing better than to move erratically or turn too quickly, he twisted himself around very slowly to face Jack. This time he greeted a huge fist rapidly burning down toward the end of his nose. With the contact of Jack's knuckles, he literally flew the remainder of the way into the room and rolled onto the floor. Jack walked in and stepped over Mike's somewhat twisted body to reach Renee.

"Has he hurt you?" Jack asked as he swept her into his arms.

Smiling to Jack she replied, "No, not in the slightest."

As Mike regained his composure, and not wishing to give Jack a second chance to destroy what was left of his face, he scrambled on all fours into the hall before standing on his hind legs. Once he reached a point of being semi-upright, he ran as fast as he could down the corridor with one hand cupping his bleeding nose and mouth.

Jack looked at Renee and snickered, "Who was that White man?"

She held her finger to her mouth requesting his silence. Then the noise of a slamming door filled the air.

Gone, she thought, *but not forgotten.*

"What was he after? The artifacts?" Jack squeezed her body closer to his.

"That's it. Besides being an asshole, Mike wants what we found."

"That figures," Jack said as he turned his head towards the open door. Throwing her arms around his mid section, she squeezed tightly. Renee lowered her head to his chest and felt the warmth and security he offered through his massive frame.

"It doesn't matter," she cooed. "You're here now and that's what I wanted most of all."

As they stood together in tight embrace, Jack broke the silence. "You really have me at a disadvantage."

"How's that?" Renee asked without removing her head.

"You're clean and smell good! I smell like a hard-worked mule."

Jack peeled her tightly gripping arms from around his body. Almost reluctantly he walked to the door, stopped just short of leaving the room and reached out into the hall. Retracting his arm, his hand was filled with his suitcase which he tossed on the bed as he re-entered the room. Picking up the phone he dialed "0" and asked for the restaurant.

Hearing this, Renee moved closer to Jack, placed her hands on his brawny arm and whispered, "We are going to eat in here, aren't we?"

"No, I don't believe so." Then, as a voice obviously came onto the opposite end of the line. "I'd like a table for two," he requested into the mouthpiece. "Yes," he replied to the unheard voice. "About an hour will be fine." Jack returned the receiver to its cradle.

Sounding like a motorboat, she couldn't help but sputter out one word several times. "But-but-but! I was hoping—!"

"Look, we've been through a lot together over the last couple of days and I didn't have you come here just to stay in this room."

Again she tried to protest, "But—!"

Taking her hands in his he kissed the tips of her fingers very passionately. "I owe you for not only my life but for being someone so incredibly special. I couldn't have it any other way than to make this something very extra special for you."

No one has ever treated me this way, she told herself in disbelief.

For the first time she could recall, she was the one that really wanted to stay in the room and do what she wanted to do. *Why,* she asked herself, *isn't he like the other men she had known? He's genuinely generous and caring.* Renee was literally overwhelmed.

Stepping away from her, Jack reached for the fifth of Jack Daniels on the tray. Uncorking the bottle, he held it to the light just the same as Renee had done with her glass. Placing the mouth of the bottle to his lips he tilted its bottom high into the air and let several huge swallows slosh down his throat. Gagging, he jerked the bottle from his mouth, gasped for air, and then coughed several times.

"Geez, that's good!" he tried to say, barely able to wheeze his squeaky words out.

Following the not so careful stuffing of the cork back into the appropriate hole, he placed the bottle down on the tray. Taking the few short steps to the bed, Jack unzipped his suitcase and pulled several articles of clothing from the launderer's little plastic containers. Renee was processing this little bit of information about his ability as a housekeeper, when he started to enter the bathroom. He abruptly stopped and turned himself slightly to look at her again.

"Even though I don't really know who you are—I want you to know I believe I love you, too," he said and shut the door before she could respond to such a grabbing statement.

Dumbfounded, she stood as still as a rock, not wishing to follow up what he had said to a closed door. Frustration flowed out of every pore in her body as her heart tried to beat its way into a whole new rhythm. Renee shivered and partially swelled as her hormones slobbered a silent statement of desire and a whisper of warm wetness dripped down her leg toward her knee. YUMMMM!!! Lord, how she wanted him at this very moment.

Not wanting to wear the towel down to the parking lot, Renee slipped on the sweat suit she had bought at the gift shop in the lobby. As she was scurrying past the registration desk she obtained the assistance of a resort employee for security purposes. With no real explanation the two returned to her car. Pushing and pulling things here and there, she found a plain black skirt and four-inch pumps along with a creme colored Granny blouse with lots of lace. The same clothes she had worn to dinner in Lone Pine the night before she had entered Saline Valley. With renewed hindsight she wished she had brought better with her. But then again she had little choice but to be satisfied with what she had. Thanking the employee who was confused to why she had requested his help, she knew he'd be watching her hips sway back and forth as she danced her way back toward the door leading to the hall and her room.

Good! She thought when she pushed open the door and scanned the room. *He's still in the shower.*

Renee laid her clothes out on the bed in preparation to looking as a real woman wanted to look for her man.

"Rats!" she said out loud when she started to slip into the blouse. She suddenly realized she had forgotten her nylons. Without them she knew she would feel half-naked and not near as classy as she wished.

With nothing else to do that would change her circumstances, she completed her dressing. Admiring herself in the mirror she decided that buttoning all the buttons, including the collar, was appropriate for not only the fashionable restaurant downstairs, but more importantly, for Jack. She wobbled momentarily but still could not bring herself to wear the beautiful blouse half unbuttoned, as she usually liked in that more casual manner.

Renee tried to sit patiently and wait for Jack to come out of the bathroom. The stress of the situation didn't allow that to work well at all. She moved to the matching chair across the little table for a better view of him as he would enter the room. Her nerves again overcame her. Cocking her head slightly to the side, her eyes squinted slightly as she mindfully surveyed the bed's dust cover. Without any further arguments with herself she decided to try lying as seductively as possible on the bone-white spread. She positively knew that when he returned to the bedroom, he would easily find himself so impressed he wouldn't dare want to leave the room that night. Spending many more minutes trying several positions on the giant mattress, Renee found she still could not be happy. Not a single pose met with her acceptance or satisfaction.

With a determined push and very much unladylike grace, she stood, only to find her shirt tail had partially pulled out of her skirt on one side. Unbuttoning and then unzipping her skirt, the material slipped from her fingers and fell silently to the floor. The little pile of broken dreams surrounded her high heels and ankles in a most disturbing manner.

Just as she bent over straight-legged to retrieve the elusive material, Jack flung the door open and penetrated the room. Arms spread wide, he in his own way modeled seductively the finest old Western cut blue suit he owned. But now, in its most heart rendering splendor, was a white-laced and bikini-clad fanny that would disrupt anyone's best planned entrance.

Startled by Jack's sudden entrance into the room, Renee stumbled forward. She found her feet trapped in her skirt as if Providence had tied her ankles shamelessly together. Jack abandoned his somehow picturesque pose for her between the doorjambs and raced to her aid. As he rounded the corner of the bed too closely he hit the mattress with his leg. One foot was thrown into the path of the other. Off balance and tripping himself he stumbled and fell to the floor along side her.

Unable to control herself, Renee roared in near hysterical laughter at the spectacle they must have made. With a mountainous laugh, Jack tried to sit, only to fall back onto the carpet and crank himself into a ball of cackle. It took several attempts to calm down enough to speak. But each time they looked at one another, they would again erupt into near eye-watering hysterics. After several attempts on Jack's part to control himself, he was finally able to stand. With an extended hand he grasped hers and assisted Renee to her feet. She tucked in the shirttail, buttoned and zipped her skirt while intermittently breaking into a barely subdued giggle. With a quick tie of a large black velvet bow in her hair, she took his hand and they walked out the door, their smiles echoing through the halls of the resort.

• • •

"Two New York cuts. One well done and the lady's bloody rare," Jack told the waiter without moving his eyes from hers. "The lady will have salad tossed with house dressing, baked potato with sour cream and chives and the same for myself."

"Very well," the wine steward replied. "I shall send for the waiter."

Jack thrust an evil eye of contempt towards the wine steward. Renee watched him walk away toward the kitchen while Jack appeared to continue scorning the poor man silently.

"What a wonderful place!" she said while she scanned the room and attempted to take his mind off the minor mistake.

The restaurant was nearly full with people quietly chattering among themselves at their tables. Subdued lights from little candles were flickering through little red glass globes on the tables. Here and there lone couples smiled at each other with their eyes. Now hers longed for his and her smile returned to Jack.

"Have you been here often?" she asked.

A little embarrassed that this was his first time at the resort as a guest, Jack thought it would not be lying if he were to say yes.

After all, he told himself, *I've eaten in the employee's dining room a couple of times when I worked criminal cases here at the Inn.*

"I enjoy it, too." he replied before he sipped his water.

Out of nowhere the wine steward reappeared at the table. They seemed to smile at one another for the briefest of moments before he handed Jack a hard-covered wine list. The steward rocked back and forth on his heels, silently waiting for Jack to make up his mind. Talking a short moment to look at the list, Jack turned his head to the steward and pointed at what he hoped would be a terrific wine. The steward turned and left without a word.

Although the room was nearly filled to capacity, Renee felt completely alone with her man. She painted a mental picture of how he had probably done more to prepare himself for this moment with her than he had for anyone since before his wife had passed away. Renee, bubbling over with a long forgotten pride, was beside herself just to be with him.

Jack broke her thoughts when he spoke. "You know I don't know a thing about you. You're really quite a mystery to me."

"You know my name and my hobby; that's a start," she said, continuing with nearly her entire life's history.

Listening, but only occasionally hearing while she spoke, Jack was fascinated by her personality. He was overcome with her poetic style and her beautiful looks. And to top all of it off, a very intelligent woman to boot. It would have taken very little in his imagination to see her sitting across from him framed in the glow of a golden halo.

"You're an angel!" he said a little too loudly from his thoughts.

Renee instantly quit speaking. Reaching across the table she pressed her hand under his. Renee heard herself moan with pleasure when a tingling sensation raced back and forth between them. With unexpected speed for a second time, goosebumps rose up her spine to the nape of her neck. She thought she would faint when she suddenly started to hyperventilate and become short of breath. She was gasping for more air for no good reason.

Neither one knew how long the wine steward had been standing beside them when his words broke the spell that had fallen over them.

"Your wine, sir," he said while he passed the bottle over Jack's right shoulder and poured a small amount into his tulip glass. Following the swishing of the crimson liquid around a little before he took a small swallow, he seemed to purposely wait a second or two before nodding his approval. It seemed like only seconds had passed after the bottle was left on the table then the steward disappeared. Now being placed before her from a large bowl on a wheeled cart, was her salad.

My God, she thought, not realizing what the waiter was doing, *I'm really lost. Things I should be seeing aren't even registering.* Out of the fear all this would be a dream, she leaned toward Jack and spoke very softly. "Please make love to me tonight," Renee begged of him.

Hearing exactly what she had said, Jack gulped and seemed to become deaf. "What?" Then feeling like an idiot he tried to stammer words more fitting and found himself saying "WHAT?" one more stupid time.

He nearly spilled his wine from the glass as he grabbed the stem and took a quick swallow to quench the sudden dryness that had invaded his mouth. The waiter left the table with a small chuckle that was heard by Jack and likely everyone else in the room.

Renee repeated in a louder voice as she gritted her teeth as if trying to lower her tone, "I need the feel of you in me tonight."

A hush fell over the nearby tables when several people turned their heads and smiled at the two of them as the waiter was laughing even louder. Renee thumped her elbows on the table and dropped her face into her hands to conceal a muted whimper.

"What have I done?" she was heard to say into her fingers by still more snickering guests.

Finishing the meal as quietly as possible, Jack signed the bill the waiter had given him with his name and room number. Feeling more than a little embarrassed, he left an extremely generous gratuity.

Renee could almost feel his need to compensate for the spectacle of near floor show proportions she had produced.

Stepping away from the Captain's station, they almost ran from the restaurant into the lobby. Trying not to show his desires for her were nearly out of control, he did his best to convince himself that he would not act like an idiot again that night.

"Come with me," he said, dragging Renee behind him.

They left the lobby and crossed the drive at a rapid pace with extra long strides that were almost beyond her capabilities. Taking the narrow walk way and down some stairs, he led Renee into the inn's botanical gardens below the parking area. Slowing a little, he became more bewildered, having forgotten the chill of the night air and the stupidity of coming outside in the first place. Taking off his jacket, he wrapped it over her shoulders and buttoned the topmost button. When he started to walk again, she tugged on his arm to let him know she wasn't interested in going any farther. Renee pulled harder, expressing her desire for him to kneel with her onto the deep winter grass. Renee knew this was perfect spot between some palms in the pale yellow of the garden lights for what she required.

"Don't be afraid," she said as she lowered herself down while pulling him along with her. "I've got to have you now."

Her voice rasped out the words which were closely followed by her mouth wantonly seeking his. Their tongues lashed out and touched. They found each other as their arms tightly entwined around one another. A fierce embrace compelled by burning passion tore into their souls. Each moaned their desire to immediately couple with the other. Not knowing where her strength came from, she forced Jack onto his back. Deftly, she unzipped the fly of his trousers and reached into the opening she had created. All the while her kisses lavished his lips. She found it no easy endeavor to expose him to her with what she speculated as being a not so gentle pull.

"It will break in half!" she cried in a worried voice while trying to bend him enough to free the massive erection through an obviously too small opening.

She loved feeling he didn't need to be coaxed and was fully aroused without the slightest of foreplay. Still she couldn't resist keeping her fingers wrapped around him. The feeling was exquisite to let them slide up and down his length for a few tantalizing strokes.

"Please respect me in the morning," he pleaded with some sort of wicked smile.

Ignoring him, Renee hiked her skirt and his oversized jacket up to her waist and swung her leg over his muscular form. Her eyes closed tightly as she felt she was about to straddle the barrel of a great cannon. Almost in the same motion she pushed her panties to the side and slipped him into the wet confines of her body. Deeper, she lowered herself upon his erection. Her hands grasped each side of his shoulders as she screeched out a moan as he completely filled her spasming tunnel. Her head reeled back in nothing less than pure ecstasy. Her legs involuntarily vibrated with the newly found pleasures that rippled through her super heated body. Renee knew nothing could stop her union with him now. She held her eyes tightly shut while she undulated her hips back and forth over the length of his crowned scepter.

Rapidly Jack's hands pulled her blouse from her raised skirt. Moving his hands up along her smooth sides until his fingers rested upon her breasts. Round and full with nipples erect, he massaged her and felt the meaty firmness that he so desired to take into his mouth.

Renee moved her hips faster with the taking of short and wanton strokes. Screams of delight filled her throat while his manhood pulsated deeply forcing her fluids out upon himself. Waves of pleasure dominated them both.

Jack's long awaited release tore into her with the surge of a bucking horse. She filled the night air with a long scream of wonderful delight. Renee tightened her grip around him and rode out the storm at a continued gallop that consumed them both.

Renee felt as if she had been completely robbed of her wind. She gasped for air. Her short erratic breaths mingled with his as her arms buckled and her breasts slipped away from his hands. She lay upon him, reveling in the beauty that had just occurred. She kissed him most briefly. It wasn't until now that she allowed her head to rest along side his. Renee's nostrils filled with the sweet smell of the winter grass below her lover.

"I love you, my darling," she blew into his ear.

"For all that is wonderful on this earth, I love you more," Jack whispered in return.

They lay together for several more minutes until Jack's softening organ fell free from her.

"Let's go to the room," he whimpered into her ear as she felt a spasm of resurrection lifting against her.

Doing her best to stand on shaking legs, Renee stepped from over him and smoothed her skirt. Jack, feeling the world had changed directions, found it just as difficult to tear himself away from the now warmed grass below his back. Standing beside her, he tried to brush away the small pieces of finely cut grass from his pantlegs and fanny. Suddenly he stopped his aimless brushing and bringing his head closer, he touched his lips tenderly to hers.

They walked slowly back up the path for no more than a dozen steps, then stopped in surprise. Out of the silence of the desert night they heard the clapping of hands directly above them. Simultaneously they looked up to see a half dozen men and women looking down from the parking lot safety rail. Each of the spectators was applauding their act of uninhibited lovemaking. Faster and faster they continued their walk up the long path to their room while laughing quietly to one another. Neither cared who could give testimony as to what had just happened. Each only wanted the company of the other and nothing more.

Jack fumbled with the key as he unlocked the door marked 210. When they entered, Renee rushed directly into the bathroom and closed the door behind her. Jack lifted his suitcase from the bed and set it quietly on the table under the window. Grabbing the ice bucket he noticed all that was left was the water and not the hint of a single cube. Moving toward the door he looked at himself in the mirror. What he saw surprised him. His knees were wet and had been stained green where he had been pulled onto the grass. Turning slightly to the side he tried to see his back. The stains were on the seat of his trousers and on his right elbow as well.

Saying out loud, "She was worth it," he opened the door and headed to the ice machine at the end of the hall. The door automatically swung closed behind him as he left the room.

Halfway down the hall, Jack realized he had neglected to dump the melted ice water from the bucket. When he had reached the ice machine he found nothing sufficient to pour the bucket's contents into.

"Ah ha!" he said, opening the exterior door to dump out the water. The water splashed onto the asphalt sidewalk below. For some unknown reason he took a moment to look toward the parking lot and saw the faint form of a man looking into the window of one of the small cars. When the figure became clearer with his vision adjusting to the darkness, he recognized the man to be Renee's boyfriend.

"That S.O.B. Why doesn't he just go away?" Jack said out loud.

Quickly he filled the bucket from the chipped ice machine and went directly to the house phone on the opposite end of the corridor. When he lifted the receiver the switchboard automatically rang.

"Desk," the voice said when the ringing stopped.

"This is 208," Jack said. "There is a strange-looking man in the parking lot trying to break into one of the cars."

"Thank you!" the voice replied with the line going dead almost immediately.

After hanging up the receiver, Jack returned to his room, grinning as he walked.

Jack immediately set the ice bucket down on the tray and went to the window. He drew back the drapes in time to see three of the Inn's employees wrestling Mike to the ground. Following a virtual hail of punches and kicks, Mike was finally pulled to his feet and led off toward the maintenance building. A man on each side held him by the arms as he jerked from side to side. The third man following close behind seemed to take some pleasure in pushing them along. Laughing to himself about what he had done, Jack wondered how Mike could take a beating three times in one day and come back for more if given the chance.

• • •

Renee stood before the bathroom mirror, looking at the new rosy color of her cheeks and the warm glow of her skin that highlighted her face. Slowly she undressed while she reminisced about the past hour and a half.

Her eyebrows raised as that clear memory took hold one more time in her loins. "Especially that last part!"

Involuntarily her body shuddered with her thought of their lovemaking. Wrapping the large bath towel around herself she groomed her hair with a small brush. Turning to face the door, she stopped momentarily to wonder how much better it could get. Twisting the knob with a still shaking hand, Renee swung the door open and stepped into the room.

Her foot hadn't touched the floor when Jack said, "Get dressed, we have to leave as soon as possible."

Looking at the giant unused bed, she was again at a loss for words.

"Let's go," Jack demanded as he finished packing his suit case and then zipped it shut.

"Why?" Renee demanded. "What happened?" thinking she had offended him by her aggressiveness under the palms.

"I just turned your boyfriend in as a burglar. Mac, the substation deputy will probably be here soon. I'm sure Mike will talk him into coming up here, and we just don't need to be here when the deputy arrives. Besides, we would have to turn over the artifacts we found." Pulling the towel from around herself, Renee tossed it onto the bed. She really had to nudge herself to return to the bathroom to dress. She took but a moment to change back to her skirt and blouse.

Gathering the Scotch and Bourbon from the tray, she shoved them in a pillowcase. After stuffing her dirty shorts and T-shirt in to keep the bottles from clanging together, she said she was ready. They left the building quietly by way of the rear stairs and crept around the corner and into the parking lot.

She passed the keys to Jack, and he quickly unlocked the doors and stuffed everything into the rear seat. Slowly and without headlights, so as not to attract attention, Jack backed from the parking space and headed her car down the resort's asphalt narrow road to the highway.

"Do you think he's going to follow us now?" Jack asked, hoping she would say no.

"Without a doubt," Renee replied, "I told him in a note where we are going."

8

"A Change of Venue"

Leaving the resort road, Jack swung Renee's little sedan onto the highway towards Corkscrew Peak, Daylight Pass and the Nevada border. It is a narrow ribbon of asphalt that is primarily used for tourists taking in the sights of the valley or heading to Scotty's Castle and Tie Canyon. At best, it's a dangerous road when driving the speed limit and then becomes even worse at night, with the occasional wild burro and predators or visiting speeders hogging the highway.

Glancing briefly to Renee as he drove a little slower than the fifty mile per hour speed limit, he queried her, "How did he know we were there?" Jack just didn't seem to understand why she had told Mike about their final destination in Pine Ridge and the reservation.

"He followed me here from the valley. And to make things worse, I kind of left him a note telling him we were going to the Battlefield."

"Kind of? You really did that?" Jack asked with a sour expression.

"Yeah, and something else. Mike told me about some Indian who also had read the note before he had gotten to it."

"What Indian? Describe him to me," he said, trying to be patient with the surprise disclosure and such an illogical move on her part.

"He probably was just some curious guy touring in the valley," she replied in a somewhat casual manner. "All Mike said was it looked like a police car he was driving or something. I don't believe he was even sure about that."

Jack watched as the headlights of another car took up more of the narrow highway than it should have. The vehicle flew past them before he spoke again.

"There is another person I need to tell you about who wants the artifacts. Probably more than Mike wants them."

"Who is that?"

"A Tribal cop named Nick Whitewater. I worked with him on the Dakota reservation several years ago."

"What does he want to do with my stuff?" Renee asked as she pressed herself a little closer to him.

The fingers of her left hand slid over his polyester pant leg to the edge of his crotch. She slowly slipped her fingers to the inside of his thigh and squeezed him lovingly. Jack seemed to enjoy her gentle caresses as the touch of her hand made him pulsate and strain against the fabric. With each light stroke of her finger, his member danced with more enthusiasm.

For a moment he remembered back to the time so long ago when his wife had sat beside him just as Renee was. His beautiful wife's fingers would brush against him and tease and she would smile.

That was so long ago, he thought. "I believe he's a pot hunter who diversified," Jack said, trying to break his thoughts of the past and a rising erection. "You do understand the stuff we found could be worth hundreds or even thousands of dollars to a private collector?"

"Sure do," Renee replied with renewed confidence in her voice. "Mike told me that he had talked to someone who felt it could fetch a million dollars or more to a European buyer."

"Damn!" Jack blurted out in surprise. "I know of some pots and baskets that have been sold for more than fifty thousand on the black market. But a million! Wow! Why that's almost enough to make an honest man have second thoughts," he added in a tone of real curious sincerity.

"Anyway, you were telling me about this Nick Whitewater," she said with eyes closed and her head resting on his shoulder. Renee opened her eyes momentarily and looked ahead to the road and then closed them again. Jack didn't know whether he should tell her everything about Nick or as little as possible. He knew he didn't want to scare her to death, only give her a firm warning.

Instead, he compromised by saying, "Besides being a crook, he's a mean cop who wouldn't mind hurting anyone to get what he wants. If he read the note you left, you can bet he'll be waiting for us at the battlefield." Thinking about the possible danger he would be placing her in, he continued, "I have some friends you can stay with while I'm there."

"Why?" she asked. "As you said, we're in this together. Besides, you need to have more faith in me and my abilities."

"I have to protect you from him," Jack said, reasoning with her. "I just have to. I know what he can do."

"Don't you want me with you?"

"Certainly I do. I just don't want to place you in an already tricky and dangerous situation."

"Look, to do this the safest and best way we need to be together. No matter what confronts us."

Jack didn't say anything in reply to her statement letting his eyes focus on the road ahead of them.

"Jack?"

"Yes?" he responded with a lifted eyebrow.

"I want to apologize for taking advantage earlier. I hope you don't feel like I raped you or something. After all,

I don't want you to think I'm some kind of woman's libber or lady of the night or something."

"I believe you should allow me to apologize to you, for not being more for you during those moments in the grass. I want you to understand, I haven't been with a woman since my wife passed away. I made a promise to myself a long time ago that I wouldn't make love to another woman unless I intended to marry her."

"You practiced celibacy all this time?" she shrieked in confusion over his admission. Renee raised her head to look at him with a questioning gaze in the dim glow of dash lights.

"Well!" he replied. "Let's just say I worked the problems out by hand."

A small giggle slipped from her lips.

"I couldn't help it," he added in an attempt to show he wasn't some kind of basket case. "I am a man, you know! And I do have urges like normal people."

Renee felt a change in his expression with his somewhat aggressive statement.

Jack thought about how stupid that statement sounded knowing a woman in the same frame of mind might resort to her own stimulation.

"Believe me. I know you're a man," she said letting the air out of her lungs as she spoke in a long purring sigh.

Resting her head back on his shoulder, she felt his embarrassment over what he had said.

Changing the subject, she went on. "Do you think Nick will try to hurt you when we get there?"

"There's no doubt in my mind," he replied when the car started down the Nevada side of Day Light Pass. "How's a cup of coffee sound to you?" he asked and then added before she could answer, "I know I could use one."

"Great!" Renee replied enthusiastically and sat up straight to look around. "You got some in your pocket or something?"

She again looked to the front and saw the light from her own car's headlamps. Only a few blinking stars in the black sky were brighter than the glow of the lights and that was about it.

"Over there." He directed her attention by pointing into the distance off the right front fender of the car.

Several lights were in fact where she thought the horizon should have been. One light, a red one, was slightly brighter than the stars or the other lights.

"That's Beatty. We'll stop at the Exchange Club."

"What's that one bright red light for?" she asked, straining her eyes to see better.

Renee thought she could feel Jack grinning in the darkness before he answered.

"That's a Cat House. You know, a House of Ill Repute."

She thought better than to ask if he had ever visited the place even before she remembered his statement of working out his own problems. Trying to be a little sly, asked, "What's the place called?"

Jack paused a long moment before he decided to answer. "I don't know for sure." he added, "The one down the road a ways is the Shamrock Ranch." Then it dawned on him that was also a stupid answer. He wondered if she thought he frequented those kind of places and had lied to her. Jack remained silent and tried to figure out how to explain to her his work had taken him there.

For the next few minutes she sat with her head against him. Her hand remained resting on his leg and her eyes closed. Nothing more was said between them as the miles slipped past. The only sounds either of them heard were the low groans of the engine as it pressed on toward their destination. Renee made herself more comfortable against his strong arm, feeling the security and safety of his presence.

• • •

Her eyes opened when she felt the wheels of the car leave the edge of the pavement onto the gravel berm as it slowed to a stop.

"Are we there?" she asked while trying to focus her eyes before a brightly lit motel sign. "Is this the Exchange Club?"

"No. It's not. I think sleep is more important to both of us right now than coffee. It's been one hell of an exhausting day and to be honest with you, I'm busted."

Leaving the engine running, Jack stepped from the car and went into the motel office.

Renee knew he was right. She also knew she was at the end of her endurance and could use some of that much earned sleep. Picking up her purse from the passenger side of the floorboard, she searched around the car for anything else she might need to take into the room with them.

Within a few minutes, Jack returned and drove around to the side of the building. As if in a daze, he got out of the car, shuffled to her side and opened the door. Almost holding each other up, they entered one of the rooms whose door faced out onto the slot Jack had just parked in. She was so sleepy the number on the door didn't even register with her when she tried to read it. Renee walked up next to the bed and looked through her glazed and blurry eyes at all the wonderful comfort it offered.

This one is a lot smaller than the one at the resort! She thought to herself.

Jack moved around her and drew back the covers and sheets and fluffed the pillows. Leaving her standing by the bed, he returned to the car to secure it from the type of itinerant individuals he knew passed through the area late at night.

As Jack left the room, Renee fumbled with the buttons on her blouse, her eyelids half closed. She felt she didn't even have the strength to politely cover her mouth when she yawned widely.

It took Jack a moment to retrieve the bundle from the trunk and to finish locking the car. Renee was still standing beside the bed when he again entered the room. Still fumbling with the same buttons she had started with, her fingers seemed to have lost their sensitivity and made that simple task take on a mind of its own. Placing the artifacts on the bureau the TV was on, he returned to her.

"You poor beautiful thing," he told her as he lowered her arms to her side. Jack unbuttoned her blouse and slipped it off her shoulders. Looking around for a place to drape it, he tossed it toward the only chair and missed. Even in his exhaustion, he couldn't help but let his eyes take in her firm upturned breasts. In her best attempt to help him undo the button on the waist of her skirt and then her zipper, their fingers seemed to get in the other's way. The black skirt fell limply to her feet.

Renee noticed his fingers were convulsing before he nervously stepped away from her to double lock the room door. At almost the same time Renee lowered her panties down her legs and stepped away from them and onto the bed. She was slipping under the briskly cool covers when Jack turned. He patiently watched her eyes flutter briefly and then close. Her head sank silently into the pillow.

Without releasing her from his admiring gaze, he undressed. Jack couldn't believe her beauty, or for that matter, understand why she had become attracted to him. He continued to watch for a long time as she found her way to a deeper sleep. Jack flicked the light switch off from the wall near the door and made his way to the opposite side of the bed in the small room. Breathing shallowly and moving slowly he lay down as quietly as he could beside her. Reaching out like a small boy who had been told to stay out of the cookie jar, he scooted himself closer to feel her warm body against his own. Like a python moving through the grass, he allowed his hand to cross her side and stomach before he allowed the weight of his arm to rest on her. He tenderly nibbled a kiss her on the neck just below her ear. With his own exhaustion overcoming him, he started his short fall into a deep sleep upon the closing of his eyes. The warmth of her side pressed firmly against him was the last sensation before he slipped into darkness.

• • •

The aroma of fresh coffee opened Renee's eyes as the morning light sneaked through the cracks between the heavy drapes and walls. Sitting on the side of the bed, Jack held one of those plastic motel cups in one hand, while he fanned the swirling steam directly under her nose with the other.

"Hmmm!" The sound of awakening taste buds evolved from her mouth.

Renee felt her nose sensors like fingers beckoning her to the edge of that scrumptious cup. She tugged it away from Jack after she allowed her fingers to curl around its circumference and feel the inviting warmth. As her head quickly closed the distance to the plastic rim, it seemed she was expecting it to run away and hide from her. Her lips stood poised and ready to sip long before they had reached their objective. A small swallow passed over her teeth and coerced its way across her tongue to awaken her as only coffee was meant to do.

"Good morning, Renee," Jack said with a smile while watching her awaken like the petals of a desert rose.

A second swallow brought her starter motor into full rev, telling her the real engine would soon kick into play. Unexpectedly, and just as suddenly, the little girl matured into that of a vibrant woman.

"And good morning to you, too!" She smiled back in happy reply.

Renee tried to sit up fully while retaining some resemblance of her respectability. The cup balanced in one hand while she pulled the sheet around her nearly exposed breasts with the other.

Jack fluffed and patted her pillow up against the headboard with his free hand. After taking the cup from her, he took a shallow drink from his own and set them both down on the night stand. With his help, she managed to slide herself toward the headboard and leaned back. When finally comfortable she extended her hand to allow Jack to hand back her coffee.

"Are you ready for a long drive?" he asked her.

"No, I don't think so." Leaning forward on the bed, she kissed him.

Parting his lips from hers by only a fraction of an inch, he spoke again. "It's almost eight o'clock, you know. How long does waking up take?"

"A while."

Setting the cup on the night stand near the lamp, she left Jack sitting patiently to watch her leave the room. Rolling herself off the edge of the mattress nearest the bathroom door, Renee stood, dragging the bedspread behind her. On tiptoes, she hurried off to the bathroom to relieve the pressures that had built up in her during the night. When she passed the dressing counter she saw the little courtesy coffeepot boiling water for two more cups. Renee yanked the cord from the socket and continued her way to that urgent mission.

Jack smiled one of his devilish little grins while he watched her slip from the room. Taking another sip of his coffee, he put his cup down beside hers to wait for her return. Wanting something to break the silence and his own tension, Jack rose and went to the television. Turning on the set, he switched it from picture to radio and began playing the dial back and forth. He attempted to search out a decent radio station for not only the news but possibly some music. Not finding exactly what he was looking for, he settled on one of the distant Las Vegas country and western stations. After adjusting the volume to a quieter level, he returned to the bed and sat quietly to wait. He was just reaching for his cup when she stepped out of the bathroom.

Renee stopped at the edge of the bed, glanced toward the radio and announced, "That will never do."

She felt she really wasn't in the mood for Willie Nelson singing something about being on the road again.

"I hope you understand, I have nothing against western music," she told him.

Renee turned the dial back and forth several times until she found some music more to her liking.

"Elevator music?" Jack asked in bewilderment. "You've got to be kidding!"

"Well, it is more soothing than rock and roll or that stuff you had on," she replied after she returned to where he was sitting.

Renee extended her arm around Jack's neck and lowered herself onto his lap.

"I think you did this last night," he said while using his strength to lift and readjust her more comfortably on his legs.

Teasingly, Renee kissed the outer edge of his lip. Each time he would move his mouth to find hers she would torment him further by touching her lips to a new place. Squirming just a tad, she felt the yardstick of information that told her she tantalized him all the more. Both laughing and acting silly, the battle of lips consumed them with the joy of their playfulness. Without innocent exploit their manipulations didn't diminish to anything less then heated excitement. Their lips locked in passionate suction as their tongues fought out the battle of control over the other's.

Jack's strong arms held securely as he stood, turned and gently lowered her back onto the bed. As if they had been attached to one another by some magical means, their kiss did not break. Swinging his muscular body above her he slowly crossed to her opposite side. His scepter wickedly cut a path searing torment across her lower tummy. Once he had adjusted his position his lips kissed their way to her eyes and lingered there for the briefest of moments. His succulent mouth gradually worked its way down her cheek to her neck where he licked and sucked in her fragrance for what seemed like forever. Her eyes closed taking in the incredible sensations he bestowed on her passions. In fantasy, her mind begged him to have his way with her in any manner he wished.

Her breathing became heavier each time his tongue would flutter against her neck or touch her ear. Her anticipation grew when his hand slowly glided its way to the underside of her breast. He let his fingers gently stroke her velvety skin. With each movement, the tips of his fingers came closer to the large pink areola and her erect nipple. Her chest rose to greet him and urge him closer to her goal.

Jack moved his nibbling kisses to her ear and probed deeply with the tip of his tongue. The sudden stabbing sensation to her inner ear caused her to squirm harder under his unrelenting torment. His finger lightly drew a path to her other breast and gently massaged all around but never quite touching her most sensitive place.

Renee started to rotate her hips while pressing herself closer to him. She arched her back and offered up her breast to be lavished by his warm and wet lips.

His kisses became small licks and prods with his tongue, jabbing out to her left ear then delving quickly inside again and again, only to retract it one more time.

Her hand rose slightly from the bed between them and she wrapped her fingers around his rock hard and throbbing penis to feel his strength. Slowly she stroked the pulsating organ from the base to the crown. Several times she clenched her fingers even tighter and tried to pull him closer behind the leg she raised for him.

Jack was more than aware he could not take much of her sweet caresses or he would shoot an endless flow of ejaculate with very little effort. Moving himself slightly down and away from her, he pulled himself free of her clenching fingers. Still lower he inched himself down her flawless body, his lips and tongue feeling the smoothness of her skin, all the while leaving a small trail of saliva. Very slowly he worked his way to the breast that was surrounded by his caressing fingers. Squeezing her breast lightly, the nipple rose from the pressure. As his mouth neared the side of the large globe, Jack pressured his tongue to slide up and barely touch the bottom edge of her nipple.

Her moans became much more audible from deep within her throat. His hand moved across her chest to caress her other breast while at the same time his lips surrounded her nipple and pulled her into his mouth. His warm wet lips pressured tightly around the firm little bud and pulled with an increasing sucking delight. Her hips undulated harder against him. Not wishing his manipulations to stop, Renee pushed her fingers into his hair as he kissed his way across the valley of her chest.

He again replaced his fingertips with his lips and tongue. Jack sucked her into his mouth and repeatedly lashed his tongue over her little bud and dragged it across the sensitive tip.

Renee moaned still louder to the pleasures he was bestowing upon her. Jack knew he had gained near total control as her head thrashed from side to side.

Possibly without even her own knowledge she continued to move her hand on top of his head and run her fingers through his long hair beckoning him on.

Jack licked small circles around first one nipple then the other while his hand massaged down the outside of her firm leg. Renee squirmed with more intensity when he drug his fingers up the inside of her soft inner thighs. Invitingly close, his fingers passed just to the side of her womanhood through the outer fringes of her pubic hair. Several times he repeated this same motion from one leg to the other and then circle back to the first. Jack sensed her inferno raging with a superhuman desire to be cooled with the spray of his essence.

Leaving her breast, his mouth gently slid between her milky white globes where he lingered with a deep kiss before proceeding on. Ever so slowly his lips and tongue worked their way down the shallow curve of her stomach. His mouth traced a wet path and swirled around her navel before he thrust deeply into her several times.

Renee now had both hands on his head. Her fingers entangled with his hair she gripped the long strands firmly to coax him on faster.

He lingered with the little licks and kissed lower with her insistence as her hands pressured him further. Succumbing to his lover's urgency, Jack gradually positioned himself totally between her legs. All the while his mouth continued to work little happy things on her molten flesh.

Kissing with more pressure through her coarse hair near the crease of her leg, he allowed himself to trail off the inside of her thigh and leisurely stroke halfway to her knee.

Renee bent forward slightly to hold his head and watch his perfect ministrations. Not wanting him to slide from her grasp she pulled his hair harder toward her place of her desires. Again the long wet strokes of his tongue caressed her skin and then down the other side to repeat his movements. Her hips bucked with each approach of his mouth to her dripping wet tunnel of love.

Jack reached up with his hands and cupped both her breasts. He massaged them with his fingers and found her nipples. He rotated each one between thumb and forefinger as waves of enhanced pleasure from his wonderful technique overcame her.

"Please! Please!" she moaned "Please do me now!"

Jack ignored her wanton cries for satisfaction. Instead of moving to her demands, he kissed her solidly upon her swollen lips.

Her body began to shake violently. For a moment his mouth remained against her as her moans became muffled screams of delight as she bit into the back of her left hand. Renee forced her hips up to meet his sucking manipulation of her lust-filled needs. She was quickly becoming a frenzied and uncontrollable animal.

Without moving further, his tongue lashed out and sank deeply inside her to find the salty sweet taste of her cascading lubricant.

Renee recoiled with surprise and then pushed forward in an attempt to grasp him.

"Please. Oh please put your cock in me now," she begged.

Renee was almost in hysterics begging for him to rise above her and lunge into her depths. Yet, at the same time her hands pulled his face tighter into her mound for more of his mouth and tongue.

Jack knew he couldn't oblige her since he did not wish to bring her to the quick end she craved. He knew she wasn't completely ready for that moment of complete release. Lifting his head but a fraction as she pulled his hair with her desire, the tip of his tongue found that special place. His mouth wet from her, glistened in a beam of light from the window. Jack sucked her clitoris past his lips. His tongue traced back and forth and all around causing the bud to become harder with each wet stroke.

"I'm coming!" she cried out knowing she had reached her point of no return. "Please! Oh God! Oh please, don't stop!" Tears of delight appeared near the corner of her eyes and then dropped down her cheek. Her hips vibrated relentlessly as he sucked her in with greater pressure. Jack now knew she was ready for him to take her. His lips pulled and then released her little organ as if masturbating her for one last suck before he raised his muscular body over her.

Uncontrollably she thrust herself up to meet him, her hands seeking out his hardness and she tried to pull him into the mouth of her waiting organ.

Jack had never before felt the sensation she was giving him through the grip of her inner muscles. As if tiny fingers were wrapping themselves around him to massage his engorged penis, it pulled him in deeper. Fighting back the sensitivity she bestowed on him, he dipped his thick hardness in slowly just a fraction of its length and then retract it. Each time he moved away from her, Renee's back would arch to hold him and her moans would grow louder. Her hips rose further still so he would not leave. Tears roared down her cheeks in wanton ecstasy while she begged for all of him again.

Now it was time. He entered her with a single lunge to the bottom of her depths. Fluids gushed from her as he pushed deeper, ever deeper to the bottom of her soul. She was a woman gone mad with lust. When he tried to withdraw his hardness he felt her rippling muscles pulling him in again. Jack increased his tempo with each new lunge. As with the surge of the surf he pounded effortlessly in and then slowly pulled out of her tide pool. Slowly at first, then faster and faster they bucked opposite one another. Renee exploded in the flames of her desire just as Jack unleashed his pounding fury deep, deep inside her.

Renee's fists clenched the sheets of the bed, and her neck muscles strained to near the breaking point. The waves of her orgasm engulfed her. Her vagina sucked him as a calf takes milk from an udder. Very slowly this tremendous orgasm subsided through lessening peaks and smaller valleys. Jack withdrew himself and sat upright between her legs. His fingers moved tenderly from her breasts down her stomach and below her navel. There he massaged her ovaries through her very taut spasmodic skin.

It took Renee longer than she had ever known to recover and regain her breathing. She was truly amazed that Jack had again robbed her of breath.

Opening her eyes to him, she tried to speak, "God, how good you treat me! I've never felt anything like that so wonderful in my life."

Before he left his place between her legs, he leaned forward and played his mouth over her hot wet lips for a long time and provided her with many tiny orgasms. Jack finally gave up his position to lay down along side her. "Did you hear any applause that time?" he asked. Renee didn't reply to his question. Her hand filled his as they looked deep into each other's eyes.

Several minutes had passed as they lay closely wrapped in each other's arms before Jack spoke again. "As much as I don't want to," he said quietly, "It's time to leave."

"I want a shower first," she sighed back. "If I'm quick, will it be all right?"

"Sure."

Renee slid to the side of the bed and sat upright. On wobbling legs she stood and found her legs were totally uncooperative as she made her way to the bathroom. After she adjusted the shower to her liking she stepped in closing the curtain behind her. Eyes closed, she allowed the steaming hot water to splash on her face and then trickle down her body. Renee knew she had never felt so complete or so good in her life.

She did not hear the rustling of the shower curtain when Jack stepped in. His hands slid around her waist and she leaned back slightly, folding her arms over his. Renee tilted her head back to meet his as she sought out his lips. They kissed with as much passion as any other time.

When their lips parted Renee told him, "I'm glad you changed your mind about leaving straightaway."

"I didn't," Jack replied with a determined look. "I thought I would save us some time by showering together."

Their lips touched again as she felt a growing pressure against her back side.

•   •   •

They had been driving for almost a hundred miles when they reached Tonapah, Nevada on Highway 95. Pulling into an unmarked space in front of a small cafe just off the roadway, Jack shut off the engine. While Renee pushed a comb through her hair, Jack looked across the road and recognized Nick Whitewater. He was talking to someone he hadn't seen before near the outermost island of pump in a service station across the highway. Straining his eyes to see the unknown man in better detail, he watched them for several moments before they separated and got into each side of Nick's car.

"I wish I knew who that is," Jack said out loud.

Renee stopped what she was doing and looked past Jack and asked, "Who?"

"The two guys over there pulling out of the station."

Renee looked but couldn't see them clearly enough to help. "What did he look like?" she asked.

They watched the car pull onto the roadway toward Highway 6 and out of town.

Jack described the second man. "He was about five foot ten to six foot, with receding short gray hair. A little on the portly side," he added after thinking about it for a second. "He was fairly nicely dressed with a gray suit and maybe a white or light colored shirt and a tie. I don't think I've ever seen him before."

"I just don't know," Renee said as Jack was getting out of the car. By the time he had opened the passenger's door for Renee to get out, she added, "You know, that kind of sounds like my professor at the University.

"What does he teach?" Jack inquired when he opened the door to the cafe for her.

"Who, Mr. Palmoroy?" she asked.

"I guess," he replied.

"Oh, he teaches my archaeology class. But it couldn't be him. He started a sabbatical just before I left San Francisco to come to Saline Valley. He's somewhere in Europe."

Sitting down at the table, they ordered lunch from a happy little waitress dressed in cowboy boots and snug-fitting, well-weathered Levis and a Western shirt. Renee watched the woman as she bounced from table to table taking orders or clearing away the soiled dishes. At times, the waitress would take a moment to pass the time of day with her customers and dazzle them with a bright smile and flirtatious manner.

"I certainly wish I was that happy at work!" Renee said while watching her closely.

"What do you do?" Jack inquired while wondering if he had ever been told.

"You mean you forgot already? I told you last night."

"I guess my mind was on other things. I just don't remember!"

"I work in one of those computer sweat shops eight hours a day. You know, garbage in—garbage out."

Trying to be helpful, Jack suggested, "Why don't you work in archaeology or something like that?"

"For two good reasons. First, there isn't enough money in it to make a living."

Jack interjected, "Unless you're a pot hunter!"

Renee continued without commenting on his remark, "And the second reason is I've never had a need to live outside San Francisco."

"You mean you wouldn't give up the city and its bright lights?" Jack asked with a combination of sarcasm and hurt. He didn't know why he had used such a harsh tone to his voice.

Renee observed Jack wasn't smiling as he spoke. "Oh I see what you mean," she said, taking a slightly more defensive stand than she had intended. "You mean the smog and pollution, let alone people cramming the streets and the high crime rates?"

"Well, I didn't exactly mean it that way," he replied in a somewhat apologetic tone of a double-edged sword. "I can see you're very proud of your city. Maybe that's why you came to dig things up in my desert."

Renee felt her blood pressure starting to rise and a tingling of anger over his absurd insinuations. "It's got to be better than living in some bumpkin town and not having anything to do but fuck on Saturday n—."

Jack interrupted her before she could finish her sentence. "You're a fiery little thing, aren't you?"

Just as soon as the last word had cleared his mouth, she replied loudly, "You can bet your sweet little ass I am!"

Jack saw the waitress look at them both and smile. In an attempt to sink his big frame under the table to hide from the tiger sitting across from him, he found he was only able to slouch down a little lower into the seat. Jack knew she had gotten everyone's attention with that last comment.

All he could think of was to say a little less loudly than she had, "Your father must be Irish—who else would raise a redneck devil with an attitude like—!"

"Enough!" Renee shrieked.

● ● ●

They had hardly said a word to one another for over four hours.

About sixty miles before reaching Wendover, Utah and U.S. Highway 80, Jack said in a squeaky little voice out of proportion to his size, "I'm sorry I got you angry back there. I was only trying to find out something about you."

Ah-ha! Renee thought to herself. *What else do you do to ruin someone's perfectly good day?* Then she spoke. "Like what?" she snapped at him, not really intending to be quite so hard.

Jack, hearing her sneer, still wanted her to know. "I guess I was going about it the wrong way at the cafe," he started and was stopped by her interruption.

"If I needed an argument from anyone, I'd go find Mike."

"Damn it, Renee!" Jack said in an attempt to get her attention long enough to settle to her down, "I was trying to find out if you would move to Cuny Table and live with me!"

Several moments of silence followed his statement. Over two miles passed under the wheels of her little automobile before his courage allowed him to look at her.

Gigantic tears were dribbling out of her reddening eyes. He reached over and placed his hand lovingly on her leg and gave her an encouraging squeeze.

Renee was not able to hold back. His touch unleashed a wailing blubber from her mouth when her lips moved to form words. "You're asking me to live with you?" she finally slobbered, realizing she had taken his statement wrong at the cafe.

"That's what I wanted to say back there."

Her blubbering became louder and was shortly replaced by a wet grin.

Wiping the moisture away from the inside corner of her eyes with a bundle of Kleenex, she blew her nose loudly before saying anything more. "You really do want me?"

"Yeah," he said at the same time squeezing her hand. "I think we would be good for one another."

Renee slid across the seat and snuggled close to him with her arm over his shoulder.

Jack wasn't exactly sure what he had done to cause the uninterrupted words ejaculating from Renee's mouth. But he did realize he seldom got a sentence in edgewise before finding a place to stop for the night in Rock Springs, Wyoming. It seemed to him their entire life had been laid out before him with all the plans she had already etched in granite. Jack checked them into a pleasant little motel on the edge of town, following her dominating the conversation at dinner. For the first time in his life he discovered the real meaning of "being used" that night.

9

"Crow's Help"

It was late afternoon when they arrived in the little community of Lodge Grass. Just off Highway 90 in Montana, it was a small hamlet of fewer than seven hundred inhabitants of unequal mixture of white and Indian on the east center of the Crow Indian Reservation. Jack left Renee sitting in her car outside a small country store while he went inside to search out one of the locals he had known when he had frequented the area.

Off in the distance Renee could see bright flashes of lightning and the huge, ominous black clouds of a building thunderstorm. Fascinated, she watched as an arc of lightning careened from cloud to cloud. Other bright streaks closely followed and slashed down toward the earth in zigzag routes of silver white violence. Renee felt relief the storm was as far away as it was from her. She would just as soon watch from this safe distance than to find herself a traveler in anything of that intensity.

Her thoughts returned to Jack when out of the corner of her eye she saw him exit the door he had entered a few moments before. As he turned to walk up the same side of the street, he raised his hand toward her to let her know not to move from where she was. Renee followed his movements as he stopped occasionally along the dirt path to talk to one or two of the Indians for a few seconds before continuing on. Still farther up the street, she watched him hesitate at one of the brown yards. This particular yard wasn't any different than all the other ones with the many trees that had turned dormant for the winter. She was barely able to make out the form of a very old person, possibly that of a woman, who was sitting under a skeleton of an oak. She seemed not to be paying attention to Jack as he spoke and was looking away from him toward the storm. Renee knew she must hear and see him as he had moved a few feet into the yard from the rickety gate. It seemed to her that he knew the woman well enough to talk to her for about ten minutes even though he didn't appear to be getting much of a reply.

A strange sensation crept over her while she watched Jack converse with that woman. Another one of those feelings you can't really explain to yourself, when your senses are letting you know you're in some sort of impending trouble. A most uncomfortable feeling that made her glad she had followed Jack's directions and stayed exactly as he had requested. Ever so slowly she rotated her head and neck from one direction, then to another. Straining her vision to any possible blind spots, she was unable to locate anyone near her little car. Renee expanded her field of view across the broad street to satisfy herself that her feelings were fallacious. It was then that she saw in the shadows of one of the buildings three young Indian men looking in her direction. She hoped they would not think she was watching them with an eye of concern. The more she looked to see what they were doing the greater her level of discomfort grew. Without thinking she automatically started to formulate her own evasive plan to overcome any possible emergency. Even in San Francisco she wouldn't allow herself to remain in a place where she didn't have better control over her own security.

Without trying to attract the men's attention, she leaned slowly over to the driver's side door and extended her left arm to push in the lock on the door panel.

As she was making her move back to her original position on the seat, two of the three men started to walk across the road directly toward her. A shiver of fear twisted its way deep into her gut when she saw the blond color of a baseball bat held close to one man's side. Looking quickly up the street to find Jack, she discovered he was not where she had last seen him talking to the old woman. When she turned back to the Indian men Renee found the two had separated. One had moved to the rear of her car while the other one with the ball bat stood at the front. Renee knew she could not open either of the car's doors to run as they would surely catch her. Frantically Renee searched for some sort of defensive weapon. Finding only her spiked heels on the floor she clandestinely placed one on the seat near her leg as her breathing became shallow and rapid and her pulse raced. She very badly wanted to scream for Jack to come and rescue her from the deadly potential that these men had to offer.

Then the worst possible scenario began to unfold with alarming horror. The Indian with the ball bat left his position near the front of her car. It took him only a few deliberate steps to reach the passenger side window next to where she was sitting. The man leaned down with his face almost touching the window and looked menacingly into her eyes. He gave a hideous smile that left her with the feeling she should definitely not wait for Jack's return. A ragged diagonal scar cut deep across his nose and lip, then down his cheek almost to his throat. His long dark hair was held in place by a red handkerchief rolled into a bandanna and pulled tightly around his forehead. Renee jerked back toward the center of the car when the Indian tapped the window with the blunt tip of his ugly bat. Even though she had tried to prepare for what she knew would come, she still jumped back nearly a foot when he hit the glass a second time. With her mouth feeling suddenly dry beyond belief, she felt a scream starting to swell deep down inside of her throat.

"Please Jack, where are you?" she pleaded to no one but herself in a crackling high-pitched voice.

The Indian motioned with his hand for her to lower the window and then he held his index finger to his mouth as if making a request for her to remain silent.

Her eyes widened and her mouth opened partially to say no silently while her head moved a small distance from side to side. Renee tried to say no again, but still managed no real sounds past a whisper. She wanted to yell as loud as she could but those words just wouldn't leave her lips. The Indian would have to be satisfied with her best unspoken response.

For a third time the Indian rapped at the window. The difference this time was the horrible sound as the bat seemed to try the integrity of the glass. Even though she watched him trying to break in, she still jumped on each consecutive strike. The expression on his face had not relinquished that terrible smile. He kept smiling and staring and hitting, time after time after time. The other Indian walked up beside him and grabbed his arm and pointed up the street. The second man said something Renee could not hear through the beating of her heart, which was now lodged in the lower part of her throat.

Now is my chance, Renee thought to herself.

Since both men were on the same side, Renee felt that now was her opportunity to flee out of the opposite side of her car. She took a moment to contemplate her plan and whether to move fast to the door and to freedom or to move slowly at first and then run like hell. She sat in indecision over the possibility of being caught and severely hurt. Her eyes moved involuntarily to where the second man was pointing.

"It's Jack! He's coming back!"

Although he was still some distance away, he was moving down the street towards her. Even at that distance she believed she could see a stern look on his face. Suddenly the thought of the Indian surprising Jack with his ball bat brought to her a picture of him being viciously beaten. At a fast walk, he continued moving toward the three of them. She realized there was no way to warn him of this peril in sufficient time.

Without breaking his stride, Jack walked directly up to the man with the scarred face. His hand extended and seized the free right hand of the ugly Indian.

Renee knew a fierce fight was about to explode. She sat in white-knuckled terror watching their tightly clasped hands suddenly move up and then down.

"What in hell are you doing?" she yelled loudly enough for Jack and the other two men to hear her baffled words.

Renee rolled down the window just as Jack was letting loose of the Indian's grip.

"This is Joshua, and his friend there is David. I asked them to watch over you while I was taking care of business," Jack said loud enough so she could hear inside the car, yet quietly enough not to bring attention of others.

Renee fought back the anger that had been brought on with the relief from her fears.

Trying her best to be friendly under the current circumstances, she sneered in a reasonably calm voice, "Hi."

Simultaneously both of the Indian men answered in reply, "Glad to meet ya, lady," or some such thing that went past her enraged mind.

Joshua turned to look at Jack and then back to Renee and apologized to her. More in an explanation to Jack than her, he explained he was knocking on the window to see what was wrong. Before he turned back to speak to Jack, he added, "You looked awful scared in there, lady! I hope it wasn't us that did it."

Renee held herself in check the best she could and thanked Joshua and David for their concern without addressing his question. Still feeling her anger over Jack for having had her watched and not telling her about it, she rolled her window closed. Renee looked straight ahead and sat quietly waiting for him to get into the car.

The sounds made by Jack's door shutting hadn't subsided when Renee's heated words started.

"Why didn't you tell me you were going to do that?" she roared out in a huff still coupled with disbelief. "Didn't you realize I was on pins and needles thinking you would have been hurt?"

Jack allowed her to continue while he sat behind the wheel watching the huge billowing clouds ease their way towards the town. Not really wanting to ignore what she had to say, he listened to her every word. He thought he would be better off not to make the same mistake at some later time or cause her to increase the tempo of her arguments.

Renee slowed in her point making and gave Jack a tiny opening and a chance to try and settle her down. He leaned over and kissed her on the cheek during this most opportune break. Without moving her head from facing the front of the car, a nasty leer from her eye shot sideways toward him with the points of so many daggers. She knew what she was saying put him where she wanted him.

"You know, you're absolutely right. If I were in your shoes I'd be pissed, too. Please forgive me. That was entirely my fault," he said apologetically as his head lowered onto his chest like a little boy caught in some wrongful act.

She wasn't exactly sure how to handle his actions, let alone his statement.

Turning her whole body to face him she spat, "The next time I won't help you when you're confronted by the likes of those men."

On her closing word she winked to him to let him know she did appreciate what he had meant to do and that she bore no lasting hard feelings.

"What did you find out?" Renee asked.

"A couple of things. First, the man we want to talk to is some thirty miles from here on bad roads in the ruins of old Fort Smith."

"Will this car make it?" Renee inquired with a real measure of concern for her little sedan.

"Only as far as the Big Horn Mountains. After that we'll have to pick up a four-wheel drive or maybe some horses."

"Horses!" Renee sputtered, "Horses? I don't know how to ride any horses! Are you crazy or something? What makes you think I like to ride horses?"

"It won't be that bad," Jack said, appealing to her sense of getting the job done while allowing her to settle back down again.

"I have a better idea. Let's walk. Besides, walking is better for your health. Don't you know their brains aren't any bigger then a walnut or something?" Renee offered in rationalizing her sincerity to an obviously stupid suggestion.

Jack gave a small chuckle while he smiled at her argument.

Jack started her car and pulled out of the parking space toward the south end of town. Not quite clear on the street layout and after traversing several paved side roads, he finally found the way to Lodge Grass Reservoir Dam.

"What's the other part?" Renee asked when she remembered he had said he had been told two things.

"What other thing?"

"You said you found out two things."

"Oh yeah. The other is some pot hunter was in town. He was looking for information about several artifacts that had been stolen from the Black Hills going back to about the same period of time as ours. From the description the old woman gave me, I'm sure it was the guy with Nick Whitewater. One of the men I tried to point out to you in Tonapah."

Renee interrupted. "What did she tell him?"

Jack thought for a second before replying. "She told him to go to the Tribal Center over on the Pine Ridge Reservation."

Trying to be a help in her own way, Renee spoke up, "If that is my professor, then that's where Palmoroy must have met your man Whitewater!"

"Yup! Got to hand it to that old gal, though. She's got enough sense not to talk about Indian matters to strange White eyes. She sent him away and out of her hair."

Renee looked at Jack curiously for a long second before she asked, "You don't have anything against white folks, do you?"

"No, I don't think I do."

"Good!" Renee replied as she lowered the visor to look at her eyes in the small courtesy mirror.

Jack snickered at her.

Renee twisted around in the seat and said very seriously, "You got to remember, I am the minority here."

If it hadn't been in front of them in the first place, Renee felt sure she would have been drawn to it anyway. It was a beautiful sight as they drove towards the raging storm ahead of them. The clouds appeared to be touching the low hills not far off in the distance. Above the black gray of the massive storm the nimbus clouds abruptly turned light gray, fluffy and billowing white above that to reach higher into the sky. The tops of the clouds looked as if a painter had smeared their edges with pale yellows and pinks and then reds lower down and closer to the blackening storm. A hundred blots of lightning streaked down to the ground or bumped against each other from the black gray masses. Even though the sun was shining, the sky was nearly cobalt blue between the splattering of clouds directly above them. Great drops of water started to smash upon their windshield. First slowly and then gradually their number increased until the rain seemed to be driven at them by eerie, supernatural forces. A sudden gust of wind drove the ever-increasing size of the drops harder into the front of the car and onto the roadway ahead of them.

"It's going to be a bad one," Jack told her. "There's a blizzard right behind this."

"A what?" Renee asked hoping she had misunderstood the word.

"This is winter, you know." Jack pressed the accelerator closer to the floorboard, and the car moved forward faster on the bumpy dirt road. "It won't be long before we reach a sheep camp where we will get out of this storm." He hoped his explanation would relieve her increasingly bothered thoughts.

"Sheep camp?" Renee said, questioning herself as much as she was questioning his idea of where to spend the night. *What am I doing here?* went through her mind several times.

The wind had barely died down with a mixture of rain and ice as her little sedan made its way into the darkness. Time seemed to pass slowly before Jack told her they were there. Flakes of snow larger than Renee had ever seen were falling all around them and wasn't melting off as she hoped it would. The correlation was definitely there. The longer it fell, the deeper it piled on her worries. When the car finally slid to a stop, Jack took a deep breath and told Renee to get out and hurry into a mud-and-stick hut ahead of them.

"What if someone's in there?" Renee asked in a loud voice filled with questions about his logic and her strong desire to punch something.

"There shouldn't be," Jack said as he reached across her, yanked her handle and opened her door. "There isn't anyone in their right mind out here this time of year. Now go!"

"What a wonderful fucking feeling of reassurance!" Renee said when she grabbed her purse and started to run toward the old structure. "With my luck this is Freddy's House."

Jack thought she had mumbled some unintelligible thing after taking a few steps from the car before the door slammed shut.

Even the tread of her tennis shoes wasn't giving her traction enough as she fought her way the few yards she had to go to the door. In the cold biting wind that had again come up, an occasional piece of hail stung her face and head. When she reached the door she found it to be nothing more than old boards nailed to a frame of dead limbs and hastily thrown up. Sliding a stick to the side that held the door secure, she swung the rickety door frame open with a hard pull. Stepping onto the threshold she was immediately confronted by an unseen musky old blanket which hung from the top of the doorsill to the dirt floor. Pushing it to one side she glimpsed at a flicker of light from a small fire in the center of the dimly lit interior. A little column of yellowed smoke swirled up to a hole in the center of the ceiling and out into the wind. Renee was astonished when the warmth of the room gently pushed against her face. She wondered how so much heat could be produced from such a small blaze.

Turning her head back toward Jack she shouted above the noise of the quickening wind. "Someone's in here!"

Over the whistle of the wind Jack was not sure what Renee was trying to tell him. He waved her to go on in before he closed the door of the car. Picking up her pack and his suitcase, Jack made his way to the still open door and moved the woolen blanket aside. As soon as he was past the blanket, Jack pulled the wood door closed behind him and shoved the stick that held it closed into place.

The first thing he saw was an aged Indian man sitting next to the fire on what looked like an even older hand-woven rug of maybe Navajo origin. Beside him was a somewhat younger woman kneading some flour for squaw bread on a flat board. Behind her, lying on a raggedy 1940s vintage mattress, was a beautiful young woman staring up at Renee. Off to his right, up against the wall and to the side just behind him, stood Renee. She was quiet and motionless while she curiously watched the old Indian. Behind the old man was a larger mattress with a couple of beat-up blankets haphazardly piled on one corner.

Jack stepped further into the hut and stood opposite the old Indian. Jack spoke first, asking if he and Renee could take shelter from the storm with them. The old man nodded his head and put his hand out in what appeared to be an offering for Jack to sit. Renee started to step forward to the fire from where she had been standing.

Without looking back to her, Jack admonished her, "Stay there."

Renee stopped abruptly and stepped back and against the adobe wall.

Renee looked at the thin old man thinking he must be near ninety years old. However, he did look healthy to her, regardless of his age or his tremendous amount of wrinkles. He sat cross-legged before the fire with a heavy red-and-white striped blanket over his shoulders.

He spoke. "I am Rick Sun."

Jack, making sure to be polite, closely followed without hesitation, "I am Jack Barlow. When I was growing up on Pine Ridge they called me Little Walking Horse. Later I became known as Watching Buffalo."

Renee had not anticipated him using a nickname in his reply let alone the discovery he was called anything other than Jack. She thought to herself that nicknames were used only in the movies or television or in the old days, not by a modern day Sheriff's Deputy.

The old Indian spoke something to Jack that was completely foreign to her. She thought at first it was some dialect of Spanish, but by the fourth or fifth word dismissed that idea. All she knew was he had to be speaking in the tongue of his nation as she did not recognize the language, let alone the dialect. Renee wanted to ask Jack what he was talking about, but remained still and quiet following Jack's directions as best she could. There was no doubt in her mind that he would tell her what they spoke of when he had the chance.

The conversation between the two of them seemed to go on and on and on. It must have lasted a good five minutes before Jack reached back and extended his hand to her without raising himself from the floor. Stepping away from the wall she grasped his hand and took one more step forward. She complied when she felt Jack gently pulling her down next to him. Astonishing even herself, Renee knelt obediently to his side and slightly behind him.

As Jack started to speak to the old man again in the tongue of his nation, he gave her a strange look apparently brought on by her sudden willingness to cooperate.

In the mishmash of sounds she heard her first name a couple of times. The old man apparently gave his approval of her through his bright eyes and a wonderfully wrinkled smile.

Jack turned only his head toward Renee and requested that she find whatever food was in her backpack and give it to the woman, who had not stopped her preparations.

Renee fumbled through her pack, finding almost a half dozen freeze-dried food packets and one Baby Ruth. She handed them to Jack who then offered them to Rick Sun. Almost without hesitation, Rick Sun handed them to the old woman, who inspected the packages with a larger than life grin. Seeing this, Renee decided to offer her candy bar to the girl who had thus far remained absolutely quiet.

But then again, perhaps sometime after diner would be better, she thought and put it back where she found it. The girl's eyes alternated between herself and Jack.

Without being asked, Renee squatted beside the old woman to help her prepare the packaged meal in an old skillet. Occasionally she looked to Jack for some sort of acknowledgment or for his approval. Every now and then she would see his eyes smile at her, even though the rest of his expression changed very little.

During what seemed like a short lull in the conversation with Rick, Jack said to Renee, "These good folks are willing to have us stay the night and they thank you for sharing our food. This is kind of a treat for them since they have been in the mountains several days and were really short."

Renee asked Jack to tell the old man that it is more than her pleasure. He winked at her for her request and returned to the conversation with Rick.

"Shit." Jack said a word that Renee and everyone else in the room seemed to understand and take with some exception. "The man we wanted to see is no longer at the old fort ruins! I'm not sure who might help us now."

"Rick looks like the kind of person that would have some really decent ideas. Why don't you ask him what he thinks?"

"Can't hurt."

Little more was said to Renee by Jack until the meal had been served and eaten. Jack and Rick talked for a long time with Rick doing most of the speaking. Jack would say something occasionally, but mostly nodded his head or made some gesture with his hands to the old man's non-rhythmic language.

Having helped stack the well-used tin plates and pan near the fire, Renee stood and went to the blanket covering the door. She thought she would look out through the cracks between the boards of the door to see if anything had changed from the storm's rampage. In the two hours they had been in the structure almost a foot of snow had fallen. The wind had stopped blowing and a quarter moon shown through the clouds that were breaking up overhead.

"Storm's over!" she told Jack and everyone in the room, hoping they would understand what she was saying.

It seemed as if no one was listening except the girl who cocked her head to one side with a kind of little kitten look of confused neurons. Jack and Rick hardly took a break in their conversation to look toward the door where she was standing when she spoke. Slipping the stick holding the door to the side, she stepped out into the crisp air. Just enough light from the moon reflected off the virgin snow for her to see the landscape. The scene in front of the hut was blue-white with darker gray and black shadows. A few feet farther out the door Renee kicked at the powdery snow. The little flakes flew high into the air and slowly sparkled their way back down. Although Renee had been skiing at Lake Tahoe every winter since she could remember, the phenomenon of nature's beauty stunned her anew every time.

Only a few moments had passed before Jack swung the door aside and stepped out to join her. They stood together quietly contemplating the shadows from the cloud's movements revealing the calm of winter in all its splendor. Wrapping his strong arms around her, he pulled her close and kissed tenderly on the side of her neck.

"What will we do now?" Renee asked.

"Do you have chains in the car?"

"Yeah! They're in the trunk under the spare."

"Good. In the morning we'll make our way back to the highway and then to the Little Big Horn battlefield."

"Why? What can we do in this kind of weather?"

"The old man is very knowledgeable in the ways of the Sioux. Even though he is Crow, he feels the best way to handle this is to free the evil spirits held in the artifacts before they are returned to the sacred place."

"Do you know where that is?" she asked.

"I have a reasonable idea, but I'm not absolutely sure. There is a Medicine Man on the reservation that will know. There are very few who are allowed to know the secrets of the Sioux Nation."

"Like what?"

Jack smiled. "Things you archeologists will only know by accident."

"Like what?"

"You don't take hints well, do you?"

"No! Like what?"

"Like where Yellow Hand is buried!"

"You know that?"

He said nothing more and looked out into the silent landscape.

Even though Jack gave her warmth, the bite of the air made Renee shiver. "Let's go back inside," she told him through the chattering of her teeth.

Once inside, Jack pushed the blanket firmly around the edge of the door sealing the room from unwanted drafts.

"Jack! Look!"

The fire had burned down and dimly lit the room. From where he stood Jack was barely able to see the old man and woman lying on the mattress the girl had been on. The girl, who couldn't have been more than eighteen or nineteen, was lying on the floor curled tightly under a beat-up old blanket.

Jack shrugged with a kind of that's-to-be-expected attitude and proceeded to unroll Renee's sleeping bag, which he removed from her pack frame. Unzipping it, he laid the bag full width over the unused mattress, took off his shoes and nothing else and lay down.

Renee noticed he nearly filled one side of the mattress but still left her plenty of room.

As if beckoning her to him, he held up the other half of the bedroll for her to crawl under.

"Now that's a neat idea. So you want to be close and share our body heat! I suppose you're going to let that poor girl freeze? Huh?"

Renee tried to whisper in a firm and strongly suggestive voice. "This will never do," she told him as she stepped over his offer. The girl moved the blanket from over her head to look at Renee when she shook her lightly.

"Huh!" was the more or less grunt that came from the girl's lips. Renee motioned her to follow while she snatched the girl's blanket. When the girl did not move at her request, Renee pulled her to her feet and led the way to the mattress where Jack lay. A little coaxing with small pulls and pushes was all it took for the girl to comply. As the girl was slipping under the covers she saw that the young woman was wearing only bikini underwear and a plaid hunting shirt. Renee pushed her shoes off and slipped in alongside her. Before finding the most comfortable position, she assisted Jack in adjusting a blanket over the bag to cover all three and bade them good night.

Rick, without moving or saying anything smiled in sincerity for her kindness before he closed his eyes again. It was then Renee thought she heard a small giggle slip from the petite person between them.

Jack didn't seem to mind Renee's gesture because it was, after all, the right thing to do and they were infringing upon the household. It also seemed to Renee that the ability to sleep with a good-looking girl pressed back against him was a new and different situation for him to contend with. Judging from her size and position, her warm behind had to be pushing into his abdomen and would soon be transferring an enormous amount of heat to keep him warm. Then again, maybe vice-versa went through her mind. Renee felt him squirm and thrash around trying to make himself more comfortable. It took several attempts until he found he could adjust his left arm and hand under his head.

"What on earth do I do with this?" Jack asked out loud about his right arm.

No one replied.

That problem was soon remedied when Renee reached over the girl and took his hand. She pulled his fingers over the girl and onto her own side. Gently she rubbed her fingers over his momentarily to ease his apparent discomfort. At almost the same moment, the girl wrapped her arm over Renee as well and molded her fingers onto Renee's hand. It was apparent that Jack would find that real sleep wouldn't come to him until he himself figured enough was enough. It really didn't have anything to do with the comfort of the mattress or the warmth from the girl. Renee surmised that if anything was to get to him, it would be the tingling in his groin that would demand the immediate change of sleeping arrangements.

Quietly, Jack slid out from under the covers and had Renee and the girl change their position to his side of the bed. Jack then slid in beside Renee and found being that close to her led to even greater difficulties for him. He tried to force his eyes shut to find the sandman and a reasonable night's sleep. For almost an hour, neither would find that magic place due to the lodgepole between them.

• • •

Jack awoke from his most fitful night with the sounds of movement in the room. The old woman was building a fire not far from where the three of them lay. He quietly rose and pulled on his socks and boots. He opened Renee's pack and searched through it until he found the little jar of instant coffee. After he removed the lid he gave the bottle to the woman and spoke a few words she could understand. Jack warmed his hands while he knelt close to the fire and watched the forms lying under the bag and blanket he had just left. Since he had risen, Renee and the girl had rolled together with the girl in a little ball and Renee wrapped soundly around her. Their heads were close to one another and their eyes remained closed in peaceful slumber.

Now that's a wonderful sight, Jack thought to himself. Standing, he silently went to the door and pushed the blanket aside to look out. No new snow had fallen since he and Renee were out before retiring.

• • •

Jack had the car running and was finishing putting the chains on the tires when Renee came through the door of the lodge.

"You look exhausted," she commented while closely inspecting the bags under his red eyes.

"I'd rather not talk about it," Jack said as he fumbled with the clasp that held the chains in place.

"Did you have a problem with me sharing our bed with the girl?"

"No, I did not have a problem with sharing our bed with her," he replied in a tone that was more indignant and abrupt.

"Turned you on a little, did it?" Renee smiled, making fun of his somewhat vengeful attitude.

Jack smashed his fingers against the fender well of her car when the rubber chain tightener slipped from his grasp.

Renee fought back a small laugh at the sight of him trying to stuff his injured pinky finger into his mouth.

"No, damn it!" he yelled out in frustration and his words mixed with the minor pain of the injury.

Renee smiled wider and followed with a little left hook of her own. "I thought so. Maybe we're going to have to talk about that someday."

Jack replied in a voice showing his dissatisfaction with the present topic of conversation, "There's absolutely nothing to talk about. Now leave it alone."

Walking beyond arms reach from one another, they returned to the lodge to say good-bye to their new friends, especially the old man. Renee started gathering her stuff to pack while Jack rolled the sleeping bag. Renee could see the old woman watching her as she collected some of the stuff that had somehow spilled out. Stopping what she was doing, she dug back into her pack and removed her Buck sheath knife and a pretty red silk scarf.

Handing Rick the knife and the scarf to the old woman, Renee inquired of the older woman. "What is your name?"

No reply was uttered. The woman looked at the scarf and remained silent.

Rick spoke up in very clear and nearly perfect English, "No one knows. Neither she or her daughter has ever spoken."

Jack thanked them for their hospitality and started out the door with Renee close behind. When Renee was just passing the girl, she handed her the Baby Ruth she had forgotten about the night before.

• • •

Jack was driving slowly through the finely powdered snow toward the main highway when Renee told him the hurt she felt for their benefactor in the night. "That's so sad. Isn't there anything that can be done for them?"

Jack replied without much hesitation, as if he related an everyday event, "Two things have to happen before they get any help at all from anyone."

"What's that?" she asked looking back through the rear window.

"First, someone has to offer help and, second, they have to accept it. Those are proud people who don't want handouts."

Following a long pause, Renee asked why Rick hadn't spoken English instead of Indian.

"Crow," Jack sighed. "Not Indian. Besides, this is his turf and if he wants to speak in the language of his people that's his own business."

On top of everything that made Renee feel bad that day, she started to regret the hard time she gave him over his hormones.

"I'm sorry for what I had said this morning." Renee offered while she was tracing her fingers on his leg. "I didn't mean to make you angry like that."

"Ah, it's OK. This whole matter has me upset and to top it off, I know you were right. I was turned on."

Renee squeezed his leg again at his honesty with her and changed the subject, "Where do we go from here?"

"The Little Big Horn."

"Why? Is there something special there we have to do?"

"Yeah," Jack replied when he regained control of the car after it started to slide sideways on the icy road. "Rick Sun was very concerned that the evil spirits of the dead be removed from the artifacts. He suggested the ceremony be presented by someone who had recently been through the Sun Gazing Ritual."

"What's that? The Sun Gazing Ritual?"

"It's a ceremony where the body is cleansed and the warrior establishes his purity and devotion to the gods, his nation and his clan."

"Is all of that necessary?" Renee questioned him. "It's only going to be put into a museum, isn't it?"

"I don't think so. The old man believes the one who possesses this stuff will have the power of demons. If it is used wrongly, a revolution might occur on the reservations and spread from there."

"You have to be kidding," Renee said in the form of a somewhat worried question.

Jack's response filled her mind with many new questions she didn't believe he himself could answer. "Don't you believe in the power of the mind?" he asked.

"Sometimes I do. But this is a little far-fetched in a day and age of television and jet planes," she added.

"Let me put it to you this way. If enough people believe in something strongly with their hearts, minds and souls, and it has been the same belief since before memory, then don't you think it could be possible?"

Renee wasn't exactly sure how to answer that. "Is that why Whitewater wants the artifacts?"

"I don't really know. Either he wants the power or the money, maybe even both."

• • •

In Lodge Grass Jack found a phone booth where he made several calls to people Rick suggested he contact for help. Renee sat in the car watching while Jack dialed and redialed many telephone numbers. During one of his more lengthy conversations, she slipped into the little store and bought two cups of real coffee and a package of Ding Dongs. Jack was already back in her car when she hurried out of the store. Taking a swallow of the bittersweet liquid before he started the motor, he explained that several people would meet them at Custer's Monument and the enclosed grave-yard. Turning North on the main highway, they discussed what the battlefield might hold for them.

10

"Twenty and One"

Both, for their own reasons, had gorged their minds with anticipation by the time Jack pulled the car off the road onto the snow-covered shoulder. Renee supposed the eight or more cars and pickup trucks that had already converged there were Jack's doing. Off in the distance and further up the slow grade, she could see several people standing around a bone-white monument against a clear blue sky—a shivering reminder rising in the snow that marked one of the 1876 battlefields.

Taking Renee's hand in his, Jack leaned over and kissed her lightly on the lips.

"Much will happen here today."

Renee leaned back slightly and started to ask his meaning, but before she could speak, he continued dramatically,

"What the old man said last night makes me wonder if your safety isn't more important than going up there."

"Do you really believe that much power is in the artifacts?" she asked before she could be interrupted again.

"I'm not absolutely sure about anything. What I do know is for the first time in my life I'm really scared. More than that, I worry that something might happen to you. Before I go up there, I want to tell you some of the things Rick Sun told me last night."

"Very well. If that makes you feel any better about us going up there," Renee responded while nervously trying to hide her enthusiasm to get the show on the road.

"Rick told me of a time many years ago when he had a dream of the battle. He couldn't make much sense of it since many people had gathered around a great white tree to dance. They were not dressed in blue as the long knifes were. Nor were they dressed as were the warriors of all the Indian Nations who had come to do battle. He said he saw the women of the village wailing over the fallen warriors as so many had fallen like sticks in a child's game.

"Amid the destruction, twenty and one people stood around that white tree to watch a Medicine Man perform the ceremony of the dead. He said he tried to look hard with his old eyes, but did not understand why the twenty-one people were transparent. Rick said he watched his dream unfold with much curiosity because he had never seen anything like that before in his visions."

"That's not so weird. Sounds like a regular dream to me. Let's go." Renee excitedly reached for the door handle.

Jack stopped her with a slight tug on her arm and then continued with a lower and almost whispered voice. "Riders on horseback rode through the twenty-one people with great speed. More than that, the hillsides for miles were awash with flames and flashes of white and yellow. He spoke of the smell of sulfur that was thick to his nostrils while a haze lingered low to the ground all about him. He told me these things to keep you from being there."

By now Renee was fascinated with the story Jack was telling. She listened intently to his remaining rendition of Rick's fantasy before she spoke. "That's nonsense," she said with a look of very little concern. "Why on earth would he not want me there? You have to remember, Jack, that it's only an old man's dream." Renee started to reach for the handle again. "Let's go."

Again Jack pulled her toward him slightly before continuing. "Rick said twenty and one for a reason. The one is you."

"What do you mean, 'the one is me'?" Renee changed her attention from the hillside to looking into Jack's eyes.

"He said you would see the flow of blood and would be captive in all the horrors of death. You," Jack added, "will fall victim to the curse on the white soldier. This is why I'm not sure you should go up there."

"I've come this far. No matter what you or he says, it doesn't make a bit of difference now. Not only that, I'm here to do what is necessary for both of us. Do you understand?"

"I didn't think you would buy all that," Jack said. His laugh was a little too phony for realism.

"Now can you tell me the real reason you don't want me over there. Huh! Jack?"

"To be honest," he related, "The Medicine Man doesn't want you there for the ceremony since you're white. He doesn't want the contamination, so to speak."

"Bullshit!" Renee blurted out. "You're not leaving me behind. After all, look at what we have been through together to get here. Did the old man really tell you that?" she again questioned him with a more hostile glance.

"Yes, he did. Not only that, I was requested to keep you away from the ceremony for all those reasons and then some."

"What if I'm not at the ceremony? Maybe off a little ways in that direction to watch. Maybe hiding?" she asked, pointing off onto the distant rolling hillside.

Jack looked up the low hill as if deep in thought. But before he could answer, Renee pointed to some high grass and bushes about a hundred feet from the stone monument and just outside the picket fence.

"How about me hiding over there? The old man will be happy, the Medicine Man will be happy, and most of all

you'll have me happy. Besides, if you don't know whether to
believe the premonition or not, why should I?"

*There's not a man around that can beat a woman's logic
no matter how hard he tries,* Jack thought while he was
walking up the hill carrying the bundle of artifacts.

He moved slowly to allow Renee enough time to find
herself a place to hide and watch the ceremony. Glancing
over his shoulder he half expected to see her slipping
through the wild grass that was pushing skyward from the
snow, but she was nowhere to be seen. He felt sure Renee
could be trusted not to give herself away to anyone from her
hiding place. He also knew she had all the abilities and
determination of a self-made woman and that nothing
would stop her.

• • •

Staying low, Renee made her way silently up a shallow
draw almost parallel to Jack's direction of travel. Every
now and then she would stop, rise and look long enough to
locate her position to see if Jack had reached his goal.

Crawling on hands and knees, she worked her way to
under a hundred yards of the Indian men, a position where
she would have an unobstructed view. Almost instantly,
Renee became dissatisfied with her hastily selected place.
Although it provided a good view, she was unable to hear
anything below a yell. Silently, she continued to crawl several yards closer toward the monument and along the fence
to an even better hiding place.

Moving slowly like a cat stalking her prey, she snuggled into a shallow snow-covered indentation in the ground
a little longer than she was tall. There she pushed the dry
grass aside to look for Jack and was surprised that a relic of
a gravestone blocked her view. Pushing the thick grass from
the side of the marker she created a sort of window.

Boasting a smile of serious accomplishment, she felt
genuinely pleased with her hiding place. However, something very strange and personal seemed to crawl on her

flesh. Dizzy momentarily, the fence and the monument tangled with each other as if caught in the rising heat waves of a hot summer's day.

• • •

Jack was still a fair distance from the memorial when he counted seventeen men near it. Each one of them was watching him while he pushed his way through the soft snow and brittle grass to the monument. About half were sitting in a semi-circle while others were milling around a newly created fire on the snow. A narrow pillar of gray-white smoke rose from between them and high in the air.

With the distance closing, he could see a large drum with five of the men sitting hunched over it as if secretly speaking to the tight drumhead. Each of three other men in the semi-circle had smaller drums and were watching him watch them.

"The singers," Jack thought out loud. "They don't even know the importance of what I'm bringing."

Jack wondered why so many had shown up unless it was out of curiosity. Trying to remember how many calls he had made at Grass Lodge, he could definitely say he talked to seven people.

"I guess friends beget friends." Jack continued talking to himself out loud while raising a questioning eyebrow.

• • •

Jack was cresting the little rise when Renee first saw him. The men sitting in the semi-circle stood with his approach. The others left the fireside and walked over to where he had stopped and circled closely around him.

Renee was not able to hear the conversation since the speaker was speaking in a very low voice. What she believed she was watching appeared to be no different than a crowd of men discussing something slightly more important than the weather.

If this is some sort of ceremony then it isn't much of one! As she finished pondering that point and was about to stand in defiance, the group of Indians suddenly broke up. She observed five of the men return to the big drum where they had originally been sitting.

As if by command of the thump from a single drum, Renee realized the men had started the ceremony, just as the other Sioux War Drums suddenly joined in. A rush of adrenaline pushed the hair on her arms and neck up straight from a million rising goose bumps. The beat was low at first and become louder as the tempo increased. The high pitch of a man singing out unidentifiable words began to rise over the pounding of the drum.

Some of the men who were standing faced each other. Dipping their fingers into what looked like little clay pots, they then wiped colorful substances on the faces of the men facing them. The pounding of the little drums became louder as did the singer's voice.

Other drummers began to join in the singing. Though her heart was racing from the fear of discovery, she wanted to be more involved. She would have gladly given her position away to learn the meaning of the chant and the significance of the ceremonies dipping of fingers into those little colored pots. Even the mystery of the face painting had to be a story that would fill a little of the emptiness she felt from her lack of knowledge. Almost numb with fascination over what was materializing in front of her, she did not notice the cold from the snow on which she lay.

The big drum joined and began to beat out a rhythm with the smaller ones. The chants of the men connected together and failed to make anything but a strange harmony. The beat became louder and then louder still. The men around the fire removed their coats and jackets and started to shuffle their feet and packed down the snow in cadence.

Each dancing man seemed independent in his moves, yet exacting in movement with the others. Renee could now see the faces of the men with their legs marching or bending and rising only to bend again. Each man wore his paint differently from all the others. Although some distance from them, she was able to see the colors of red or pale yellow. Some wore black covering half of their face, while others masked themselves with white dots or lines. It was just as she had seen in paintings by some of the masters of the Old West.

If it were not for the bone white stone markers and cars parked in the snow, she knew she was witnessing something that had occurred some hundred and twenty years before. An eerie feeling crept over her. She couldn't help but believe that a ceremony, just like this one, had happened before the General's last battle. Maybe Sitting Bull's Sun Gazing Dance at the Sacred Tree Trunk, maybe when he was cut over a hundred times for his vision of the impending massacre. Renee's mind reeled with thoughts she had never considered before.

The scene before her seemed clever yet unreal as she watched. The pounding of the drums became louder with every fall of each hand. What once was a deafening silence had become an almost unbearable noise banging through her skull. With each second that passed, she had greater difficulty taking her eyes from the spectacle playing out before her. A thin mist rose from the ground where the men danced and spread slowly out to engulf everything in its path. The legs of the dancing Indians were becoming hazy to her through that ever-thickening fog.

Blinking several times to adjust her vision, she squinted and was able to see a dark figure clad in heavy fur near the circle of men. He had not caught her attention before and left her with no idea where he had come from or how he had gotten there. His face was painted half black from about the tip of his nose up to the horned fur hat on his head. The rest of his face was pale yellow with whiter spots haphazardly smudged on his cheeks.

This man, this Indian, was not tall nor was he short; he wasn't big nor small. He was a man of no particular description at all, yet, no matter how he seemed, she could not look into the company of men without seeing him standing out from the rest. A giant of a presence.

The whole spectacle was taking her to the brink that she had to suppress her urge to jump up and enter the circle. Praising herself for her own fortitude, she steadfastly held herself in check.

Looking up to break her self-induced trance, she could see devastatingly black clouds gathering overhead; storm clouds that had seemingly appeared from nowhere. They were ugly and menacing, far worse then the ones she had seen the night before. They swirled above the ceremony on the hill as if drawn especially to her by an unseen force. Dazzling rays of light plowed through cracks in the multitudes of gray and black and then filtered through the smoke from the fire and the foggy mist. The view flashed and turned to what seemed like a fiery laser light show.

The ceremony had truly become a beautiful yet eerie spectacle. It was as if the center of the world was here and dragging her in closer and closer.

Shutting her eyes momentarily, she reopened them to see that more men had joined the dancers. Renee found it difficult to believe what was happening. The men who had joined in braved the cold wearing only loincloths and moccasins. Some had on feathered headdresses while others wore funny hats of fur or leather and feathers.

Glancing down the side of the hill she saw many more men running up to the expanding circle of dancers and drummers. Fifty or more had arrived now and still many more continued to come.

Above the chants of the singers Renee was barely able to hear the wail of women. Screams of agony of lost loved ones mingled in the air. She could see deerskin clad woman of all ages moving over the side of the hills, the valleys and flats. Some were dragging young boys by the arms behind them as they cried out their torment. The movement of their legs was hidden by the ever-thickening ground fog. Some would stop and kneel into the mist while others seemed to continue their search as if for something unknown.

Renee felt the whole town of Lodge Grass must have turned out to participate at Jack's request. Literally hundreds upon hundreds of men, women and young boys were now all around her. Everywhere she looked about her, the people were looking and searching for something not even she could see. Many were sitting in the fog while others lay down and disappeared secretly into it.

The chants were mixed with more yelling while the sounds of the thundering clouds rumbled violently above. With those sounds came the clickity-clack rhythm of horses being ridden at a hard gallop.

Flashing past her closely as she lay in the snow was an Indian on a spotted horse. Renee recognized a dappled and wonderfully muscular Appaloosa, lathered and sweating profusely as if it had been ridden long and hard. Swirls of dust followed the fetlocks closely and disappeared into the mist.

Suddenly another galloped past her, then another, then many, many more. Warriors yelled and hollered as they raced across the field in all directions. Lightning flashed across the sky then down to the ground near the monument in great zig-zagged streaks. A terrible scene of carnage began to unfold before her.

Men in blue with white gantlets and fedoras turned up above their eyes, stood in small groups or lay upon the ground. Some hid behind the corpses of their mounts, while others used their fallen comrades as barricades from the torrents of bullets and arrows.

The smell of sulfur tore into her nose with the awful odor of rotten eggs. Everywhere Renee looked a pool of blood stained through the white virgin snow. Even under her elbows she watched as crimson blood bubbled up from below her.

The report of a handgun caused her to look over her shoulder and behind to a tall soldier. With sweat flowing into his eyes, he stood firing revolvers with each hand directly over her. A bloody bullet hole was through one side of his cheek. Broken teeth and jaw were showing through ripped and torn flesh where his other cheek should have been. With-

out warning another bullet struck his left arm and mangled it
above the wrist. He pointed his remaining pistol at an Indian
on horseback, fired and missed and fired again.

Renee watched in fascination when his body was hit
again and wheeled around against his will. His back was to
her as she lay on the ground behind him. From another direction a shot was fired into him. His back blew open spraying
her with the valiant soldier's blood and shredded pieces of
organs. At the same time it was as if he had been lifted from
the ground and thrown backwards to cover her with his body.

Renee could not see anything but the dark blue of his
tunic when she looked sideways over her shoulder. She felt
her breath had been bashed from her lungs from his impact
upon her body. She felt his weight as he smothered her with
his own quivering flesh.

Renee squeezed her eyes closed in fear and then opened
them slowly hoping this fanatical fight would end. The noise
of the battle now felt distant to her senses. Her sight was
foggy and her body was numb. The snow had turned pinkish
red all around her and she wretched from the turmoil of her
nerves.

Awkwardly she looked to the gathering of men at the
monument. She could see through the translucent bodies to a
white man lying on his back. He had been stripped of his
clothes. His fair white skin shown brightly in a single ray
from the sun that seemed to have forced its way through the
clouds. His hair was long and almost blonde and his face was
heavily tanned under a thick mustache. He looked strange
and did not fit with the others standing over him. Squinting,
Renee saw a huge amount of blood had dried on his left side.
Just above his head a lone Indian stood.

"My God! That's Sitting Bull!" she yelled without a
sound coming from her throat.

Suddenly she felt an evil presence near her. Looking up,
she saw standing at her side a toothless Indian woman and a
young boy of no more than twelve years.

Renee fought with the weight of the dead soldier. She
strained to roll onto her back and appeal for help. Renee tried

to speak without raising herself further. Words still would not come from her mouth.The woman, dressed in skins, raised her arm and struck down at her in a mighty blow. When she raised her arm again, a long rusted knife was in her hand. Blood dripped copiously from the blade.

Renee tried to scream when the blade came down again and slashed across her arms and then her legs. She could feel cold air rush in the opening created in her pants by the blade of the knife. The woman grabbed at Renee's lower stomach with one hand and slashed with the knife in the other. The Indian woman's yells echoed through her mind as the hag stood.

High in the air she held the flaccid penis and dangling testicles of a man as if to show her strength. In absolute horror Renee screamed. But again, she made no sound. The toothless woman stuffed the genitals into a bloody hide bag and started to run from her. Within a short distance the hag stopped to squat into the fog with her grinning son beside her. The Indian woman's knife slashed out again at some other unseen form.

Sweat rolled from Renee's face while her body convulsed. She could hardly control her hands as she ran them over her abdomen feeling for the warm wetness of her own blood flowing from the gashes in her flesh. Finding none, she frantically reached between her legs and found a warm wetness covered the front of her. Renee knew she had lost it all, she had been castrated. Both hands now covered the void the Indian had left her. Her mouth opened wide emitting the scream that still wasn't there. Her head fell back into the snow. Tears rolled down the sides of her face. Renee remained frozen with fear and was too afraid to move as she prepared herself to face her death.

Trying to visualize what really had happened she fought off the panic that had just overcome her. She did not know how long it was before she tried to move or before she bent her head forward only to find she had urinated in her pants.

Almost in laughter, Renee gathered her composure and rolled over onto her stomach. She could see the Indian in the heavy fur robe holding Jack's bundle of artifacts high above his head. Jack was dancing beside him along with several other warriors.

Crazy Horse was now there with Custer and Yellow Hand and had risen a foot or two above the ground to be suspended in mid air. She could see through nearly all the Indians to Jack and the Medicine Man. Only then did she realize a few of the men were real and not figments of her runaway imagination. Renee tried to count the people who were not translucent like the others. Eighteen, she counted. The old man was wrong, she thought as she wiped the sweat mixed with tears from her face and eyes with a handful of snow. Looking down the easy sloop of the hill, she recognized one man running toward the monument through the racing horses and shouting Indians.

Nineteen, she thought, *that makes me twenty.*

"My God!" she said out loud before she realized she was able to speak for the first time. "It's Mike."

She watched him with frustration when he entered the circle of men near the monument. As soon as he had passed through them, everything fell silent on the hill. The translucent Indians disappeared along with the fog. The heavens brightened and the clouds were no longer threatening. It was then Renee realized what she had been witnessing was in her mind. It couldn't have been real.

Or could it? she wondered in confusion

What she did know for sure was that she wasn't bleeding and hadn't lost her cock and balls, and in all probability, her ovaries might still be intact.

In the deadly silence that Mike had brought with him, Renee was able to hear Jack speaking directly to him. Separated from Mike by ten or twelve feet, Jack spoke loudly and clearly with a tremendous presence of command in his voice.

"What do you want here?"

Mike pulled a short-barreled revolver from the waistband of his pants.

"I want the artifacts," he demanded back as he pointed the revolver towards Jack.

The dancers backed away, enlarging the circle.

Renee now had a clear and unobstructed view of what was taking place. She strained to hear all of what Jack and Mike were saying to each other.

Renee heard Jack speak in his casual and unnerving voice. "Don't you think you should take yourself out of here?" He paused, allowing Mike to say something. When he didn't, Jack continued. "There are a lot of witnesses."

"I don't care," Mike replied. "I only want the stuff. If I have to hurt someone for it, believe me, I will."

"Hear my words and understand, I cannot let you leave with it."

"You thought you had stopped me before and didn't. What makes you think you can stop me now?" Mike insisted.

Without hesitation Jack continued, "You have no place to run. If the law doesn't find you, I believe my people will, and I can't think of a worse way to go."

"Bullshit," Mike answered before he took a few steps forward and turned the gun to point toward the Medicine Man.

"Give me the package or I'll blow your fuckin ass off." Snatching the artifacts from his hands, Mike stepped back and again pointed the gun towards Jack. "I believe I owe you something for this nose and lip." He held his face out in proud defiance.

Mike extended his arm and aimed the pistol directly into the middle of Jack's chest.

"Can you think of any good reason why I shouldn't shoot you right now?" he demanded.

"Because you're a smart man. You'll go to prison when you're caught. Or worse, they'll hang you. Have you ever seen a hanging Mike?" Jack said as he moved his head up and down.

Renee's heart stopped, started and skipped in its own rhythm. She felt flustered that Jack had such a disregard for his own life.

Mike raised the barrel to some imaginary cross he had drawn between Jacks eyes and yelled in an angered voice, "Fuck you. You Indian fucking son-of-a-bitch."

Renee could almost feel Mike's finger press against the trigger as the hammer slowly rolled back and the cylinder began to turn a fresh round into firing position.

Renee could not believe her eyes or her ears. She didn't think Mike had ever been a violent person until all this came up. She couldn't understand his apparent and sudden change from a wimp to a wanton maniac and murderer. Watching more closely as she listened, she was beside herself with the fear that Jack would be hurt or even killed by this unwelcome pot hunter.

Trying to formulate a quick plan, she decided if she stood and started yelling, Mike's attention would be distracted, possibly even long enough for Jack to jump him and snatch his gun from his grasp or knock it to the side.

Renee took in a deep breath, placed both hands in the snow below and prepared to push herself upright. The muscles in her arms hadn't yet flexed to the point she could lift off the ground when all hell broke loose. A thunderous roar directly over her head smashed into her ears. A concussion of suddenly compressed air and sound pushed her violently back onto the snow. Her ears rang with an unbelievably high-pitched whine.

Following the blink of her eye, Renee saw Mike's head explode into a thousand fragments of bone, blood and brain. His body stood headless in the crowd. The revolver in his hands barked out repeated shots while his fingers involuntarily squeezed and squeezed the trigger again. It was like watching everything in slow motion. Renee gasped as Mike's first bullet tore into Jacks upper chest. Jack's arms and head snapped forward while his body careened back before he himself smashed onto the ground. At that same moment in time, while Mike's beheaded body was falling, more bullets flew. One struck the Medicine Man in the shoulder and spun him around like a child's top. In only a second all three men were lying in the snow bleeding or dead. The other men around them ran in every direction to hide from certain injury by Mike's headless body or from the man who had shot him.

Renee jumped to her feet in horror from what she had just witnessed. Quickly looking to her rear to see where the shot had come from, she peered down the muzzle of a high powered rifle. She recognized it as the kind of weapon hunters use for big game with a telescope mounted over the breech. And just behind the muzzle stood Nick Whitewater. He was number twenty one.

The old man couldn't have been more right if he were here! she thought before reality hit her. "You rotten bastard!" Renee screamed at the top of her lungs.

She rushed toward Nick Whitewater, kicking and striking out with her feet and fingernails. With all her strength she tried her best to hurt him, but her blows had little effect against the chest of such an inhuman being.

"You've killed them," she repeated with nearly every strike that landed on him.

Nick, with the clenched fingers of one hand, smashed his fist low into her abdomen. She fell to her knees with searing pain and gasping for air. So hard was the blow that she believed she was on the verge of blacking out and fought to remain conscious.

Nothing made any difference to her now. There was only the pain and nausea in her stomach and the gray that was enveloping her.

• • •

The Medicine Man and a few of the painted Indians gathered around Jack as he lay on the ground. Others were running from the hill towards the cars and trucks. A few hid in the bushes and grass while they watched the man with Renee.

Nick yelled to the men nearest Jack, "Is he dead?"

"No," returned the answer from one Indian standing above Jack's head.

Not wishing to place himself in the middle of them in order to take the artifacts, Whitewater seemed to have decided to remain where he was.

Again Nick yelled, "Tell him if he wants the woman, I'll make a trade for Custer's stuff. Tell him I will call tonight to the telephone booth near the store."

"What time?" another man yelled back.

"Seven o'clock," Nick screamed to him as he pulled Renee to her feet by the front of her coat. "Make sure he understands I will kill her if I don't get what I want," he yelled out as he turned to drag Renee away from the battlefield.

Although she heard the words, she did not understand them. The pain of Nick's punch and her gasping breath were all she knew of the moment.

Nick pulled her away from the shallow indentation in the ground where she had apparently given herself to the past. He moved with ease while half holding her up and half dragging her along behind him as he walked across the field of snow. Renee's feet and legs buckled under her time after time as he pulled her reeling body. If not the pain and lack of breath, the exhaustion of the ceremony would have prevented her from making any easy headway. Still, she found some strength to resist and struggle with her new enemy. This was a bastard of a man, who not only had slaughtered Mike, but probably killed Jack in the doing of his awful deed.

• • •

"He's lucky. The bullet passed right through him," one of the Indians said to another when he lifted Jack to a sitting position inspecting the blood on the back of Jack's shirt.

"It entered just below the collar bone," another said.

They pulled Jack's shirt from his shoulders, but no exit wound was found. Only the dripping blood that had trickled over his shoulder smeared his back as he lay in the snow.

The Medicine Man stood beside them with his arm broken from one of Mike's bullets. He picked up some snow and packed it around his dripping wound and then held his arm up with the other hand.

"Get him to his feet," he ordered the men around Jack. "We have to get him to town."

Jack stood with the assistance of two of the Indian men who had been inspecting him. Once on his feet, he pulled himself free of them and staggered. He stumbled as he tried to follow Nick and Renee across the side of the hill. The men studied him and directed his feet toward the cars. Looking back over to where he had last seen Renee, he so wished she knew he had not been killed and would come for her.

• • •

It must have seemed a strange sight to the nurse at the little clinic in Lodge Grass when the painted Indians deposited Jack on the table.

"You really should see a doctor. I can make arrangements to get you to Hardin or Billings," she said, shaking her head in disbelief.

"Look, Marge." Jack used the name that he read on her name tag. "Please fix it here. The thing I don't need right now is to have this reported to the authorities."

"I have to. It's the law in this state and I'm not particularly fond of the idea of going to jail for you or anyone else."

Although she had given him some painkiller and shot something into wound, the probe she was using still hurt like the dickens.

"Ah, come on," she said while pushing the rod a little deeper causing Jack to recoil as he yelled out his pain. "You can do better than that."

"Like hell I can," Jack responded with a voluntary kick at her shin.

"Ahhh fuck, that hurts!"

"A doctor should remove this. It's awfully deep!" Marge said speaking to herself as much as she was to Jack while ignoring his comments.

"No" Jack reminded her. "Let's do it right here. Now."

The Indian who had worn the buffalo robe at the ceremony entered the room. "Marge," he said, "Can I talk to you
outside for a moment?"

Since she was already disgusted with Jack anyway, she
agreed. Walking out of the little room, she left Jack sitting on
the hard surface of the makeshift gurney. The probe was still
sticking out of the soft meaty flesh a half inch below his right
collarbone. The door was being closed behind her when she
heard Jack asking, "Are you going to leave this thing in me?"

"Yes," she replied as the door latch clicked closed.

"Chris, what happened to you?" she asked. "Why the
war paint?"

"It's a long story. I think I've been shot."

"There must be something wrong with all of you. How
can you not help but tell you've been shot?"

Unwrapping the makeshift bandage from his arm, she
helped him into the circuit physician's office and had him lie
down on a small couch.

"You can fix this later," Chris said while pushing himself up against the arm that was trying shove him down.

"You need a doctor, too. Did you and that other man
fight?"

"No," he replied while she was squeezing and probing
with her fingers and an especially long Q-tip.

Marge rushed out of the room and returned a few minutes later with a large tray of medical equipment and a bowl
of reddish looking fluid. While she cleaned the wound and
prepared him for temporary splinting, he explained the problems he and Jack were facing.

● ● ●

Jack thought he had been forgotten when Marge finally
returned to the room he had been left in. Removing the
probe, she set to work extracting the bullet lodged in his
chest.

During the packing and bandaging of the now gaping
hole, she said, "You've lost a lot of blood and need to be hos-

pitalized. I want you to know what you're doing here is wrong and I'm against it."

"Did Chris explain what's going on to you?" he asked.

"Yes, and I'm still against it," she stated indicating her dislike for the plan, for Jack, and especially for Chris's comments about reservation politics in the doctor's office.

"I can understand that. But please, keep it quiet for a few days until I can get her back."

"Get who back?" Marge asked.

Jack smiled and tried to stand. "Thanks again." he replied. Marge followed him out of the room to return to Chris.

Jack finished dressing himself as rapidly as possible with his wounds and left the building. He found Renee's car had been parked outside and several men were standing near it. Jack thanked them for their assistance and to determine that the artifacts had been returned to the trunk of Renee's car. He felt his confidence grow along with his strength since he was with people who cared and whom he could trust.

Jack and three of the painted men went to the rear of Renee's little sedan. Jack knew the artifacts were the only bargaining power he had for the return of Renee. For whatever the reason, he opened the trunk one more time to see the cause of so much grief. He slowly shook his head from side to side before locking the lid closed.

Feeling stiff and more than slightly damaged, Jack drove her car to the phone booth to wait, the one he'd been told Nick would call at seven that night. Fumbling through his wallet he located his calling card and dialed in the number for the County Sheriff's Department where he worked. He briefly contemplated how would he explain the damages to the Bronco and his rapid exit from the state.

While dialing the number, Jack tried to formulate a plan and an explanation of how he was involved in a murder when the phone rang on the opposite end.

"Sheriff's Office," the voice said in a quasi-military tone.

"This is Deputy Barlow. Let me speak to the undersheriff."

"Boy, have they been looking for you. Hang on and I'll get him on the phone," the desk sergeant said excitedly.

Click, the earpiece sounded as the Deputy put Jack on hold. Jack just knew he was finished as a cop.

"He'll fire me for sure," Jack mumbled to himself. "I wonder if they'd give a letter of recommendation?"

Another click and the line was alive again.

"Where the hell are you?" came the questioning voice of the undersheriff.

"Montana, sir," Jack replied in a crisp voice.

The least he thought he could do was to act official and take it like a man.

"We were really worried about you. Someone torched your trailer the night you called in. The fire even wiped out the company four-wheel drive."

Jack said nothing.

"Jack. Jack, are you there, Jack?" the voice repeated.

"Yeah, yeah, I'm here," he replied after the feeling of relief over the Bronco settled in.

"Look, Jack," the undersheriff went on. "Do what you need to do there and get back as soon as you can. I think the detectives will need you to help them in their investigation."

"This may take a while longer. Maybe a week, but I'll be back." Jack replied in a voice that didn't betray his pain.

"Good," the undersheriff agreed. "If it's longer, give me a call. Starting now, you're on emergency medical leave."

Jack didn't reply or thank the undersheriff for his offer and stood in the phone booth with the receiver to his ear wondering why things were going down this way. He knew there was something he was forgetting.

"By the way, Jack," the undersheriff remembered, "we found a bag of bones and a skull in the back of the Bronco. Bill, the evidence tech said they were really old and probably Shoshone. What were you going to do with them?"

"Oh yeah, the bones!" Jack said, suddenly remembering he had left them in the back of the four-wheel drive. "I found them in Saline and was taking them to the Reservation in Bishop. Kind of thought they might like to plant him some-where," he concluded, trying to sound uncaring.

"I'll have them sent up. Remember, take your time and get back as soon as you can or call."

Jack thanked him and hung up the receiver. Thoroughly amazed at Nick's stupidity or incompetence, let alone his own forgetfulness of the bones, Jack did at least feel he was off the hook for part of his problems. Not much remained for him to do but wait for Nick's call.

What he did know was he had to formulate some sort of a plan. Some way to assure Renee's safety and allow him to retain the artifacts for his people.

For crying out loud, he thought, *I'm starting to sound just like him.*

• • •

Renee sat across the front seat from Nick, handcuffed to the handle on the door of his big sedan. Behind her she heard a cough. In her suffering and pain she had not noticed the older man sitting in the back seat when she was violently pushed through the open front door.

"I hope you're feeling better, Renee," the voice announced from the rear seat.

Even though dazed and shaken, she recognized that unmistakable raspy voice.

"Mr. Palmoroy!"

Before she turned herself on the seat to look at him, she swallowed hard against her dry throat and asked herself why it had to be her college professor of Early American Cul-tures.

"Wh—what are you doing here?" she stuttered.

"What do you think?" he answered briskly. "My associ-ate Nick here has promised me some items you found."

"Do you mean you're behind the slaughter at the monu-ment?"

"Hardly. It's a shame such things happen. But what can you expect?" he gave Nick one of those looks a teacher gives a bad child as he answered her question. "I was prepared to pay dearly for those things. Perhaps you would enjoy telling me of your find."

"Go to hell," Renee snapped. "I'm not telling you a thing."

In a smug voice, Palmoroy advised her, "I don't need your cooperation as much as I think Nick needs it. Due to the circumstances, you might consider what you're saying."

Nick grunted out a laugh. Renee thought it sounded like one you would hear in a horror show.

Within minutes, Nick swung the big car into the drive of an old, dilapidated farmhouse. When he opened the door for her she kicked out at his crotch with her right foot but missed. Dismissing the minor blow Nick drew back his arm and drove it forward. He back-handed her across the face and knocked her half-senseless. Quickly regaining her composure, Renee figured a better plan would be needed to free herself and avenge Jack than to take another slap for a stupid move.

Mr. Palmoroy led the way from the car to the door, while Renee made a small attempt to pull away from Nick. Turning and twisting, he dragged her by the chain connecting the handcuffs into the front room. It was very apparent there was no use crying out for help since the nearest house looked to be a good half-mile away. From the way things were going down and the lack of her kidnapers' preparedness, Renee believed her abduction had not been planned. This became evident since Palmoroy was busy looking through the house as Nick dragged her around the floor searching for a place she could be tied. Eventually he pulled her up to a post separating the kitchen from the dining room and cuffed her to that. In her defiance, she knew she could not show her weakness by crying, nor could she assist such evil bastards.

11

"A Book to Burn"

For the few moments Renee was alone, the thought of Jack being shot tormented her painfully. If he hadn't been killed, he had to be mortally wounded. For him to be hit so hard at such a close range horrified and sickened her.

"He has to be alive. But how, just how could he have survived it?"

Renee was in her own agony, wishing she could have held him in his final minutes of life and comfort him, to let him know how much love had grown in her heart and soul for him during the few short days they had been together. Tears of tremendous pain poured from the depths of her inner being.

"I have to pull myself together. I can't cry. I have to destroy them," she told herself.

Not even the artifacts were of importance any more. The only way to rectify what these pot hunters had done was to cause each of them the anguish they had brought to her.

Renee pulled at the base of the post to which she had been handcuffed. Not a fraction of a movement of the wooden pillar could be felt through her trembling hands.

"Christ," she moaned in utter desperation. "Why did the damn carpenters have to build this thing so freaken solid?"

As she pulled harder, her thoughts wandered to her little apartment and why the cabinets seemed to fall off the wall if she were to touch them wrong. "Not here, not in this freaken place. But there must be a way."

Her eyes played around the kitchen area for anything within reach to aid her escape. But the house had been thoroughly cleaned out of usable items long ago and nothing close enough existed to help her. The floor was littered with garbage, old clothes and discarded books. Cursing silently to herself, she kicked away some weathered and water-stained periodicals from under her feet. The magazines flew across the kitchen with most of them slamming up against the wall where a stove had once stood.

Only one old crumpled magazine remained in the circle she had cleared beneath her—a copy of *Look Magazine*. Bending over as far as possible with her hands at the bottom of the post, out of curiosity she strained to see the date.

"1938! Shit," she said in a voice that was just a scosh to loud. "A damn collector's item."

"What's the problem in there?" Palmoroy yelled from another room in the back of the house.

"Not a fucking thing," Renee hissed back and in a lowered voice added, "Nothing a dickless asshole like you would want."

Renee kicked that last magazine with the energy of her hatred for Nick Whitewater and especially for that slime ball prick Palmoroy.

The pages tore open as it shot into the air and hit the kitchen wall just under the window. It wasn't the thud of paper as she expected, but the tinkling sound of metal striking the wall. That peculiar sound was closely followed by the clinking of something onto the tattered hardwood floor.

Whatever it was that made that noise, it bounced on to a filthy and soiled shirt not far from her. Renee immediately recognized the curve of a old rusted beer can opener as it lay in the ragged folds of the material. The church key was similar to the one Jack had used in Saline Valley. Renee wanted to shout to the Mother of all Beer Bottle openers that her accidental find was the key to impose her revenge against these men. Stretching out with her foot she tried to touch the shirt and drag it to her. Hooking it with the toe of her shoe, she pulled it closer. Renee recognized she was now confronted with the real problem.

Renee weighed the situation as best she could and considered the most logical method to lift the opener from the floor to her fingers. Bending over at the waist and resting her head between her outstretched arms, she stared down at the rusty thing.

I certainly couldn't get them to give it to me, she thought. *If only I can roll the shirt into a ball with my foot so the opener won't fall out. Maybe I can work my foot under it.* Renee grunted her anxiety while she labored with her feet and silently muttered instructions to herself. Half sticking her tongue out the side of her mouth, she continued. *If all goes well I will be able to lift it to the counter top and I will have—*

The wadded shirt fell from its perch when she had lifted it only half way to the top of the counter.

"Well, fuck! Maybe—toss—the—sucker—up—with—my—foot."

Renee hoped she could balance bundle long enough for her to lift her leg and kick, briefly stopping to think about what she looked like in such an uncomfortable position.

Now that's a lot of ifs! she thought again as she stuck her tongue out through her teeth while not forgetting that her first two attempts had failed miserably.

Using both feet she managed to work the fabric over itself and the object of this whole exercise. Sliding the wadded pile into her left foot, she again folded the old shirt over itself one last time.

Perfect, now if I can—get it—back on top of my foot, balance it and—lift.

A broad smile emerged when she realized she was going to work herself loose easier than she had imagined.

The voices of Palmoroy and Nick were becoming louder along with the sound of their footsteps. Renee scooted the shirt containing her passport to freedom away to be just within a long leg reach. Her maneuver was just in time as Nick walked into the room and directly up and next to her.

"You're going to be fun tonight," he told her as he shook her hands against the wooden pillar, making sure the cuffs were still secure.

Palmoroy tramped through the discarded papers and magazines she had kicked against the wall to look out the kitchen window and across the field. "I think she will be all right here." After a pause for what seemed to Renee to be of considerable thought, added, "Maybe you should gag her anyway."

"Yeah," Nick agreed. "Now is not the time to lose what Barlow wants most." With one swift motion he reached down and picked up the rolled shirt and snapped the folds out as if cracking a whip. The rusted can opener flew through the air and glanced off Palmoroy's back. Again it clinked to the floor after bouncing off the edge of another counter. Even though Renee wasn't surprised when Palmoroy bent over and picked it off the floor, her heart stilled and then sank along with her means of escape.

Holding his glasses just off the bridge of his nose, he inspected the opener with the thoroughness of a well-trained archaeologist before he placed it neatly near the edge of the counter.

Renee fought back her smile as best she could. *Thank you, you S.O.B,* and once again, with the allegiance of the ancient god of bottle openers, Renee thought she would hear the fat lady start to sing.

Nick tugged a folding knife from a shiny leather sheath on his belt. Pressing some sort of bar on the back strap of the handle to release the blade, he snapped the evil instrument open. The wicked-looking weapon nearly doubled in its length. Placing the razor sharp blade in the armpit, he easily dragged the blade through the material. The arm separated from the bodice with a single slow pull.

"We know you'll be quiet till we get back," Nick said as he moved the back of the blade across her throat just under her chin.

Renee's head reared back, trying to avoid the feel of the brutally cold steel while she swallowed hard in her suddenly drier throat. She was astonished that someone like Whitewater was such a creature of habit when he took a moment to wipe the blade onto his boot before returning the knife to the scabbard.

The care and cleaning of the tools of the trade, she thought. Stepping behind her, Nick lowered the cut off arm of the shirt over her head and pulled it back and into her mouth when she tried to protest. She could feel her hair as it became tangled with the fabric as he tied a simple overhand knot tightly behind her head.

Renee's first sensation of the gag was the oily, gritty feel of sand and dirt, long embedded in the fibers. The bitter taste of salt along with what little saliva she had mixed in the material. The impact to her senses was sudden and violent when the faint odor of dried urine entered her nostrils. Renee retched deep in her gut and fought back the rising vomit.

Nick laughed at her spasms and the sounds she made through the cloth. He pushed his face against the side of hers and sucked in the rotten smell into his own nostrils.

Her gut-wrenching feelings grew worse as she felt the middle finger of his right hand push against the fabric covering the tight crack of her ass.

"When I get back, I'll give you something to suck on you'll really like."

"Go outside," Palmoroy demanded, disgusted with what Nick was saying. "I'll be out in a minute."

"Fuck her a good'en fer me," Nick encouraged him as he turned to walk out the door to the car.

By now Renee's stomach had started the slow recovery from the vile gag.

"I'm sorry this had to go badly for you and your friends. You don't understand the gravity and value of the things you've discovered." Stepping behind her, he untied the knot and dragged the material from her lips.

Renee tried to spit out the foul girt from her teeth and mouth before she tried to speak.

"Why?" she begged. "Why are you doing this to me?"

"Like Nick tried to say, you're our bargaining chip. Nothing more, nothing less."

"But, why me? You could have used the same information to recover the stuff yourself."

"Let's just say when you're a man who has reached my station, you let the enthusiastic do the work."

"Then you believed in me. You knew I would eventually find the artifacts, didn't you?"

"I was hoping you would. I spent a lot of time and effort making sure you would have the diary and Custer's letter."

Renee suddenly remembered poor Mike lying on battlefield with his head torn to tiny bits and some larger pieces. Silently she asked herself if he wouldn't still be alive had she been a little less inquisitive while looking through the diary.

"You mean you even knew about the letter? I'd bet you haven't told Nick everything either, have you?"

"Certainly not! Would you trust someone like him with all the facts in an endeavor of this great of importance?"

Renee leered at him. Palmoroy started to replace the gag in her mouth.

"Please, I promise I'll be quiet. Pleaaaaa…" her words not finished were reduced to a muffled mutter with the material twisting back into her mouth.

"You do understand. I can't afford to become a suspect in any of this. Mainly, we can't have you sounding an alarm, now can we?"

After clinching the knot just a little tighter, Palmoroy stepped away from her toward the sink. Unbuttoning his shirt just above the belt buckle, he reached inside and unhooked something. Renee watched in wonderment while he pulled a long nylon money belt from around his belly.

Renee gave away her real look of surprise. "It's really hard to believe you were a tenured instructor! You hiding another gun in there or something?"

"Bearer bonds, my dear. Just bearer bonds."

Mr. Palmoroy carefully rolled the belt into a small ball, stooped down and pushed it under the sink to a place where it could not be seen.

"I'll bring you a sandwich or something. Kind of a last supper," he told her smugly.

"Kind of stupid letting me see where you put those, isn't it?" she did her best to be heard through the gag.

Before he walked out the door to the car where Nick was impatiently waiting, he slipped his hand over her crotch and moved his middle finger back and forth the length of her vagina. Almost tenderly at first, he felt the soft folds of fabric covered flesh. Stopping the movements he pressured his finger harder into the center of her womanhood. As he did this, he told her, "I'll bet you could be a lot of fun. It's too bad we couldn't have gotten together under better circumstances."

Although her own mind was filled with rage she constrained her lower lip and said nothing. Renee noticed Palmoroy's face had turned red with a blush before he completely finished what he was saying.

You old son-of-a-bitch," her muffled words came through the vile rag. "You embarrassed yourself. I'll bet you're too shriveled up to do a real woman any good."

The expression on his face changed to a sneer letting her know he understood exactly what she had said.

"I would find it kind of erotic to have intercourse with a woman whose family tree doesn't fork," he said in some childish attempt of retaliation.

Renee kicked hard at him before he had a chance to move outside of her reach. But her blow just glanced off his lower leg with little, if any physical damage.

• • •

Renee waited until the engine started and the sounds of the car moving out of the drive had died away before she tried to again reach the opener. Stretching as far as she could, her fingers were almost a foot short of having it in her grasp. Moving around to the side she raised her leg and set it down on the cold surface of the counter. Lifting herself slightly, her other leg dangled down and didn't quite touch the floor. This precarious position gave her no leverage whatsoever.

"For crying out loud. Why couldn't I be two inches taller?" she moaned.

With about as much difficulty as could be expected, Renee inched the opener closer to her hands with the side of her foot. As luck would have it, the combination of her slick nylon Jacket and the awkward position caused her to slide from the counter.

Her wrists ached with the sudden twist of steel digging into her skin. At last she was able to wrap her fingers around it. Although they were cold and somewhat numb on the tips, she manipulated the bent and pointed end of the opener. Just as Jack had instructed her at the hot pool, she worked the opener under the spring steel that hid the release. Forcing the point into the ratchet with her right hand the lock smoothly dropped open and swung free. As quickly as she could, she tore the gag from her mouth before she freed the other half of the handcuff.

Renee's stomach retched as her search for water became foremost to her needs. If only the faucets worked. Anything at all and she would wash out the vile filth coating her mouth. Following a brief search of the rooms, nothing was found to satisfy that most urgent need. Cautiously, Renee slipped through the front door to make sure Palmoroy and Whitewater had left and to continue her search. The ankle-deep snow was all that could be had.

"It will do for now," Renee told herself as she took a handful, bit into the hard little crystal and swished them around. Somewhat satisfied, she tried to spit. This simple act was like trying to whistle with a mouth full of crackers, but her tongue did feel a little more tolerable.

Renee entered into the kitchen through a ragged opening where the rear door should have been. Squatting down, she recovered the money belt from behind the rusted drainpipe.

Deftly, she stretched the belt out on the counter and dragged the long zipper completely open. Taking a brief second to look out the window and listen for any unwanted noises, she opened the pouch.

Using as much caution as possible while believing Palmoroy had probably tricked her again, she slowly removed and unfolded the papers. Nothing less than a handful of beautifully printed American Bank Notes that Palmoroy had hidden from Nick's greedy eyes. Five, one hundred thousand dollar bonds were wrapped around ten, one hundred dollar bills. Her eyes nearly bugged out.

"Wow!"

• • •

No one had the faintest idea where Renee could have been taken. This left Jack at a loss for something to do in order to rescue her from Nick Whitewater. If there was no other way, he knew he might have to put Whitewater permanently out of his misery and self-induced shame in order for her to be saved. In his weakened state, Jack sat watching the phone booth trying to organize a plan and hoping it wouldn't come to that. Exhaustion, lack of sleep and hunger added to the effect of the painkiller as well as the loss of blood. Stepping out of Renee's car, he felt he could at least take care of that "hunger" part. With a throbbing in his chest he painfully made his way through the front door of the store.

Walking through the isles, Jack stacked a loaf of bread and small jars of peanut butter and jelly into a hand-held shopping basket. Near the checkout counter, a generous selection of candy bars was in the rack with one in particular catching his eye. Picking out a half dozen Baby Ruth's, he set them on the counter along with the basket and tried to act as pleasant as possible. Putting his hand to his shoulder, Jack squeezed the bandage tenderly to slow the ache where the bullet had been extracted. Although he still felt dizzy, he knew he would have more strength after he gobbled his dinner.

"You can do better than this stuff, you know," the clerk said while skillfully placing the groceries into a medium-sized paper bag.

"Huh! What?" Jack asked as his eyes rose up from the counter to locus on a slightly over weight and middle aged Indian woman.

"I said, you need something to eat better than this."

Trying to be polite, Jack smiled and tried his best to respond intelligently. "That's about all I can afford. Don't worry about it. It will do OK."

A look of irritation rolled over the clerk's face. "You're on my reservation now, and you'll do as I say. Understand?"

"Ah hell," Jack muttered, thinking this was no time for rivalries between tribes or clans or whatever.

"Follow me," she said as she made her way from behind the counter.

The woman led Jack out through a rear door to a travel trailer some fifty feet behind the store.

Nudging him to sit at the small table after she removed his coat, she turned around and reset the thermostat to a higher and more comfortable temperature.

Without turning to face him, she talked into the wall "Everybody knows what you're doing here."

Jack didn't attempt to make any excuses since he knew only too well that this tight-knit society was aware of what was happening practically before it took place.

"I will feed you, then you sleep."

Jack heard her words, but they really didn't sink in for a second or two.

"Thank you," he responded to her kindness. "But I don't have time for sleep."

"You will take time. I will wake you in a couple of hours."

Jack started to speak in reply to her command, but before he could say anything, the woman held her index finger to her mouth and told him to "shush."

One can of chili con carne, four slices of bread, a large glass of milk and a cup of nearly boiling coffee filled Jack's stomach to near bursting. Moving over to the small bed he flopped himself onto the soft mattress. He knew too well from the way he felt that not even the throb in his shoulder would rob him from of sleep this day.

The kindly woman unbuckled his belt and opened his pants. She removed a moth eaten, gray wool military blanket from a cabinet over his head and gently covered him from toe to throat.

"I'll wake you at five-thirty."

"Make it five o'clock," Jack responded through a wide-mouthed yawn.

He closed his eyes momentarily and felt the trailer shake as she moved around doing one thing or another. A little for-eign sound caught by his ear caused him to force open his heavy lids and look. Her hand was just pulling away as she left a Baby Ruth candy bar on the pillow near his head. With the best smile he could muster for his condition, he closed his eyes and immediately faded into sleep. However, his sleep was not as quiet as he wished.

Nightmares woke him several times and were inter-spersed with visions of a panting wolf moving swiftly over a grassy field. Even in his dreams he knew he had been there before. The place had to be what his nation still called Greasy Grass. The place not far from Custer's Last Stand.

• • •

Renee wanted to spend as little time as possible around the abandoned farmhouse. Her first and utmost fear was the possibility of Palmoroy and Whitewater returning before she could leave or find help. She quickly packed the money belt with the bearer bonds and stuffed the lot into her coat pocket. The hundred-dollar bills were a different matter; she wadded them into a roll and stuffed them into her pants.

Taking one last look around the kitchen, a kind of a part-ing shot in her escape crossed her mind. A message for Pal-moroy. A quick look through the living room and kitchen led her to a discarded "Bic" lighter in one corner of the room. Judging from a scorch mark on the wood floor, some kids or transients had built a small fire there and left the lighter. Renee rolled her thumb over the striker and a small flame appeared. Quickly she removed her thumb from the little piece of plastic, and the fire extinguished just as fast as it started.

Renee needed something to burn of similar size to the bonds.

The Look magazine! she thought. Picking the battered pages from the floor, she compared them for correct size. *Perfect!*

She tore five pages from the back of the book and wadded them up before placing them in the sink. Smiling, she ignited one corner of a page. While watching the fire build in its intensity, Renee decided this alone wouldn't be enough to convince Palmoroy of what she had done to him.

But how will they positively know?

Another and more substantial idea came to her. Renee pulled the wad of hundred dollar bills from of her pocket.

"No. I really shouldn't. That's a Federal offense," she snickered out loud. "Then again, who would tell?"

Tearing one bill in half, she held the two parts to the fire. Renee blew out the flames when about a quarter of each section remained and placed the singed pieces in the sink near the charred paper.

"Boy, is he going to be mad as hell over this," she laughed as she headed out through the yard and across the road from the farmhouse.

Renee tried to open the distance between her and the place she had been held captive. Over the entire distance to the opposite side of the field, she repeatedly looked over her shoulder. Even though she was somewhat certain of her freedom, she still had a compulsion to make sure they hadn't returned and witnessed her flight.

Renee stopped when she reached the skeleton of a long dead tree along some forgotten irrigation ditch. Making sure she was at a safe enough distance to stop for a moment to rest and regain some wind, she leaned back against the rough bark of the tree's trunk. Looking back over the ground she had crossed, she figured she must have walked or run better than a mile. Renee shuddered when she discovered Palmoroy would know exactly what direction she had taken.

"Damn it. They can follow me wherever I go," After taking a moment to think about the probability of being caught again, she yelled, "Hell, I can out run either of you fat sons-of-bitches."

Several beep breaths and a leg stretch or two, and Renee started her jog to the little town of Lodge Grass off in the distance.

• • •

In that murky place between consciousness and sleep, Jack saw the quickening pace of the Coyote as it pursued a maiden in flight.

It took several moments of the store clerk's massaging Jack's back before his mind cleared enough to realize that someone was administering to him.

"Who? What?" And then the reality of where he was dawned on him. "What time is it?" he asked dryly.

"Five minutes till five. I have called some men who will help you."

"Here?"

"They're in the store," she said as she helped him off the mattress and assisted him with his belt, button and zipper. Jack rubbed his face with his hand, trying to brush the sleep from his still heavy eyes. He wished that all this were a bad dream. Jack made his way out of the little trailer into the general store while making his Baby Ruth last for three bites. He still felt miserable as his shoulder ached with an almost unbelievable pulsating throb.

Several men were waiting in the store and he recognized only three of about seven of them. Joshua, David and Rick Sun were standing closest to him and near the counter when he stopped beside the bread racks.

The old man spoke first. "It is not good, a brother turning on a brother in the way Nick Whitewater has."

Jack couldn't help but agree with him.

"We have come here to help you get back your friend and make sure you go to your counsel with the ancient ones at Pine Ridge."

"Where they have taken her?" Jack asked, hoping his question didn't sound like he had just made a demand.

"We have been watching and have not seen them."

Even though there was nothing that could be done at that point, Jack instructed all of them at once, "I do not wish anything from any of you for now. However, if the men or their car is seen, I want you to tell me as soon as possible. Another thing. What has happened to the body of the man who has been killed?"

Another man replied, "You shouldn't worry about him. He won't be found before it is time."

"Has anyone called the FBI, or the Federal Marshal yet?"

"No." Several of the men replied in near unison or shook their head in the negative.

"That's great." Jack nodded while he was checking his watch for the time.

Except for Joshua, the other men left the store to start their search for Renee and her kidnapers.

Joshua drove Jack back to the clinic in Renee's car. Once there, Joshua went inside to talk to Marge while Jack searched through his suitcase for his .22 caliber automatic. It seemed like only seconds had passed before both Marge and Joshua returned to the passenger side of the car.

"I told you, you should've gone to the doctor," Marge admonished him with a really stern and matronly I-told-you-so voice.

"I need something for the pain!" Jack pleaded with her seemingly stonewall attitude.

Marge looked up and down the street before she reached into the pocket of her white smock. From it she produced a small container of tablets and passed them through the window to Jack's eagerly awaiting fingers.

"You have no idea where you got these," she instructed him before she turned and walked away.

"What now?" Joshua asked.

"Back to the phone and wait, I guess," Jack responded before swallowing one of the tablets without water.

Impatiently Jack sat in the little sedan praying for the phone to ring. Over and over he tried to formulate a plan that would separate Renee from Whitewater and Palmoroy. None would come to his exhausted mind. Joshua had excused himself and left him alone for almost an hour before he finally returned. Jack watched him running from behind one of the houses not far from where he himself had talked to the old woman earlier. As close to a dead run as he was capable, Joshua raced up close to his window and bent over as if to speak to him. Panting, he hurriedly pushed through the opening a large caliber revolver as if trying to keep anyone from seeing. Inspecting the big blue chunk of iron and hefting it in his right hand, Jack felt its tremendous weight.

"That's a .44 Magnum. What do you want me to do, hunt elephants or something?"

"I thought you might like to even things out a little, that's all." Before Jack could say anything to him, Joshua continued, "It's hot. I just stole it from that retired tribal cop's house."

"Take it back right now," Jack snarled at him. "I don't need more trouble than I already have."

Joshua snapped the gun from Jack's grasp while nearly taking his trigger finger with it and ran back up the street.

I hope he does what he was told, Jack thought while he smiled his appreciation for the thought. "Kids!" Jack sniffed the wetness back up his nose.

"Ring. Ring. Ring." The phone in the booth seemed to clang just loud enough for Jack to hear at that distance. He hurried from the car and picked up the receiver by the end of the fourth ring.

"Yeah?" Jack said into the mouthpiece.

"Is this Jack?" The question came after several seconds of silence. "I'm glad you're still alive."

"Yeah."

"You got the stuff we want?"

"Yeah," Jack replied and immediately added, "You have her?"

A deafeningly long pause occurred before the man on the opposite end replied. "Unless you want her dead, you should listen to what I want you to do. I'll make the exchange with you at the Visitors Center at Sharps Corner. You know it?"

"Why in South Dakota? Why not here? You've killed her, haven't you?"

"Don't be stupid. I have my reasons for doing it this way and it doesn't concern what you want."

"Then let me talk to her right now," Jack demanded into the phone.

"If you aren't there in twenty-four hours from right now, she will be dead. You'll have nobody to blame but yourself."

The line went silent.

Jack stood with the receiver pressed hard to his ear. He prayed the unknown caller would come back on the line. Several seconds passed before he gave up his frivolous wait. Stepping away from the booth, he bumped directly into Joshua. He hadn't seen him return or heard him standing there breathing hard from running.

"I'm sure they've killed her."

"What makes you think so?"

"Because they want me to meet them on the reservation in South Dakota."

"Any particular place?"

"Yeah," Jack responded thoughtfully. "At Sharps Corner."

Joshua thought a moment, then asked, "Don't you live around there someplace?"

"About twenty-five miles out on Cuny Table. They must be after my mother!"

"Bright Moon!"

"Look Joshua, tell everyone where I'm going. See if you can find the remains of the girl I was with and lastly, have Rick Sun get a hold of the Medicine Man at Porcupine. Have Rick fill him in on what has been happening here."

Before Joshua could reply, Jack turned away and went back to the phone and dialed his home on Cuny Table. A recording automatically answered.

"The number you have called is temporarily disconnected or is not in serv—"

Jack hung up the receiver before the message had completed. He rushed to Renee's car before Joshua had an opportunity to ask if there was anything more he wanted done. Starting the engine, Jack slammed the shift lever into low and the rear wheels spun on the slippery snow. A quick look over his shoulder allowed him to see Joshua running into the general store to do as he was told. Jack knew nothing must stop him from getting to his mother's house without delay.

•   •   •

The distance was far greater than it appeared. Because of this, her trek had taken infinitely longer then she had wanted. Her remaining minutes of light were being used up rapidly. Finally, on reaching town, she quickly found a hiding place behind one of the small ship-lapped sided houses. This was her first opportunity to catch her breath and try to settle down and still feel somewhat secure. Checking her watch in the very dim light from a window over her head, she saw that it was three minutes to seven.

Why seven o'clock? Why does that mean something?

Try as best as she could, she just couldn't remember what. Renee crept around the side of the old house and closer to the street. Hoping she wouldn't be mistaken for a burglar or some foul vermin of the night, she tried to stay low and behind the bushes even though they were void of leaves and offered little in the way of camouflage to her.

From the corner of the little house she was able to see two men standing under a covered, dimly lit boardwalk near the center of town. The distance was too great to recognize the men to be Whitewater or Palmoroy or anyone else she had recently met. Even though the danger of discovery increased with every step, she slowly and cautiously made her way forward until she was sure it wasn't her abductors.

God, I hope they can help me, she thought to herself.

It took her several minutes to close the distance enough to clearly see the car parked next to the men. Renee was delighted when she discovered it was in fact her car! A breath of freedom filled her lungs. Double-checking both ways on the pot-holed road she still did not see her abductors or their car.

Stepping from behind a tree near another house, she continued slowly toward her car. Renee dropped to the ground when one of the men moved quickly to her sedan and jumped in. At about the same time, the other man just as suddenly turned and ran into the building.

"Crap! That S.O.B. is stealing my fricken car!" she shouted.

Renee jumped to her feet and ran as fast as she could toward the sedan while it moved away from her at an ever increasing rate.

Momentarily forgetting her safety, she yelled in desperation, "Stop! Bring back my car. Stop, thief!"

The further the automobile moved away from her the slower she ran toward it, until she stopped where her car had been parked. She looked about her and then up and down the street. Not a soul had opened their doors to see what her commotion was all about.

"Why don't you people help me?" she yelled as loud as she could, in disgust, anger and feeling sure she was going to chew up and spit out the next person that said the wrong thing. As she ran into the general store, the squeaky door slammed against the outside wall with a crash just after she stopped a quarter dozen steps past the threshold.

Behind the counter an Indian woman stood. Not far from her, Joshua was using a phone at the end of the counter nearer the cash register. Neither one said a word to her as she raced in gasping for breath. They stood silently staring at her and she at them.

"You're supposed to be dead!" Joshua said in a loud voice breaking the silence.

"Not hardly."

Before she could say more or question either of them, the woman asked her, "Are you the girl who was with Jack?"

"Yes I am. Where is he now?"

"You just missed him by a minute. He's on his way to South Dakota."

"Thank God. Then he is alive!"

"Yeah! Why shouldn't he be?" the clerk replied with even less concern than when Renee had first came in. She felt the rush of relief drain her of strength.

"Shit. I need a car. Can anyone around here help me?"

The lady behind the counter tried to explain that Renee would have a hard time finding anyone on the reservation who would want to get involved.

"Why not?" Renee pleaded with a renewed feeling of contempt.

"There has been death over what you and Jack brought here. It is the evil you have brought to us. Things that should have been left alone with the dead."

The clerk left Renee with little or no hope when she spoke those words.

"What about you, Joshua? You're Jack's friend, aren't you?"'

"Truck's broke."

The clerk interrupted Joshua. "Maybe you can find someone who will give you a ride to Billings. There you can rent a car."

Renee hesitated with the door handle in her hand and looked back toward the clerk. After a second of alternating looks between both of them, she finally said, "It's worth two hundred dollars for the ride." Joshua started to speak when the clerk put her hand on his arm and quieted him. Renee stood erect and shrugged her shoulders, turning her back on them and left the building. Standing in the light in front of the store, Renee bent over slightly with a feeling of hopelessness. The only recourse left was to use the phone to call for a cab or something from Billings or somewhere closer.

The figure of an inconsequential and frail person emerged from the darkness and leaned toward her.

"You're Rick Sun." Renee worried momentarily why she didn't jump at his unexpected approach before she continued. "The people in there don't want to help."

"That's because she is a witch." Rick said matter-of-factly in somewhat broken English.

"I know she is," Renee sneered in reply while looking back toward the closed door of the store.

"I mean a real witch." He thought a moment then added, "She reminds me of my wife. You need a ride, don't you?"

"Jack has left to go to South Dakota and I need a car to follow him." she told him with an unmistakable tone of pleading.

"I think I can help you. Follow me." The old man started a slow shuffle down and then across the street.

Renee tried to walk with him but found his slowness extremely difficult. The urgency of getting on the road pushed her adrenaline through her system.

Please. Oh, please hurry. She begged to herself.

They had walked a little over a city block to an old single-car garage. Rick fumbled with a ring of keys as he tried to work one into the lock in the darkness. Renee wanted to snatch the key from him and do it herself. But somehow she found the strength to hold back that urge. She realized that the last thing she needed was to anger the only person in town who was trying to help. After what seemed like forever, the lock finally dropped open. She couldn't take it any longer and reached across Rick's hand and pulled the padlock from the latch. With a mighty jerk she swung the door open on her side. As Rick walked into the building, she opened the opposite door and forced it across a pile of snow.

The engine fired without hesitation and started to run at a fast RPM. Rick switched on the lights and illuminated Renee directly in front of the truck. She ran her hand over the smooth, nearly dust-free hood in appreciation of his modern vehicle.

"If it's not brand new, then it's a good-looking newer Ford," Renee said to herself.

Quickly she moved around to the open driver's door.

"Is this yours?" she asked Rick.

"Yes. I use my allotment checks. The B.I.A. bought it for me," he replied with the pride of his eighty or ninety some odd years. "Don't know how to drive though," he added with a sorrowful tone in his voice. Rick slid out of the seat onto very springy legs and told her to get in when he regained his balance. As they passed each other in the small space between the truck door and the wall, Renee kissed him on the cheek then slid behind the wheel. Rolling down the window, she again thanked him for his help.

Renee reached for the shift lever on the steering column to put the truck into drive. There wasn't any. Again searching around, she found the interior light switch and turned on the overhead courtesy light.

"It's a floor shift?" she screamed with utter lack of hope. "I don't know how to drive a damn stick shift."

Rick gave a very concerned look and started to speak. But Renee's methods cut him off when she slightly depressed the clutch and ground the floor shift into third gear. The horrible noise was closely followed by her depressing the accelerator to the floor causing the motor's scream of agony. The truck suddenly bucked forward when her foot slipped off the clutch pedal. The nearly new Ford shot forward, stopped, then bucked again. The sequence of bucking and momentarily stopping continued until she rolled onto the road and started to gain speed.

She was half a mile out of town before it had dawned on her she didn't know which direction Billings was in. She told herself she wasn't going to turn around until she reached a place where she could rent something she could drive a lot more easily.

12

"Nobel's Prize"

Renee had driven a little under forty miles when she reached the road sign she didn't want to see: "Billings, 31 miles."

"Good grief! I'm driving the wrong way."

To make matters worse, the inexhaustible amount of snow on the side of the roadway was becoming higher and thicker. Over the next half mile, Renee argued with herself about her ability to make a wide turn with such a large truck.

Maybe slow down just right and then lock the brakes. The truck just might slide around a hundred and eighty degrees.

Renee tossed the idea around until she had convinced herself she wouldn't lose the much needed momentum to keep the truck from stalling.

On the other hand, if I lose control, I could be in worse shape than if I just stalled on the road. I'll bet there's an owner's manual that will explain all this, she told herself, attacking the problem scientifically.

Renee leaned as far over as she could to reach the latch on the glove box. As everything else had gone so far, the little door remained just past the tip of her fingers. To compensate, she scooted herself to the middle to be within reach of the release. Her left hand held the top of the steering wheel while the toes of her left foot were on the accelerator peddle. Renee extended out in the darkness with her right hand to feel out the latch while maintaining a lop-sided vigilance of the road.

Damn. They couldn't put it where a short person could reach it, could they?

Renee stretched herself a little bit farther than she had intended. Her left foot slid off the accelerator pedal with an agonizing, Oops! Quickly she pulled herself upright with her left arm and at the same time shoved her foot against the wrong pedal and accelerated the engine. The truck started to slide slowly sideways as she pulled the wheel towards her while trying to sit up. There was little doubt in her own mind that she had done a sensationally stupid thing. The original plan surely would have worked. However, she was sincerely happy that no one was around to see her now.

Renee covered her eyes in disbelief as she sat in the middle of the seat while the truck slipped sideways, all four wheels spinning wildly on the ice. There was nothing for her to do but watch the catastrophe that was headed her way. Renee really wanted not to watch the spectacle that was intensified by the crunching of ice being thrown against the underside of the vehicle. When her eyes would not stay shut any longer, she drew in a deep breath, grabbed the wheel tightly and did the only logical thing: she hung on.

Great white spears with ever-enlarging black centers extended themselves from their sockets as the truck spun around several times. As if guided by divine providence, Rick's Ford slowed to a stop in the middle of the roadway.

"At least you're pointed in the right direction!" she yelled at the windshield.

On its own, the truck began to jerk forward as the huge tires tried to find their traction. The engine had not died as

expected and the truck was at a fast idle, trying to gain
momentum back in the direction of Lodge Grass. Renee
took stock that she hadn't gotten the instruction book as she
had intended, but was completely satisfied she didn't presently need the thing anyway.

The miles seemed to tick away with less frequency
than the minutes following the episode at the milepost sign.
She drove slower than she really wanted to, causing the
engine to groan along at less than the required revs. The
truck seemed to be doing just fine in what may well have
been the fourth gear and fifteen miles per hour.

As she passed through the little town of Lodge Grass,
she saw Rick Sun standing in front of the general store. He
had a look of quivering excitement about him while his slim
arms were suspended above his head and danced to and fro.
It seemed to Renee that he was yelling something at her.
Renee wished she could explain to the kindly old man, but
dared not stop. She just knew Whitewater and Palmoroy
would be nearby and lying in wait for her return.

She heard herself apologizing to him as she added
more power to move faster past him. Even though she did
feel more than a little obligation to Rick for the use of his
truck, she decided an enthusiastic wave to him would be as
consoling as anything else under the present circumstances.

"Strange!" she laughed out her anxieties. "He doesn't
look real happy. But I do understand. I really do understand
how he feels."

The fear of driving this tank on icy roads and the
thought of not being able to catch Jack just seemed to make
things worse. Renee fought the urge to cry.

• • •

She was only about five or six miles short of Sheridan,
Wyoming, and heading toward Buffalo when she saw a dark
figure walking on the side of the lonely highway. He looked
strange to her and didn't seem to be dressed appropriately
for the freezing air. In the quick glimpse she had of him, he
appeared to be hugging himself from the cold. Renee

ignored the man for a short second before the image of Jack corresponded with this man's approximate height and size. Renee turned her head and looked back through the rear window of the pickup to make sure her fatigued mind hadn't been playing tricks on her. There wasn't enough light for her to see him again. Squinting her eyes didn't seem to help her vision at all.

As she turned her head back to see what was coming up on the road, she discovered she was bearing down on a little white sedan left sideways on the right side of the road.

"That idiot left his damn car—MY CAR!"

Renee jerked at the steering wheel hoping she would have room to maneuver around her car and not hit its rear end. No such luck. The right front fender of Rick's truck smashed her little sedan squarely on the right rear fender and spun the little sedan around behind her.

Completely out of control, the pickup careened into the bank of snow on the left side of the road and then rico-cheted back to the right. The front of the truck plowed onto the snow bank at the edge of the road and stopped abruptly. Bouncing back from being thrown against the dash, Renee sat frozen. In some sort of weird fascination, she watched the sparkling snow flakes fall back to the earth in the bright glow of the remaining headlamp. Her heart pounded furi-ously and her breathing was rapid when she was finally able to swallow her stomach back to where it belonged.

Renee kicked open the door and stepped out onto the slippery roadbed. She caught herself from falling as her foot instantly lost traction and tried to leave without her. Had she not been hanging on to the door handle, she knew she would surely have been hurt bouncing off the ice. Correcting her stance as best she could, she looked up and watched as the engine decided it had enough and died on its own.

"Goddamned stick shifts anyway!" she screamed at the truck and then kicked at the door panel, almost losing her balance one more time.

Somewhere out in the darkness was a man's hurried footsteps crackling and crunching on the icy surface of the road.

"Jack! Is that you?" she whispered into the darkness.

"Renee? Are you OK?" Jack yelled back with considerably more force. She did not answer his question. Again he shouted but to no avail. Not a sound came in reply; not even a whimper from the direction of the truck. Jack started to run the fifty or so more yards to the pickup while yelling her name several more times. He had just reached the mangled rear end of her car when he saw her silhouetted by the truck's headlight. She was trying to run toward him, repeating his name over and over silently through her sobs. Emotions she had been fighting all day intensified her feelings from the accident and seeing Jack once again.

Each hardly had time to encircle the other with their arms when their lips smashed together. A long and passionate kiss filled with immediate concerns and worried desires for each other consumed them.

"I thank the gods they didn't kill you! Are you hurt?" he whispered in her ear as he squeezed her tightly to his body.

"Jack—Jack, I saw you shot. I thought you'd been killed by Mike!"

Before he could speak again, she was on her toes pressing her mouth savagely to his through her new tears of happiness.

"Rick said you were going to South Dakota. Were you leaving me?"

"Like I said, I thought they had killed you."

"You only thought, and you were leaving without making sure?" Sounding a little hurt, she pulled him toward the warmth of the truck.

"I think Whitewater is headed to Cuny Table to kidnap my mom. I must get there as soon as I can," she said.

After he assisted Renee into the truck, Jack walked to the front and looked over the damage she had inflicted from striking her own car. It was still drivable, with minimum damage to the front fender and grill. The front wheel and bumper had not been pushed into each other, and the tire turned freely.

Jack hadn't shut the driver's door before Renee was all over him, hugging, squeezing and kissing. Through his shivering, she felt his enthusiasm and reluctance to push her away in order to start the engine and continue to his destination. She could tell he wanted to say something really important to her.

"Did Joshua steal this for you?"

"No," she replied feeling a little disappointed as she hugged him tightly again. "This is Rick Sun's truck."

"Rick doesn't own a truck—and he can't drive," Jack said. "Did you or Joshua steal it?"

"No, honest! It's Rick's. Why'd you park my car in the middle of the road like that?" she questioned him in retaliation.

"I didn't park there. That's silly. I went to sleep behind the wheel for a second and woke up as I spun out."

"I'm so happy you weren't hit by Mike's bullet." She tried to prompt him into talking about the wound.

"But I was. I got it in the shoulder just under the collarbone," he explained, showing a little pride.

Renee gently placed her hand over his wound to show her concern. She felt him wince with her touch, but he said nothing.

Jack started the engine and pulled forward to Renee's sedan. While she remained in the truck, he retrieved the artifacts and their luggage and pack from her car. Once back, he shoved a small lever on the floor making sure it was locked in four wheel drive and started toward South Dakota. He hadn't gotten fifty feet when Renee asked if it was a good idea to leave her car in the middle of the road like that?

"I suppose not," he replied and stopped again. "With the rear end damaged so badly, I don't think it's movable. I really don't think this truck will push it over that snowbank either."

"We can't leave it in the middle of the road. Someone will come along and hit it just like I did," she insisted.

"Do you have any highway flares in your car?" he asked while stepping out of the pickup.

"Sure. They're under the front seat, driver's side."

"You also have insurance to cover the damages, don't you?" he quizzed not waiting for her answer.

"Sure do," she yelled.

From the glow of the Ford's remaining headlamp, Renee watched Jack search through her car. He quickly found and struck two bright red flares alongside her sedan, but he didn't walk down the road to place them as she thought he would. Again she yelled out to Jack telling him the flares would last only about fifteen minutes and to hurry so they could report the accident.

"OK," Jack yelled back. "I'll do something to make them last longer."

Renee was startled beyond belief when she saw him throw the brightly burning flares into her car. The one he tossed onto the front seat burned the fabric almost instantly and the other onto the rear floorboard took only a moment longer.

Renee was holding her hands over her face by the time he got back into the truck and started to drive away.

"You're burning up my car!" she yelled at him, in total bewilderment of his actions.

"You said you had insurance, didn't you?"

"What's your point?" she growled with lips pressed tightly together. Renee turned around and sat on her knees to look through the rear window to the destruction of the sedan. She had little difficulty in seeing her beautiful interior was already raging with flames.

"Don't worry about it. That will burn for a long time and now no one will run into it." he reassured her with a smile only an insurance investigator would appreciate.

Renee turned her head towards him and cocked it a little sideways. She couldn't think of anything appropriate to say and barely found the strength to move her head from side to side in disbelief.

● ● ●

They had hardly entered Buffalo, Wyoming when Jack told Renee he couldn't go any further. He told her that she had to drive since his eyes were once again failing him.

"I don't know how to drive this thing!" she responded to another of his really dumb requests.

"But you were driving."

"Why do you think I ran into my car?" she tried to explain to him in an exasperated voice.

"Well, I thought you knew—."

She cut him off again. "I can't drive and you need rest. So let's find a room for a couple of hours and sleep. There isn't anything you can do in the condition you're in now and Palmoroy isn't going to do anything until he talks to us," she assured him.

Jack started to argue with her over the urgency of the situation. Again she cut him off and did her best to make him understand what she says, she means.

Jack remained in the vehicle while Renee registered them into the quite respectable looking motel on the north side of town. By the time she had returned to the truck, he was already asleep behind the wheel. Once again Renee found it difficult to handle Jack's muscular frame. Little pushes, shoves and rousing encouragement were used to make him drive to the parking lot and to walk into the room. She hurriedly helped him out of his clothes and into the shower. He was almost beyond himself with exhaustion by the time she had him dried off and sitting on the edge of the bed. Removing the soggy bandage that had partially fallen away from his wound, she did her best to clean around the still seeping hole.

Leaving Jack lying on the bed, Renee raced down the exterior walk to the motel office and borrowed a small first aid kit from the manager. She explained to the clerk and his wife, her husband had cut his hand on a broken cup. From a vending machine in the rear of the lobby, she purchased a package of sanitary napkins and rushed back to the room.

Jack was totally out of it when she opened the door and saw him stretched out on the bed. A small physician's packet of pills was still clenched in his fingers.

It wasn't hard for her, let alone for anyone else, to determine that he was still in substantial pain and had taken at least one of the pain killers. Renee dressed his wound with the Kotex and lots of medical tape to hold it in place until something better could be found in the morning. Although exhausted and tired herself, she remained awake beside him for most of the night. When he became fitful in his sleep, she massaged his legs and feet or his hands and arms in an attempt to calm and comfort him from the foul dreams. From the deep recesses of his mind, he did not seem to mind her loving touches.

During one particular moment she saw his eyes moving rapidly under his heavy lids. His fists would clench and open then clench again. At times, his legs would jerk and move abruptly as if they had a mind of their own. Renee dearly wanted him to alter from whatever he was dreaming about to anything more pleasant. She, herself, felt the hurt for him each time she saw his face twist in discomfort.

Not being able to endure his pain any longer and out of her desperation to help him, she cupped his testicles in the palm of her hand. Renee rolled each of the hard globes around in her fingers ever so softly and felt their firmness through their sack of confinement. Even in his medicated sleep she felt him starting to respond to her gentle ministrations. His fingers were slowing their clenching and he was relaxing more to the way she wanted him. Even with him in this drugged slumber, she didn't have any doubt that she could make him succumb to her sensitive palpitations of his awakening genitals. But now her only desire was to make his unconscious senses relax and find tranquillity.

Still fondling his testicles, she wrapped the fingers of her right hand around his semi-flaccid shaft and felt the velvety texture. So smooth and soft it glided as she slid the skin over the crown and pulled it back down tenderly. With each consecutive stroke his penis strengthened and became firmer in her hand. Jack's almost immediate response to her ministrations surprised her. She would have believed a combination of a painkiller and exhaustion would have prevented anyone from having an erection.

In but a few strokes his penis became swollen tight and pulsated to its full length against her palm. Even though she didn't really want to believe she was sexually arousing him, she found it almost impossible to ignore, let alone stop. Her own desires were dictating her to take him past the point he had now reached. Renee was beside herself with the want of him. His eyes opened slightly to look at her and then slipped closed again. Because of that simple act, she knew he did not wish her to stop. She found herself longing for the taste of him more than she had ever wanted anything like this before.

But he is so peaceful and quiet now. Why, he even has a cute little smile on his lips! she argued to herself with a grin.

Renee pulled his almost transparent skin down the shaft and lowered her head over the bulbous end of his member. She flicked her tongue across he tip of his penis and tasted a tiny drop of nectar that had formed. She started salivating profusely before her lips surrounded his swollen crown. Closing her mouth around him firmly, she circumnavigated her tongue ever so slowly around his sensitive point. She allowed her lips to flutter around and over the top of him. Gently she raised her mouth up and then back down his shaft while increasing speed and depth with each consecutive stroke. The hand cupping his testicles kneaded and manipulated them through her fingers and from side to side.

She did not care how long it would take her to satisfy him; it wouldn't be enough to give back what she felt she owed him. Soon he pulsated and enlarged with the additional flow of his blood rushing into his already engorged organ. Blood that continued to fill his already enormous penis to almost bursting proportions.

"Nothing less then a real 'Blue Veiner' or a 'Diamond Cutter'," she said as she briefly pulled it sideways only to have it snap upright again. Renee stopped momentarily to take note of and watch his expression for any changes due to her incredibly insensitive act.

Maybe I could raise myself over him? she thought for a brief second. *Maybe he doesn't like someone to give him his pleasure this way.*

Without any further vacillation, Renee decided she should continue with what she had started and leave her own needs unsatisfied. She replaced her mouth on him and began her assault with ever increasing ferocity. His pelvis involuntarily reacted and slightly followed her lips with each lifting stroke. As if she was drawing from an immense straw, Renee received his precious bodily fluids when each drop splashed thickly onto the back of her throat. She remained with him this way for many minutes, not wishing to relinquish the sensation he had unknowingly given her. As his spasms grew smaller she lavishly drank every drop of the semen she longed for.

She knew she had done good for her man and was proud of the abilities she had bestowed upon him.

It's too bad he will never know how good that was, she thought before she fell to sleep with her head on his leg and her hand holding him as he retreated.

When Jack stirred, Renee was already dressed and moving around. Looking at his watch, he discovered he had slept far too long for the distance they needed to travel. Shaking the sleep from his head he looked over at Renee who was standing by the bathroom door. He rubbed his shoulder very gently, feeling the thick pad Renee had taped on him. Although the pain of yesterday had subsided considerably overnight, the throb had returned and was still very much with him.

"I had the neatest dream last night!"

"I know." she looked away from him and smiled.

• • •

Jack told Renee it would take nearly a half day of continuous driving to reach Rapid City, South Dakota. From there they would take Highway 44 to Cuny Table and his home. As if guilt had overcome his most positive thoughts, he explained to her over and over there was little or no chance to reach his mother ahead of Whitewater and Palmoroy.

"If only this weren't Whitewater's patrol area and he didn't have a long head start."

"Why not ask for more help?"

"I wish there was someone I could trust. Maybe even in the Tribal Police or something. Except for me, Whitewater knows Cuny Table better than probably anyone else on the reservation."

"Do you think your mom is staying in the house in weather like this?"

"I have no idea, and I won't know until we get there. You have to remember the weather has been this bad only the last few days. The phone and electric lines are downed easily in this country. I just don't know if she would be all right or not."

Renee started to unbutton her blouse while she talked. "Boy, do I have something special for you."

"Are you a sex fiend or something?" Jack asked when he caught a momentary glimpse of her breast.

"No, really. I've got something here you can use." she repeated herself.

"Yeah, right!" Jack's eyes left the road to watch her pull a long nylon belt from around her stomach. "What's that?"

"Quite possibly a way to bargain for your mom," she eagerly responded with a smile.

Renee unfolded the bearer bonds and held them up close to the dash so he could see them as he drove.

"There are five of these one hundred thousand dollar bonds here. I'll bet Palmoroy has to return with the artifacts—or these!"

Jack slipped the papers from her fingers and held them even closer to his face and scanned the delicate printing design.

"Anyone can cash these in?" he asked.

"For their full face value," Renee replied happily.

Renee shifted closer to Jack after replacing the bonds and tying the belt around her waist again. She could see he was nearly as full of excitement and now had something substantial to bargain with.

"These bonds are made for barter."

Over the following miles Renee explained to Jack the events she had witnessed and what had taken place at Lodge Grass and Custer's Battlefield Monument. She was sure he was finding it difficult to believe her story about the transparent people. He even went so far to say it was like something out of 'Twilight Zone.' Knowing he hadn't ever seen anything that unusual himself, he questioned her sanity in a roundabout fashion.

"Palmoroy has no idea I've got the bonds. He thinks I burned them in the old farm house," she related matter-of-factly to Jack.

"Then they have no reason to barter for them," he responded.

"Not really. But I believe I can distract Palmoroy and Whitewater with them long enough for you to grab your mom. It might be possible that you could turn them against each other with them."

"They're still going to want the artifacts regardless of the bonds or Bright Moon. There must be a way that my people can have them," Jack thought out loud.

"Hey! I've got a plan. I think I know how we can rescue your mom and return the artifacts to their proper place. If you're so inclined, we could keep the bonds for ourselves."

"I don't know. That's too much like stealing. Did you forget I'm a cop?"

"You mean like risking your life for short pay and damn little else because it's something you believe in?"

"Yeah, that's it," Jack responded with pride.

"I guess the way you do things got the better of me. Like when you didn't pay the room bill at Furnace Creek?"

"My credit card will cover the amount I owe," Jack replied with certainty.

"Then how about when you burned my car down last night?"

"That's easy," Jack replied. "Someone hit your car on the rear end and the fuel tank exploded. Probably was hit after it was abandoned by some thief on the highway," he again replied with a heavily shaded answer. This time Renee didn't outwardly object to his not so little white lie.

"Let's say I buy that one. Then I suppose you're not involved in the murder of Mike? You know, the bullet hole in your shoulder and all?" Renee said with a feeling of a little I-told-you-so building inside of her.

"You really want that money—don't you?"

"Damn right I do! Do ducks swim? Do elevators go up and down? Do Indians have brown eyes?" she demanded.

"Sometimes not," Jack answered back with a smile smeared across his face.

"You're a half bree—" Renee stopped, checking herself in what she was about to say and before she decided to continue. "Didn't really mean to put it that way. I'm sorry."

"No problem," Jack said still with a bright smile.

"Why don't you leave word in town for them to meet you somewhere to make an exchange. That way we will have them on our terms. We can set some sort of elaborate trap for the both of them," Renee said in a rapid staccato of her thoughts.

"Maybe I should have my head examined, too," Jack said, wishing she would find a better way to help.

"How about dynamite? Dynamite is good. We can use it against both of them at once," Renee responded ignoring his remarks.

"I suppose you'll throw it at them and I shoot it with my trusty Winchester?" Jack said in disbelief. *Then again, you do have the makings for a plan tucked away in there someplace.* In a patronizing voice said, "Tell me more of what you intend to do."

"I'm not sure you could hit something that small. You may not be that good. After all, you don't even have a rifle, do you?"

"What do you mean I couldn't hit something that small? You don't have any idea what I can do. For somebody who can't drive a damn Ford pickup you sure have a lot of far-fetched ideas."

"Don't like being treated back like that do you? So now, think about what I'm saying. There's nothing to shoot at. Set a trap and let them blow themselves up. Don't you understand?"

"I understand you want me to steal dynamite, set a booby trap and blow the hell out of someone in a respectable way. Where I come from they call that premeditated murder."

"Let me put it this way. Considering they have already killed once, I'm pretty damn sure they won't hesitate to kill again for what they want."

"I suppose you're right. But I still have to do this my way," he admonished her.

"I know that. We'll work it out."

The smile had left Jack's lips.

• • •

In Rapid City, South Dakota, Jack stopped in front of a house in the barrios of the inner city. Half dismantled old cars were parked in the driveway and garbage had fallen on the ground around the over filled trash bins. The yard was littered with broken toys and old auto parts partially hidden in the brown uncut grass and weeds. Renee looked up and down the street and saw most of the homes were in nearly the same condition of messiness. Telling her to remain in the truck and lock the doors, Jack went to the front of the house and knocked several times on the door jamb.

Renee saw the rustling of the heavy curtains in the window to the right of the door just before they cracked open. About the same time the front door opened less than a half foot. The inner darkness prevented her from seeing anything just past the threshold. Jack stood almost motionless as he spoke to the invisible person for several long minutes before the door finally opened to its full width. A man of enormous proportions stepped onto the porch.

"Jeeeeze! Four hundred pounds of pure slob," Renee quipped.

She watched the two men talk for several more minutes. The fat man shook his head from side to side several times before she saw him nod. With that indication, Jack immediately rushed to the truck and opened the door, barely giving Renee time to release the lock.

"We have to find a bank and get some cash. Do you still have my credit card?"

"How much do we need?"

"Six hundred dollars. There's a bank we passed about three blocks back." He pointed back down the street.

Jack was just starting the truck when he noticed Renee unbuttoning the top of her pants and unzipping them.

"For crying out loud, what are you doing now?" Jack asked less than enthusiastically.

"I forgot to tell you about the cash that was with the bonds."

"What cash?"

Renee slipped her hand deep into her pants and pulled the wad of bills out. She counted off six and shoved them into his hand. The few remaining bills were again wadded and stuffed back into the crotch of her drawers.

"Isn't that a strange place to keep money?" Jack asked as he watched her in amazement and new curiosity.

"It's safe there. Even you wouldn't take the time to look in there for money," she replied with a grin and a wink.

"Good grief," he breathed as he yanked the handle and pushed open the door.

Jack walked back to the fat man who had remained on the porch and handed him the freshly folded bills. The man must not have trusted Jack since he took the time to count out each one. It seemed to Renee the whole episode was like watching a dope deal go down on TV. The big guy went back into his house and Jack returned to the truck and got in.

"And who is that?" Renee demanded.

"Believe me, you don't want to know."

Jack started the motor and adjusted himself behind the steering wheel and waited. Inside of two minutes the fat guy walked out to the truck and opened the door on Renee's side. She slid herself as close as possible to Jack when the man grabbed the dashboard and the opening of the cab to pull himself onto the seat. Renee found herself squished between the two men. Her left arm was around Jack's shoulder while the fingers of her right hand gripped a chunk of meat inside his right leg. She seemed to have a death grip on him and was using his leg as a handle to pull herself away from the stranger. Besides a new feeling of claustrophobia, Renee couldn't help but notice the man probably hadn't taken a bath in weeks. And if things weren't bad enough, the truck's heater was on and both the windows were rolled up. Renee started to feel sick to her stomach as her senses were overwhelmed by his odor being similar to that of decaying raw chicken.

Within a mile Jack stopped the truck in front of an iron gate at a self-storage center. The fat guy grunted his vast body into movement and pushed his way out a door that was a little narrower than his width. Instead of speaking across Renee, he walked around to Jack's side before he spoke in a low and soft-spoken voice. He told Jack what he needed to do would take but a second and turned to press a code into the security box that hung on a short post. The gate jumped into motion and rolled noisily to the side.

"Number twelve," The man instructed Jack.

Renee and Jack hadn't been stopped for a second in front of the correct roll-up door when Renee asked, "How can you stand to be near that guy?"

"Personally, I don't breathe." Jack said as he pried her white-knuckled fingers from his leg and then stepped out of the truck. Before he shut the door he asked her, "That's not where you keep my credit card is it?"

"In where?" Renee asked before it dawned on her what Jack was referring to was given away by his grin. "Here," Renee said as she extended the middle finger of her left hand and she gave him a very defiant "bird."

Jack chuckled and shut the door.

The fat man waddled his way over to the roll-up door and unlocked two large padlocks. With a gasp and a pull he lifted the door exposing a room full of radios, televisions and assorted boxes. From the corner of the right side the door was tracked on, he pulled out a rifle in a short leather scabbard and handed it to Jack.

Jack opened the truck door and laid the rifle on the floorboard in front of the seat.

Next the man removed what appeared to be a heavy wooden box with faded red writing on the side of one of its panels. In a delicate fashion he handed that to Jack. The printed words were too badly faded for Renee to read even at such a short distance. Next, a very small cardboard box was placed into the larger one. Renee recognized the smaller of the two as being a cartridge box.

Probably for the rifle, she thought to herself.

Jack carried the boxes to her side of the truck and told her to open her door.

"Sit on this side," he instructed her.

Renee scooted herself over to the passenger side of the seat. Jack very gently moved the wooden box into the truck making sure not to hit the door jams or anything else.

He slowly lowered the box onto her lap and said in a whisper, "Dynamite."

Jack turned and shut the door again.

"I knew that! I really knew that!"

Renee could tell it was old by the dust covering the top layer of sticks and the faded printing. She reached in and lifted one of the sticks to examine it closer. She looked over to the fat man and Jack while the man slammed shut the storage room door and locked it.

The fat man took a double take when he saw Renee looking at them and holding the stick up in the air beside her face. Like a shot, the man was gone. Renee watched him running as fast as he could to the end of the building and skidding himself around the corner. She was caught in fascination with the strange sight of rippling of lard on the fat man's legs as he ran. Jack opened the driver's door.

"Don't move," he demanded in a louder whisper.

"What's wrong?" Renee asked as she dropped the heavy stick back into the box.

Jacks face turned white; his eyes suddenly dilated and small beads of sweat emerged from his forehead almost as quick. He dropped his head and repeated his words to her, "Don't move," as a sigh escaped his throat.

"What on earth is wrong with you?" Renee asked.

"That stuff is highly explosive. It's old," he said still sweating.

"I know that. Just look at all the crap stuck on' em!"

"No, no, noooo! Look closely at the crystals on the bottom side of the sticks. They're very unstable."

Renee again pulled one of the cream-colored sticks from the box and looked for what he was talking about.

"Put—it—down—slowly," Jack begged her. This time Renee did as he requested.

Jack's hands were shaking almost beyond his control as he tried to explain the problem with the dynamite.

Renee did know it was strange that Jack's color wasn't returning to normal as quickly as it should have.

"This stuff is nearly a hundred years old and very, VERY unstable. The slightest bump or wrong move will set them off."

"Well, why in hell didn't you get newer ones?" Renee demanded, feeling her hands starting to shake as Jack's already were.

"Good grief," was his only response.

Jack drove out of the storage lot and down the street for several blocks until he found the road he apparently was looking for. They hadn't been driving very long when he swung the truck into a fast food business. Renee was still too shaken from having to hold about thirty pounds of explosives to take note of what restaurant chain it was or what he was doing.

Jack ordered several hamburgers and fries along with a couple of soft drinks into the outdoor speaker box.

"Give me some money," he requested before pulling forward.

"Remember, I put it back in my pants."

"Don't you know what pockets are for?" Jack admonished her before he put the truck in neutral and slid himself closer to her side. He lifted the box high enough for her to unbutton and unzip her pants and then reach into her crotch to retrieve the money. In trying to extract her hand, her watchband caught on the clasps of her zipper. She gave a forceful pull in an effort to release herself. The leather band didn't slip free as she expected. Before Jack could say anything she again pulled with a force a little stronger than the first effort.

The band tore loose and her hand withdrew sharply striking the bottom of the box of explosives. The wooden crate slipped from Jack's fingers and fell on end and sideways down her legs. Ten or so sticks of sixty-percent dynamite dropped from the box and rolled onto the floorboard of the truck. Both Jack and Renee stared at the explosives as if instantly frozen.

"Please pull forward," came the voice from the order clerk breaking the silence.

"Just don't move. Please don't move," Jack pleaded with her. He bent over to pick up the fallen sticks and replaced as many as he could see back into the box.

"Please pull forward. Your order is ready," the unknown voice repeated in a more demanding tone.

Jack sat up and slid back under the wheel and drove forward to the pickup window. The dark-haired girl on the other side of the glass looked at both of them questioningly. When she gave Jack the paper bags of food she asked what they were doing on the floorboard. Jack thanked her and drove quickly out onto the roadway.

They were famished. Renee, supporting the box on her lap with one hand as she unfolded two hamburgers with the other. After giving Jack one, she bit into her own. Mustard, ketchup and mayonnaise along with a slice of unripened tomato dribbled out of the bun and onto the crystalline covered sticks of explosives.

"Why me, Lord?" Jack muttered.

13

"A Battle for Bright Moon"

Renee was at a loss as to what point of the compass Jack had turned when he left the main roadway. *Possibly South or maybe even West,* she thought to herself. Instead of quizzing him about it, she sat quietly and watched the countryside pass by. Her eyes alternated between the passing flats, hills, occasional woodlands and the wooden box pressing down on her lap. She was pleased the layer of snow covering the dirt road softened the occasional bump or sideways movement of the truck. Even the deep ruts in the road from earlier vehicles rolling through the muddy spots had been considerably dampened.

On any one of a number of particularly vicious bumps or sways, Jack would look over to her, then to the dynamite questioningly.

Why bother to look? Renee wondered to herself. *By the time this stuff goes off, it will be too late anyway!*

"Jack, why don't we dump a bunch of snow in the bed of the truck and put this box on top of it?"

Jack looked at her and again at the dynamite before a strange expression came over his face.

Feeling a little paranoid, Renee started to think she had once again said the wrong thing at the wrong time.

Jack slowed the truck from about twenty miles per hour to a very cautious stop.

Renee looked around and saw a splattering of trees here and there in the field of snow and wondered if Jack was going to follow her suggestion or had something else in mind. Looking across the flats, she thought she might see a mud and stick lodge like the one they had stayed in a couple of nights earlier. But nothing was out there to let her know they had reached anywhere important.

Jack stepped out of Rick's truck and moved around to her side in what had become near foot-deep snow. When he opened the door, he leaned in and kissed her lightly on the side of her lips.

"You're such a wonderfully smart woman! You come up with some of the most magnificent ideas!" he said in an abrupt comment that caught her completely off guard.

Jack turned and squatted down to the snow while Renee watched him try to scoop up the fine white powder in his hands and then stand. By the time he had lifted the double handful from the ground to the bed of the truck, most had fallen from his grasp.

"Why don't you put your coat on the ground and fill it up? You can get a lot more in quicker that way." Renee smiled, feeling her ideas were exactly what he wanted.

Jack started flinging a copious amount of the little crystals toward the truck. It seemed to her that his way was getting more on himself than where it was supposed to go.

"That's not very efficient," she commented out the open window.

Perhaps that was one comment too many, she thought when she heard a small growl from outside the truck. He stood and then reached across the box to her coat hanging over the back of the seat.

"You're not going to use my coat for that, are you?" she asked in a half pleading voice.

"Certainly. It is your idea."

At the rate he was going, it took Jack about ten minutes to prepare the bed of the truck to receive the box of explosives. He tossed her coat to the side of the road, swung open the door and lifted the dynamite from her lap. For the first time Jack realized that the warmth of the interior of the truck had caused some of the top layer of sticks to sweat causing a new sticky residue to form. Nothing large, only tiny droplets of a clear liquid lightly tinted yellow between a few of the older crystals. Seeing this, Jack started to perspire again. He balanced the box on his knee with his foot resting on the short running board of the truck.

"Do you see those honey-like drops? That's very old Nitroglycerin," he said while pointing at a particularly large gathering of the delicate stuff with a nervous finger.

Cautiously, he lowered the crate onto the snow and packed a layer of the ice crystals over the sticks. Jack made sure the box was adequately cushioned in the bed of the truck before he shook the snow off Renee's jacket and got back in the cab.

"You know I won't be able to wear that for quite a while," Renee said while feeling the remnants of snow melting into the inner fabric.

"Oh Jeeze, I'm sorry," Jack replied as he opened the door again and stepped back out.

He stooped to the side of the truck where Renee couldn't see him.

Renee moved over to the driver's side to try and see what Jack was secretly doing. Her face was nearing the doorjam and she was craning her neck to look around him. Before her reflexes could pull her back, Jack lifted a huge armload of snow up and tossed it into her face.

She screamed out at him, "What in hell are you doing?"

"Breaking the tension," he told her through one of those gut-busting laughs of his.

Renee clamored out of the seat and pushed him aside as she passed him. By the time she had gathered her own load of snow, Jack had beaten her to the punch. She turned around in time to be hit by a giant fluffy snowball. The handful of snow she threw danced meaninglessly in the air before slowly finding its way to the ground. Renee was just starting to bend over to build a more compact snowball in the dry snow when Jack moved up behind her and lovingly surrounded her with his arms. He pulled her buttocks back against his groin and rotated his pelvis against her in a seductive gesture.

She stood up straight while forcing her butt against him and then leaned her back against his chest.

"Have I told you today that I love you?"

"No, but I really like hearing it," she warmly responded to his unexpected remark.

"Good," he answered back and proceeded to slip his hands under her shirt.

His icy cold fingers closed over her breast and then specifically circled around her nipples. Renee jumped back against him and fought to free herself from the bitter cold that grasped her. Her hands tore and pulled at his frozen fingers. Twisting and turning she combated to free herself and rub away the goose bumps that had popped up over her arms, chest, neck, back, legs and everything else she owned.

"I'll get you for that!" she screamed. "It's get even time," she yelled repeatedly through her laughter.

"No time now. Tension break's over," Jack said while lifting her off her feet and depositing her on the driver's side of the truck. Pushing against her legs and butt she half rolled, half slid further inside. Jack got in and started the motor.

Renee touched her pointed finger against his leg and dragged her nail in little figure eights over his Levis. "Don't forget. You're mine and I'm really going to enjoy making you squirm."

"What did I do?" Jack said with the innocence of the big brown eyes of a puppy.

The road progressively became rougher the farther they followed its course to the house on Cuny Table. Many times along the way Jack found it necessary to speed up and virtually plow Rick's Ford through higher and higher snowdrifts. How he could remember where to turn to find the correct route in all this snow astounded Renee. They had traveled over twenty miles when they came upon a crossroad. A single set of tire tracks made a left turn into the same direction they were heading.

Jack stopped the truck and got out. Fascinated again by his abilities in reading signs, Renee watched him touch the edges and ridges of the tracks. It was almost as if he was trying to become one with the unseen vehicle that had passed through ahead of them. Several minutes later he finally he re-entered the cab.

"It looks like—maybe—a Jeep Cherokee. A four-wheel drive," Jack stated with the hard look of depression.

"How on earth can you tell that?" Renee asked, while looking puzzled.

"I just know," he responded with a look of real sincerity. "The track tells me they're about an hour ahead of us and moving slowly."

"Do you think its Palmoroy and Whitewater?" Renee asked, placing her hand on his arm at the same time to let him know her concerns for his mother.

"I wish I could say No, but they're the only tracks leading up there. Whoever it is, they—" Jack stopped talking and rubbed his eyes with thumb and third finger. "I don't want you going up there."

"Why not?" Renee asked, feeling she was being left out of what fate had brought them together for. "I'm afraid you have no choice but to take me with you. I'm in this as much as you are and we need to work together to bring the swap off."

Once again Jack got out of the truck. He went to the rear and stepped up on the bumper, paused and then got into the bed.

Renee watched through the rear window while he rummaged into his suitcase. Instantly recognizable to her, he withdrew a small-framed handgun from his grip. When Jack was back in the cab, he jacked the slide back and locked it into place. Renee was able to see one of the bullets ready to be slammed forward into the barrel from its resting place on the magazine.

"Do you know how to use one of these?"

"If you mean can I shoot? the answer is Yes," she responded.

"That's not what I'm asking. I want to know if you're prepared to shoot Palmoroy or Whitewater to defend yourself or my mom."

Renee hesitated too long to answer his question the way he wanted.

"I didn't think so."

"I'll do what I have to do. If shooting someone becomes necessary—I will," Renee protested.

Renee was surprised at the words she never would have believed herself to use. Never in her life had she considered the possibility of having to hurt anyone, let alone kill them with a hand gun. She had had fights with Mike to the point where she wanted to retaliate and didn't, but those were only verbal fights. Then there was the guy in Golden Gate Park that jumped her late one evening two summers ago. A good scream and a kick in the groin scared him off.

Can I kill someone? she asked herself.

Jack briefly instructed her on aiming and firing the little firearm. Not as perfect as he wished, but good enough to get by with up close.

"We're less than three miles from my home," Jack explained to her. "I want you to follow my instructions closely. I'll drive to within a mile of the house and park. You stay where I tell you and guard the artifacts and bonds until I find out about my mom."

"What if they come here before you get back?" Renee asked with some fear and doubt as the whole idea continued building in her mind.

"Then shoot the gun at them. Don't shoot quickly. You only have ten rounds."

Jack pulled the large bore rifle up from the floorboard and set it against the seat beside him.

"Do you understand?" he asked.

"Yes," Renee replied with a noticeably shaken voice. "I'm scared," she told him.

I'm scared for all of us!" Jack said, responding to her fear without looking at her. "Are you ready?"

Renee shook her head in the affirmative. "As ready as I'll ever be!"

Jack rolled the truck forward, closely following the ruts in the snow. He intentionally drove even slower than he had before. Maybe ten or twelve miles per hour while he watched the road ahead or along side into the occasional bush.

Renee did what she could to scan the area as well. She knew only too well what or who she was looking for. If they were out there, their presence evaded her as well. Renee's nerves were shot. Although not visibly shaking, she was finding it difficult to concentrate.

"Are you sure I can't drop you off before we go any farther?" Jack asked with a more understanding tone to his voice.

She took a deep breath before she urged out her answer. "I'm positive."

Jack negotiated a deep drop in the road surface. The truck bounced severely before he again stopped some hundred yards up the opposite side of the dip. Rick's truck was just inside the mouth of a small arroyo over the tracks of the vehicle that was ahead of them.

"If they try to escape from my house and back down this road, I don't want you here. I'm leaving the truck to block this exit."

Jack pulled the rifle from its scabbard.

"Hand me four of the bullets from the box," he asked of her as he snapped the bolt open with an almost sickening metallic snap and dragged it back to its stop.

The deathly sound of such a mechanism turned Renee's stomach. She knew what the gun was meant to do and was well aware it now seemed the only way to handle this matter. She was so bloody happy this sort of thing was what Jack had been trained for since joining the Army.

Renee read the caliber on the box out loud. "Three hundred Winchester Magnum." That didn't really register with her until she removed the first of four of the twenty rounds the box contained. "My God, they're huge!"

"They're good at fifteen hundred yards with a good rifleman shooting," Jack replied to her comment with seemingly satisfaction of knowing his business.

"Killing doesn't bother you, does it?"

"I do what I have to do. If they leave me with no other resolve—" Jack abruptly cut himself off from what he was saying. "Here is what I want you to do. Take the artifacts and bonds and walk up the road about seventy five yards. There you'll find a stack of rocks along the right side of the road. At that point try to make your way up to the large outcropping of boulders and hide in them."

"That means I can't help you at all, doesn't it?"

"Not at all. That means you'll be protecting our bargaining power while I'm scouting the area. Do you understand?" he asked.

"Yes," she declared and stopped pestering him with anymore questions.

"Then promise me you won't return to this truck until you see me signal you."

Renee moved her head up and down in the affirmative.

"No," Jack demanded. "Do you understand?" he repeated himself.

"I understand," she replied in nearly a whisper.

Jack and Renee stepped from the truck at about the same time. Renee gathered the bundle of artifacts from the bed after putting on her coat. She then started her walk up the arroyo as Jack had instructed her.

"Psssst!" She heard him making sounds in her direction from the opposite side of the truck. Looking back to him she saw him motioning with his arms and hands and immediately understood what he wanted her to do.

Walk low, slow and quiet, she told herself.

Renee hunkered down and did her best to walk quietly as possible while carrying the artifacts. Two steps was all it took to realize the sounds of her feet crunching in the ice and snow made tremendous noises. She couldn't think of any method to walk the cat-like way as Jack wanted her to. Instead, she ignored his wishes and hurried along to find herself a suitable hiding place.

Renee quickly found the boundary marker Jack had told her about. She looked up one side of the embankment for the outcropping of boulders and then up the other side. None were immediately visible to her from where she stood in the middle of the arroyo. After searching out a reasonable route to the top on the same side as the rock marker, she started climbing. She only made a few steps before sliding back onto the icy roadway. Her footholds on the snow-covered rocks made the climb harder than she had expected. A third attempt brought her to the top. From her new vantage point she saw the boulders Jack had told her about. They were still some fifty feet farther up the edge of the ridge and parallel to the wash and road. Once there, she located a worthy point between the large boulders where she could deposit the artifacts and still have room to sit, watch and listen.

From this position she was able to see a relatively modern looking house that was in dire need of some tender loving care. A grove of trees was on one side of the structure while open ground lay to the side and front. Renee judged the house was at least a half mile or more away from where she now hid. In front of the house, a dark-colored station wagon was parked, and two men were kneeling beside it as if they were hiding from someone. It was far too great a distance for Renee to make out who the men were.

That couldn't be anyone but those ass-holes, She thought. "Why are they hiding like that?" she asked herself so loudly that her own voice startled her.

Quickly looking around to see if anyone had heard her, she decided her speaking really didn't matter since no one seemed to be near. Looking back toward the house, she believed the men's position made it all the easier for Jack to find them. Renee watched the two men for several more minutes before she leaned back and tried to make herself more comfortable for what could possibly be a long wait. It seemed there was no need to worry about what the men were doing since they were not moving around at all. From the distance Jack would have to travel, she knew it would take him quite some time to reach them.

Renee stared at the bundle of artifacts in front of her. She knew this would probably be the last time she would have the opportunity to see these magnificent pieces of history again. Even the National Museum in Washington DC kept Custer's jock strap hidden away and out of the regular public view. But these especially, the ones she had found herself, were by far more important than most things they had there. How she wished the whole matter would have ended differently—that she would have been acknowledged as the finder and receive the notoriety she deserved. Then again, she realized she probably wouldn't have met Jack. Nor would she have come to respect and love him as she had under any other circumstances. Or perhaps it really was some divine destiny that had brought her to this place with him.

"That's ridiculous," she said to herself.

Renee positioned herself on her knees to look for the last time. She unfolded the canvas cover of the artifacts onto the snow in the limited space between the rocks. Gingerly she removed the finely painted scroll of the battlefield and hung it over one of the large rocks beside her. Then the feathered headdress was next placed over the scroll. Admiringly, she allowed her fingers to fondle the dark brown and white feathers feeling their smoothness and texture. Renee couldn't get enough of the beauty of such a headpiece. Returning her eyes to the now smaller pile she took in Custer's pennant which contained his wonderful pistol. Carefully she unfolded the little flag revealing the gun Jack had been so enthralled with. She grasped the ivory handle and slipped her finger between trigger and guard. Pointing the revolver toward an imaginary target somewhere off in the distance, she squeezed the trigger.

The unmistakable report of a gunshot echoed through the air. The sudden and unexpected noise surprised her and broke her concentration. Whether it was her nerves or an automatic reflex that caused her to jump back against the rocks behind her, she wasn't sure. Renee knew she had not created the noise that had momentarily frightened her. She was positive she hadn't even cocked the hammer back so the weapon could be discharged.

Renee raised herself until she could just see over the boulders to the house farther up the road. Both men were still crouched behind their car where she had last seen them. She was thinking Jack must have fired the shot when the silence was again broken by another, singular, loud report. This time she saw a small puff of gray-white smoke emanate from the window in the front door of the house. Renee wondered how Jack had gotten past the men hidden behind the car to get into the house.

Renee searched the terrain from the road to the house for him, but he couldn't be seen anywhere. Looking back in the direction from which they had originally come, she saw two more vehicles slowly moving up the road to Rick's truck. One was a pickup with several men sitting in the bed while the other was a large station wagon. Both vehicles stopped a fair distance from where Jack had parked. By the time all the men had exited from the trucks, she had counted twelve big men. They started to walk in her direction and toward the narrow entrance of the arroyo.

Renee frantically searched her pockets for the little automatic Jack had given her to protect herself. Confusion was replaced by memory when it dawned on her she had left the gun on the seat in the cab of the truck. Renee looked down, trying to see Rick's truck and then to Custer's revolver in her hand. She wondered if she should fire that ominous oxidized bullet to warn Jack that more men were coming. Calming herself, she decided she should wait until their intentions became obvious.

Renee remained as still as possible and held her breath when the men walked past Rick's truck and up the wash. When they were almost directly below her she was able to hear some of them talking to one another. From their facial features and language, it was all too obvious they were Indian. If only she understood what they were talking about or planning, she would know whose side they were on.

The men were moving along at a fairly quick pace and reached a point up the wash where she was finally able to see their backs. One of them seemed to be carrying firearms from what she could determine. However, the last man did carry a small drum like one she had seen near the monument in Montana.

"Could all of this be staged? How?" Renee wondered.

Her thoughts were in turmoil. There was nothing she could do but wait and watch as Jack had instructed her.

• • •

From the years of having lived and hunted around the house, Jack knew it would take him better than an hour to make his way in the direction he had chosen. If Whitewater and Palmoroy had already reached the property as he suspected, then his only chance would be up a shallow draw and through the wooded side. *If there was ever a time he needed his skills of hunting and stalking, it was now,* he thought. Jack remembered back to the many men he had pursued in the past. His quests for justice had taken him from the rugged deserts of the Eastern California valleys to Red Shirt and Sheep Mountain Table here on the reservation. But, this was different. He never would have believed he would be the adversary of a tribal cop, let alone find himself fighting on his own property to save the life of his mother. Jack did know there was some poetic justice in doing battle with a Cheyenne thief, cop or not!

His movements were as precise and well thought out as he had ever committed himself to. Slowly and cautiously he traversed the terrain, taking note of every movement in the brush and trees, both close and far. At times he would stop and shoulder his weapon to scout the area ahead with the wide-angle telescopic sight. From his current position, he was not able to see the front or side of his house or the rock outcropping where Renee was hidden. At one point, he thought he heard the muffled sound of a rifle shot, but dismissed that sound as a trick of his tired mind. Occasionally he would stop to look back and make sure no one had crept up behind him.

Although he was dressed for the cold, he felt like he was freezing. Each time he lifted the firearm, he found it difficult to hold the rifle still as he sighted through the lens. Jack tried to make himself believe the shaking was a problem with the cold and nothing as exotic as his nerves. He knew these were things he would have to overcome before he reached his destination. From his past experiences, if he were to do battle with these men, he knew he would have to be clear of mind and prepared to be the worst of aggressors.

A strange rhythm seemed to be filling the quiet air of the country around him. A near silent cadence which was not foreign, nor was it acceptable to his perceptions in this place and time. He did not wish to receive the music of a chant or the thump of that infernal drum that thundered louder with each yard he moved forward. Maybe it was his heritage that allowed the sounds to break his concentration repeatedly, or even the warrior in him that understood the ritual before the battle. Or all these things combined that his own mother had told him to expect so many years ago. Jack's mind fluttered from thought to thought against his will. He found his emotions reeling from the past and mixed with the reality of the present. Perspiration formed on his face and his hands to the point that he was constantly wiping his fingers and palms on his pants. He mused the reality of what the Old Ones had said so many times before, "Today is a good day to die."

Jack had never been able to hold his bladder at moments in time such as this. Even as a child playing stick games or hiding with the other Indian children of the village, he found it necessary to urinate during the most inappropriate times. The fullness in his lower stomach was distracting him further from the virtue of his hunt and his mission. Jack located a place beside a high tree stump where he knelt to relieve himself silently into the snow. His eyes never looked to see where he was urinating, only outwardly and across the ground he had to pass over. In his nervousness and haste he hadn't quite finished when he stuffed his penis back into his fly. The last of his warm urine wet the front of his Levis and down his left leg. Jack's concentration was so strong by the time he had finished the dampness went completely unnoticed.

He crept slowly and ever deeper into the woods. From this selected route he would be less than a hundred yards from the house when he would reach the location he wanted. From there, he would emerge with a good view of the side of the house and the front yard would be had. He released the safety and held the rifle at the ready across the front of his chest. Slowing his pace slightly, he traveled the remaining distance to his best place of visibility; a place from which he knew he would be able to take the advantage. Jack knelt and carved a shallow furrow in the snow as he crawled the last few remaining yards. From behind one old stump near a discarded wood stove, he saw Whitewater's head peering over the hood of the Jeep Cherokee. Although he was within pistol range, Jack felt he held the advantage with his big bore rifle.

Suddenly a shot rang out considerably louder than the noise of the drum or the song he had allowed to remain in the back of his mind. Neither Palmoroy nor Whitewater had fired their guns toward him or at the house. Both of the men were looking off down the hill toward Renee and the truck and the sound of the drum. Jack was completely confused as to the meaning of all this. What he did know was he had to stop the two men and end this madness.

On hearing the report of the gunfire, Palmoroy swung around and pointed a large caliber revolver toward the house. He fired a single bullet and then ducked down behind the Jeep again. Not many seconds later he again raised himself to shoot. This time Jack was ready for him. He believed his best shot would be through the windshield, to hit Palmoroy solidly in the abdomen. Jack raised his rifle, aimed and squeezed off the round that was under the firing pin. A tremendous roar erupted from the muzzle of the weapon while the recoil jammed the butt of the stock harshly into his shoulder. The shock seemed to vibrate across his chest and into the wound from Mike's bullet. The sudden pain sickened him and made him nauseous and dizzy. A flash of white blinded him for the briefest of seconds as his face dipped into the snow.

Before Jack was able to eject the spent cartridge and replace it with a live round, Nick Whitewater fired three shots in his direction in rapid succession. Clumps of snow directly in front of his hiding place sprayed violently into the air. It became immediately apparent to Jack that he had not hit Palmoroy. Even the glass windshield hadn't fractured and disintegrated from the impact of the bullet he had fired. Jack was astonished and ashamed that he had missed at such a close distance and could only figure the rifle must have been sighted in for far more than six hundred yards. That being the only explanation, he must have shot right over the top of the Jeep and Palmoroy.

Raising up quickly to see if his assailants had changed positions, he saw "Man Thing" race up onto the porch and stand in front of the door to be let in. In a blink of an eye the tip of his cat's tail separated from the fluffy shaft with the roar of several explosions from Whitewater's gun. In an attempt to find the strike of the bullet, Jack adjusted his point of aim and did not take precious time to tinker with the sights. Quickly, he chambered another round and swung the rifle to his shoulder, aimed and fired. This time he purposely aimed lower hoping he was splitting the difference. He wanted to hit Whitewater in the ass. Pulling the butt of the rifle harder into his shoulder, he squeezed the trigger and the muzzle roared out its deafening bark. Being more ready for the kick this time, his body absorbed the burst of energy into his shoulder and chest. But once again the heavy projectile missed its mark.

Jack reloaded yet another round and quickly fired. The right front tire on the jeep immediately went flat, and a copious amount of snow encrusted dirt flew into the air and sprayed down upon the men.

With a little pain and a lot of lost pride, "Man Thing" raced from the porch. Her ears were flat against her head and her back was straight as she charged toward the white jeep. In and of itself, this was not abnormal for the cat, as many of her scars and occasional loss of fur, occurred from fights with more ferocious predators then the likes of Whitewater and Palmoroy. The sight of a moderately sized house cat charging her attackers through a hail of bullets was nearly as comical as it was scary.

Jack chambered the last round from the magazine, then raised himself and fired. His adjustment of his sighting sent the bullet through the driver's sideview mirror. The hot lead exploded on contact with the vehicle and sprayed Whitewater with pieces of glass and metal. Almost at the same time he had fired his last round, the report of another shot rang through the air. Whoever was in the cabin placed a round squarely through the windshield of the Jeep. The glass splintered and shattered, flinging tiny bits and pieces everywhere.

Jack started to fill the rifle's magazine with four fresh rounds when he saw the two men start running down the road toward Renee and the truck. Palmoroy would shoot aimlessly back toward the cabin while he ran. It looked like Whitewater was reloading while his big body lumbered ahead of his partner in this crime. Both of the men slipped and slid on the snow while trying to retain their footing in their haste. For the briefest of moments the question of their retreat entered his thoughts.

"Man Thing?"

Pushing himself to his feet, Jack started his run to the cabin door. His endurance was nearly drained by the time he reached the porch and he found he had to stop momentarily to regain his breath. Still gasping for oxygen, he moved forward past one window to the door. Jack's hands had just touched the knob when he was surprised by the rusty black barrel of his old single-shot twelve-gauge shotgun. The muzzle protruding through the broken pane exploded along side of his head. The concussion was terrible and racked against a wrenching headache. His eardrums felt as if they had been torn from his head when a high pitched whine began to ring across his ears.

Jack shoved the door open in time to see his mother trying to break open the breach to pull the spent cartridge from the old Savage shotgun.

"Bright Moon! Bright Moon!" he yelled as loudly as he could at the old woman standing before him.

It was not easy for her to recognize him even in the few feet that separated them. Jack remembered she had always refused to wear her glasses and was practically blind without them.

"Walking Horse? Is that you?" she yelled back as she finally recognized his voice.

"Yes, yes, it's your son," Jack responded with what little energy he had left.

Bright Moon dropped the old gun to the floor and stepped forward to him. When they met, they hugged. His mother spoke with the best English she could manage. Even though her accent was heavy with the dialect of the Sioux, Jack found no difficulty understanding her.

"The Witches have come for me. I have fought them back from this world." she insisted to him.

"They're gone now," Jack reassured her.

Before he could tell her more, a tremendous explosion shook the building. The chants and drum stopped for a long time before they again resumed. Jack turned to the open door in time to see a billowing column of grayish black smoke rising high toward the sky. A flash of curly maple-colored cat shot past them. Every hair on Man Thing's back was sticking straight up.

The dynamite!

"Renee!" he yelled as he started to run from the house toward her hiding place.

• • •

Renee watched the fight at the little house from her well-protected position in the boulders. Her mind was filled with fear and terror while at the same time the fascination of the battle would not let her turn away. Off in the distance the drum was beating with an unrelenting measure. Chants filled the air causing her to recall in greater detail the music at Little Big Horn and the horror of Mike's exploding head. She could imagine the fight Jack was putting up with Whitewater and Palmoroy in the glistening snow of late morning. Renee wanted to rush to his side and do what she could to help. But she had made a promise to remain hidden away until his return for her.

Maybe I could hide a just a little closer.

Renee kept the Officer's Colt revolver in her hand when she stood. She began to work her way through the crevices in the boulders to open ground and a possible way back down to the road. Suddenly she stopped to see the two men from the Jeep begin to run toward her. Straining her eyes, she was able to see it was Whitewater leading the way. It amazed her that such a big man was able to cover so much ground with the speed he had on slippery snow. Palmoroy was running behind him by only a short distance. He would shoot, run a few yards farther and shoot again. She believed Jack really must have put up a magnificent fight to have frightened them away from his home.

Palmoroy fell into the snow after he fired what Renee thought was possibly his last bullet. She watched him stand and try to run again. His feet never found a firm grip on the icy rocks, causing him to fall again. His inability to continue running permitted Whitewater to reach Rick's Ford first. Not having to open the driver's door since Jack had neglected to close it, Whitewater jumped into the seat. In the back of her mind, she could see the keys Jack had also neglected to remove from the ignition. Whitewater started the engine and slammed the gears into first. All four wheels spun on the slick snow and rock barely allowing the truck to move ahead and gain speed and traction. It seemed ironic to Renee that he was leaving Palmoroy to fend for himself against his pursuer.

Renee lost sight of the truck momentarily under the walls of the arroyo as it continued its rapid exit. Seconds later the Ford reappeared being driven in an almost reckless manner.

"You son-of-a-bitch!" she yelled, having forgotten Palmoroy was nearly below her on the road.

"I'm going to kill you!" Palmoroy screamed up at her.

He raised his handgun and jerked harshly at the trigger. Seeing him, Renee dove back into the boulders. She didn't hear the report from the pistol as she thought she should have. Instead, a noise louder than anything she had ever heard in her life consumed everything about her. The massive rock she had thrown herself against for protection shook violently, as did all the ground and other boulders. The air filled with falling snow and rocks and dirt blown out from the sudden explosion of the Ford. Even if she could hear she knew there would not be any sounds. This tremendous blast should have silenced the world and everything in it.

Renee remained still. Her hands and arms over her head protecting her face from the falling debris. When everything had quieted in the sky above her she found herself in a thick cloud of very gray snow. She raised herself above the boulders to see what had taken place. The beat of the drum again started and began to strengthen in its intensity, as did the chants of the Indians. Bewildered and beaten she looked over the edge and into the wash for Palmoroy.

14

"Naked Men in a Line"

Renee knew she could not stay where she was with Palmoroy seeking to kill her at any moment. As rapidly as possible she gathered the artifacts without using the care she had previously, and abandoned her hiding place. Stepping from the boulders onto a particularly thick blanket of snow, she began what seemed like a futile search to seek out her new place of refuge. Looking all around her side of the arroyo, no place as close as she had wished seemed to exist. There was only a clump of trees a long way off in the distance and farther away from the house than where she wanted to be. She weighed the possibility of locating the Indian men she had seen walk by and place herself in their sanctuary. Once there she felt she would be relatively safe from her maniac instructor.

Renee started off into the direction of the sounds of their drum and then stopped abruptly. She remembered with agonizing pain that the presence of other men had not stopped Palmoroy and Whitewater at Little Big Horn from killing Mike. But then again, now that Whitewater had probably blown himself up, she felt sure she could evade her college professor without jeopardizing more innocent people. Renee moved back and forth in a quandary with her less than desirable alternatives. Her decision processes clouded with her very real fears for her own immediate safety and that of Jack and his mom.

"God! Where do I run?"

Her legs felt as if lead weights had been wrapped heavily around them. Her feet seemed to become truly frozen to the snow. Somewhere, higher up the plain from where she now stood, she recognized the faint calling of men shouting or singing. Occasionally the squeal of a bagpipe would become louder and then softer as if someone was raising and lowering the volume throughout the melody of their song. This squeal of the pipes easily overshadowed the chants of the Indian singers behind her. She stood motionless and listened to the muffled words and tried to ignore all the other gut wrenching feelings that had boiled up into her throat.

> We'll beat the bailiffs, out of fun,
> We'll make the mayor and sheriffs run,
> We are the boys no man dares dun,
> If he regards his whole skin!

> Instead of Spa, we'll drink brown ale,
> And pay the reckoning on the nail,
> No man fo—

The song slowly silenced with the wind whipping up from behind her. Strangely, Renee knew the words to the music and even found herself momentarily singing along and then humming with the fading singers. She had never heard those particular words before as far as she could remember, but she knew exactly what they were and who they were meant for.

"Garry Owen!" she shouted. "They're singing the Regimental song! I know that song! I've sung that song!" she screamed in near delirium.

Renee was surprised that her feet and legs moved freely now. With each consecutive step, she shuffled faster toward the place her thoughts told her was the safety of many old friends. She felt compelled by a searing need to be with them and to stand proudly among them.

The closer she drove herself to them, the more she had forgotten that Palmoroy was mad as hell and was hunting her as Jack was hunting him. She moved forward and increased her speed until she ran as fast as she could covering as many feet as possible with each stride. Unsure of her trail, time after time she lost her footing and slipped and fell onto the soft powdered snow. Righting herself, she recollected the artifacts and handgun and ran harder still, until losing her balance to fall again.

"Please! My God! Please help me reach my Autie!" Renee cried out in a strange prayer, not understanding the words from her own mouth.

Renee did not see Palmoroy pulling himself onto the embankment, as she ran past him by not more than a few feet. Nor did she see him raise his revolver and point the muzzle between blades while the hammer rolled back and the cylinders turned.

• • •

Jack covered the open ground toward the arroyo with an ever slowing pace. Again he felt the exhaustion from the wound and the physical stresses of the last several days taking their toll. Precious minutes were lost as time after time he had to stop to regain his breathing and fight away a feeling of dizziness. His legs felt as if they were on fire and his side screamed with the pain a runner feels following a particularly long and laborious sprint. Bending over at the waist and resting his hands on his thighs, Jack knew, if he sat down he would not be able to stand again to continue trek to the truck and Renee. The mile and a quarter through the field took so much longer than he would ever have expected. By the time he reached the high bank of the wash, he was suffering the increasing torment of his light-headedness and the oncoming gray fog in his vision. Off to his right several hundred yards his attention was drawn to a ring of men dancing while an unseen drummer rapidly beat out a familiar, insistent rhythm.

Jack looked down to where the truck should have been. Nothing there except the tire tracks and many footprints in the snow. Looking farther down the wash to the dip in the snow covered roadway, he saw the twisted metal of Rick's pickup truck. For a hundred feet around the debris the snow had been covered with blown up dirt and rocks. The small bushes were torn off at ground level or bent and broken and scattered around like Pick-up sticks. The bed of the truck seemed to be completely destroyed with only the rear axial sitting in the middle of the road. And now, visible tires had been torn open from the impact of the explosion and were burning. Small columns of thick black smoke rose from the rubber toward an almost cobalt blue sky. Off to the side and in the ditch that cut across the road, the lower half of the cab of the truck sat upright.

Sitting down on the edge of the embankment, Jack pushed himself forward and over into the arroyo. It was steeper than he had anticipated and almost immediately he lost his control. He started to fall over the crumbling granite and snow slick rocks. Trying to catch himself was futile. His free hand grabbed at rocks or his fingers would not find substance as they dug into the fresh powdered snow then slipped free. In an effort to catch himself, he let go of the high powered rifle to free his good hand. Jack tumbled and rolled to the bottom of the steep embankment and landed with a solid thud. He lay face up for a long time before he made any attempt to move.

Jack pushed his hand under his coat and shirt and found the fall had torn open his throbbing wound. Warm blood oozed from under the Kotex pad Renee had applied over the ragged hole. Reaching into his right rear pants pocket, he pulled his bandanna out and forced the fabric into the cavity with the tip of his finger. Breaking into a heavier sweat, Jack screamed from the pain when the material penetrated the deep wound. With ragged determination he worked his way to his feet and forced himself to walk the remaining yards to the truck's body.

Flashing dots of bright white light seemed to filter into his mind as did the remembrances of his childhood. He was six or seven when his father had taught him the art of skinning the wild animals that had been killed for their pelts as well as food for the family table. That peculiar odor of freshly slaughtered meat that had been burned into his mind was now returning to him. Although he didn't want to look into the driver's seat, he knew there was no other choice. He had to determine whether or not Renee had been killed.

Jack reached out with his hand and gripped his fingers tightly on the remaining top edge of the driver's door. Forcing himself forward, he pulled his body closer and closer. The first thing he saw was an unrecognizable mass of mutilated and torn flesh and organs. Had it not been for the tremendous amount of destroyed meat and the size of the legs and feet, he would have not been able to tell who had been driving.

"You fucking bastard. You rotten cock sucker. Ya got just what ya fucking well deserved!" Jack screamed at the remains of Nick Whitewater as he was overcome with anger and relief.

From his past experience and as any investigator could tell you, the tricks that an explosion brings always leave you wondering. This time was no different; he himself wondered why parts of Palmoroy weren't in the truck with Whitewater. He stood there stared briefly at the legs and their arrangement. It struck him as being kind of funny that the left foot still rested on the clutch peddle and the right foot was on the accelerator as if they were ready to shift gears and drive away. The remainder of the stomach appeared to have opened just like taking the lid off a cauldron of sausage, pasta and stewed tomatoes.

His speculations brought reality and returned him to the finding of Renee. Jack again slipped his hand into his wound to determine if the bleeding had stopped and readjusted the makeshift bandage. He looked up the opposite side of the bank he had slid from to the outcropping of rocks where Renee should have been hiding. Even though he couldn't see all that well from where he stood, it was apparent there was no movement at all. Jack knew there would be no other way to find her, but crawl up to the top and search her out. On unsteady legs he returned to the indentation where he had fallen to retrieve his rifle. Tilting his head back against his hand, he rubbed his neck from side to side. He felt as if all but the last inkling of remaining strength had been sapped from him. He wasn't sure he could even crawl up the forty or so feet to the top.

Placing his foot on a boulder, he grasped another with his right hand and exerted his strength simultaneously to lift himself. His arm ached and his legs throbbed with each effort to pull himself higher to the top of the ridge. Jack was only inches from the crest when he had the sensation of a dark gray fog forming before his eyes. Knowing he was on the verge of blacking out, he tossed his rifle ahead of himself. As quickly as he could he pushed and shoved and pulled his aching body over the top. As he tried to kneel, the gray fog completely consumed him before turning to blackness. Jack fell face forward into the cold snow and then rolled partially onto his side. Unable to help himself any longer, he lapsed into unconsciousness.

● ● ●

The hammer fell on Palmoroy's revolver and the muzzle jumped violently unleashing the missile toward Renee's back.

She did not feel the projectile as it cleanly sliced its way through her coat alongside her hip. As it exited, the projectile shredded the seam holding the zipper to her pocket.

Palmoroy drew the weapon back and looked at the revolver's sights as only a scientist would in trying to determine what had gone wrong.

"Impossible!" he said loudly enough for Renee to hear even though his words didn't seem to enter her ears.

Palmoroy tried to stand on the edge on the embankment and lost his balance. His legs raced back and forth in a frenzy of movements like an amateur roller skater out of control. Falling forward he landed on the back of his left hand and twisted his wrist up severely. The sudden and severe pain flashed deep into his system. The spasmodic clenching of his fingers caused him to squeeze the trigger of the handgun and discharge into the dirt below him. Although not broken, he knew his wrist had been badly sprained.

Palmoroy sat up and swung his legs around and over the edge of the arroyo. He tried to rub his wrist to relieve some of the pain when he inadvertently fumbled and dropped his pistol.

"NAKED MEN IN A LINE"   **267**

The revolver slid and bounced its way to the bottom of the wash. He held his injured hand and tried to rub his burning eyes with the forearm of his coat.

Renee was driven by forces she was unable to comprehend. Even so, she pushed herself along ahead of the increasing wind against her back. The song Gary Owen had long ceased along with the squeaky sounds of the Irish pipes. As she moved closer to her unknown destination the moans and cries of injured and dying men filled the air all about her. Almost dreamlike, she entered between two columns of men standing on each side of the route she had been compelled to take. Two hundred or more naked men with gaping holes and gashes across their arms and legs stood on each side of her bloody trail. Some were headless while others lacked their genitals and hair. Every mother's son had been mutilated in some way or another.

As she passed each man, the soldiers' arms stretched out toward her and would occasionally touch her arms or back, or the bundle of artifacts she held in her hands. Renee looked into the drawn faces of these men and saw their mouths move without uttering sounds. Of the men who still had their heads, their eyes were swollen and tired looking as if they had not slept in an eternity. It seemed to Renee the line of troopers would never end. They all seemed to have died in the agony they were still living.

Now the burden she was carrying grew heavier in her arms with each labored step she took. As she moved past each opposing set of troopers, some of the men would close their ranks behind her. Still others would gather by her sides and walk with her toward a single nude man at the end or their converging lines. The closer she came to this solitary form, the more readily she was able to recognize him.

A large hole in his left side did not prevent him from standing erect and poised with the presence and command of a high-ranking officer. This man was the only one who wore any articles of clothing. A snug fitting supporter held his genitals close to his abdomen. Although she had probably seen the man's pictures before in some history book somewhere, Renee felt she knew him more immediately than anyone else ever had.

Renee suddenly stopped her walk towards him when she saw a grimace of pain slash across his face. Using both hands he covered the gaping wound on his side and knelt down heavily to the ground. While sitting on his knees and legs he bent forward at the waist to press his cheek into the hot ground. She watched his mouth open in a silent, agony filled scream as the parched dust blew from beneath his nostrils. Renee saw the tears flow from his eyes while the wound at his side began to leak thick rich blood between his fingers. Dropping the artifacts to the ground in front of her, Renee stepped over them and inched her way closer to the pitiful sight that rocked back and forth in torment.

With his gun still in her hand, she closed the remaining few feet that separated them.

His left arm rose and his head turned more to face her. He reached out to her with his pleading, bloody fingers open and spread as if trying to grasp her and draw her closer. Renee watched as his lips moved forming a name and words she had heard in unremembered dreams so many times before.

"Libbie, please my Libbie," came the silent pleading from Autie's lips.

Lowering herself to the snow, Libbie crawled slowly on her hands and knees the last few feet to her man. She knew the pain of his wounds and cried for his soul in a loud wail. Again she saw his mouth open wide before he doubled over in his eternal anguish. Libbie reached out and let her fingers touch his long blond hair with her free hand.

She stroked him gently and spoke, "Oh, how I love you, my darling."

He once again turned his head to her and mumbled his loving prayer, "My loving Elizabeth. Bring me to you."

Libbie heard and understood the words that caused her to remove her hand from the side of his head. She stood and mopped the river of tears from her face with the back of her hand. Libbie lifted the revolver while cocking the piece as it rose higher to a point of aim. She pointed the muzzle a few inches from the bridge of Autie's nose with the bore a scant few inches directly between his eyes.

George closed his eyes and turned his head to the side while he spoke to her, "I love—"

As the hammer fell, his voice became silent. The bullet entered mercifully into his temple, and his body dropped to the earth and did not move again.

In her weakened state, the sudden recoil pushed her back while at the same time she allowed herself to fall to the snow and onto her butt. As if her act was not enough, the world around her had changed again. She felt a new and menacing presence standing directly behind her.

• • •

Palmoroy was finally able to clear his eyes well enough to see. Standing, he searched the immediate area for his weapon. Here and there he kicked into the snow in his desperate attempt to locate his means of destroying his student. Looking up and into the direction Renee had been walking, he saw her slowing moving almost five hundred meters further up the incline. Taking hold of his wrist with his good hand, he quickly followed with as much speed as possible to overtake her. With each step his anger raged as if he had become a madman whose only intent was to slay this woman. The artifacts had become nothing more than an afterthought to his intent of smashing her head as many times as he possibly could before boredom would cause him to cease.

The distance to her took some time to travel in his state of pain and anger. Along his way he would stop and pick up a stick or a rock and then move closer on to her. If a larger or better means of inflicting death upon her would come to his view, he would detour and exchange it for what he held. When he was only twenty and some odd meters from her he stopped when she knelt to the snow. Curious, he watched as she crawled a few feet further forward. When he was sure she had not heard him, he quietly continued to move until he heard her soft voice sobbing out the unmeaning words.

"I love you, my darling."

By the time Renee stood, Palmoroy had closed the distance until he was directly behind her. Palmoroy watched her stand and raise the firearm only to point it at the ground a short distance in front of her. Even with seeing that, the report of the pistol in her out stretched hand startled him momentarily. More out of curiosity than anything he looked around her to see what she had shot at.

Again he was surprised as Renee dropped to her butt and sat entranced looking to the snow ahead of her. He raised his menacing chunk of granite above his head with his good hand as she turned to him. Her eyes were red from crying, and she was pale beyond his belief.

Renee stared into his eyes with look of a child who had been devastated following the death of a parent.

It was like Palmoroy was frozen in time for just a second or two before he realized that now was his opportunity.

"You dirty slut!" he screamed into her face as he lifted the rock still higher.

She had little doubt of his intention to smash it down into her head with all the strength he had.

•   •   •

The snow had slowed the bleeding from Jack's wound to nearly a stop. Regaining most of his consciousness, he raised his head high enough to see Palmoroy walking away from him and chasing after Renee. Dragging the rifle through the snow from alongside his body, Jack brought the wooden stock loosely forward to his shoulder. Lying prone with the butt of the weapon against his upper arm, he looked through the telescopic sights. Nothing could be seen. Everything was an opaque white with splotches of gray through the magnifying tube. Releasing his aim and lowering the rifle to his side he found snow and ice sticking to the lens and along the breech. Using the collar of his shirt he wiped as much of the frozen liquid off as he could.

Again he replaced the rifle to be able to see Palmoroy through the magnifying lens. Small drips of water and pieces of ice still stuck to the glass on the forward end of the telescope's tube and distorted the images. Jack saw he would not have time to clear the lens better since Palmoroy seemed to be standing behind and slightly to the side of Renee. Suddenly she fell to the ground in a sitting position and did not move.

"I'll kill you-u-u-u!" Jack wheezed out his scream at Palmoroy with too great a distance between them to be heard.

Jack sighted through the scope of the rifle one more time and directed the cross hairs to hold in the center mass of Palmoroy's back. In an instant he knew he had to shoot when Palmoroy's hands rose into the air. Not enough time to take a breath and let half of the air out as he had been taught. Instead, Jack jerked the trigger back releasing the deadly bullet to find its own course to the target. With the recoil of the weapon Jack again blacked out and his face dropped into the smothering snow.

• • •

Libbie closed her eyes to Palmoroy when his hand seemed to reach its highest limits. She uttered not a single word in expectation of the end happening here with her beloved husband Autie. To her, the time seemed like an eternity while she waited for him to strike and rob her of her life. Her thoughts mixed with hopes of dying in the Sacred Places when the flash of Jack's face entered her mind. Reality snapped back at her to let her know her destiny was to release the regiment and Custer's souls from their torment of life in-between.

Opening her eyes in a desperate search of why Palmoroy was using his time to crucify her, she saw a strange and surprised look on his face. His eyes became glassy and dead. The rock dropped from his fingers and landed harmlessly on the snow along side his foot. Palmoroy himself then fell to the ground in a shaking mass when his legs collapsed from under him. As he was falling, she thought she heard an explosion or the report of a cannon being fired. The sight reminded Renee of someone dropping a large sack of potatoes. His head came to rest close to her side with his unforgiving eyes staring up into her own. Dazed, Renee stood and staggered away from Palmoroy toward the little house so far away.

Trying to make her way to Jack's home in a bewildered and confused state of mind, Renee roamed aimlessly across the snow. She did not hear the many men crying out to her. Nor did she see the commotion around the prone body of Jack, not far from the rock outcropping. Her adventure had left her exhausted and completely drained of her senses. She had extreme difficulty in separating any remaining truths of reality from the fiction of illusion.

• • •

Almost a month had passed since Renee had been delivered to her home by an official of the Pine Ridge Reservation Council. She had been fired from her job at the agency, the college had dropped her from her classes, and the bearer bonds had mysteriously disappeared. Most importantly, her lover and partner in the quest for the abandoned wagons didn't seem to be interested in her or else he had succumbed to his wounds.

She had tried calling Pine Ridge in her attempt to find Jack on at least twenty different occasions. The Sheriff's Department offices at Independence, California revealed there was a Jack Barlow who worked for them, but he was on special assignment and would not be available for some time. Then there were the pleading love letters she had sent to his home in Olancha which had been returned with 'No such address' written on them.

The daytime wasn't too bad for her. She could busy herself with filling out applications for a new job or reading about the catastrophe that led to the annihilation at the Little Big Horn. For that matter, her new hobby of writing the romantic novel of her adventure with Jack consumed a good portion of her time. The highlight of most days was her trek on foot to the store or checking the mailbox. Even if the insurance company was to pay off on her claim for her car being totaled, she knew she would still walk. Nights were another matter. By the time darkness fell she would sit with the dim lights of the city outside that flickered through her open curtains. Occasionally Renee would try to watch a movie on television to unburden herself of her miseries. She even found that when she tried to cook, she seemed to be trying to make a familiar stew each time. If she found a love story to read, the wounds of her heart would hurt deeply to finish it. And reading a Western story where the Indian lost was now totally out of the question.

Then there was bedtime. Although she had not slept with Jack on any kind of a regular basis, she still missed his presence. The warm and secure feeling of his muscular frame pressed close to her had been more comforting than anyone she had ever been with. If he were with her now, she knew she would surely jump his bones and make mad and passionate love to him for as long as he could take it. If she ever had him in her grasp again she was satisfied she would never let go.

When she remembered the times spent with him she would find herself crying. Tremendous sadness filled her heart to the point uncontrollable tears would flow relentlessly down her cheeks. If she slept at all, she would wake hugging her pillow and talk tenderly of her life without him. Graciously, she would play her hands across the soft fabric where his chest should have been and spoke her words of love.

• • •

The time was ten-thirty in the morning when Renee stepped from her apartment to fetch the morning's mail from the post box down the walk. Pulling on a light jacket to fend off the morning fog still lingering over the Bay, she made her way slowly to the row of mailboxes in front of the complex. As with every other day since she had returned home, inserting her little brass key enabling the door to swing open had become a laborious ritual.

Inside the dark enclosure a single manila envelope rested. Removing the letter from its place of hiding she read the neatly printed lettering in the upper left corner. Strange! Why would his county be sending me a letter?

Tearing open the flap with a renewed sense of urgency, Renee unfolded the cold feeling paper and discovered a cashiers check for two thousand five hundred dollars payable directly to her. Looking at the check in disbelief, she wondered to herself, who would be stupid enough to send that much money. Then hope faded as it dawned on her, it probably was a reward for returning the artifacts to the Sioux Nation. If that were the case, then she felt she was cheated and deserved more consideration than money.

"Cow county cops! What do they know?"

Without much further thought to the check she began to read the letter out loud.

March 11, 1992

Dear Ms. Mitchell;

The circumstances leading to our investigation of the Saline Valley incident requires your immediate assistance. Detectives have deter-mined your presence is essential to the conclu-sion of their documentation of evidence to close the case. You are to meet the detectives at the Saline Valley Hot Pool not far from the wagon you found.

Enclosed you will find sufficient funds for your transportation, food and accommoda-tions. No reply is necessary.

You will be expected no later than two p.m. in the afternoon of March 22, 1991, on the County road where you had originally parked.

Cordially,

Investigations Division

Typical of an investigator, Renee thought to herself. *They even forgot to sign the damn thing.*

Renee didn't really want to make the trip as she had been requested. She knew the journey would bring back to her some memories she did not wish to recall in the presence of others. Nor did she want to talk of her intimacy with Jack to any uncaring cold-hearted sleuth. After spending several hours of reading and rereading the communication, she couldn't see any way to get out of the request. On the other hand, she felt she would at least have the opportunity to try and locate Jack or find out what had become of him.

Renee returned to her apartment and made the required calls for a rental car and reservation for one night's stay in Lone Pine before entering Saline Valley. Following those calls she summoned a cab for a quick trip to the bank to cash the bank draft the county had sent. Then she was off to the car rental company where she selected a bright red four-wheel drive Toyota. Once back to her apartment she found the remainder of the day went slowly. Every thought of an investigation and what was about to come made her cry. The memory of her relationship with Jack was almost more than she could cope with. Many times she found herself in near hysterics with her grief.

Renee intended to wake at eight in the morning. Instead, she rose closer to three o'clock after a fitfully short sleep filled with nightmares on the reservation of Custer's Battlefield. She turned endlessly with the fear of another horrible dream. All these things prevented her from remaining in bed to wait for the alarm to go off. Dressing in black pants, a white blouse and brown shoes and belt, Renee gathered the remainder of her clothing and went to the waiting rental car. Tormented, she started her travel across the mid-section of California.

• • •

Renee parked her rental in almost the same spot as Mike had parked his Buick more than a month earlier. This was the spot under the cottonwoods where they would start the investigation of these things she felt should be best left alone. Renee was in the process of locking the driver's door when a Sheriff's truck raced up beside her along with a cloud of dust.

The deputy yelled out of his window, "Are you Miss Renee Mitchell of San Francisco?"

"Yes," she replied meekly, feeling the tears starting to gather in the corners of her eyes again.

"Get in. I was sent to give you transportation."

It seemed to Renee the deputy was a little more cautious in his driving than Jack had been in crossing the desert floor.

The only similarity was that the deputy seldom spoke to her while he maneuvered across the rocky and brush covered terrain. It had taken nearly an hour before the driver brought the sheriff's vehicle to a stop. She opened the door and stepped out behind a very large military style tent only a few yards from the hot pool.

The deputy told her to make herself comfortable and that the detective would be there momentarily to talk with her. The sheriff's truck pulled away and headed back in the direction it had come.

Walking to the front of the olive drab tent, Renee stepped under the awning and found a large folding table with two camp chairs slipped neatly under it. On the top of the table were all five of the Bearer Bonds she had stolen from Palmoroy's hiding place under the sink. They were held down by a large dusty rock fouling the beautiful scrollwork. Beside those she recognized the silver locket and chain that held Libbie's lock of hair. Renee reached out but did not quite touch the silver chain that had once belonged to Custer. And lastly on the table was a Gold star of a County Sheriff's Deputy. Renee picked the badge off the table and let her thumb run over the smooth belly of the California Bear while she held it in her palm. She didn't know how she knew; she just did when she spoke the words out loud to the brightly shined gold star.

"There can never be anyone else, Jack. I'll love you forever."

Tears overflowed and cascaded down her cheeks. She lifted his badge and touched it to her cheek letting her tears wet the golden surface. Her mind was loving him while she looked off to the mountains he enjoyed so much.

She saw a dark figure standing several hundred feet away from her among the Peterborough and creosote. The distance was too far to tell who the man was, but she did sense he was Indian and he was watching her intently. Renee wanted to move forward and toward him to bring to an end her roll in the investigation. But suddenly, as in the trick of her mind, the figure of that man faded and disappeared completely leaving only the harsh environment of the Valley.

The door flap of the tent swung to the side and a man stepped out behind her without sound or her knowledge.

"Is there something I can do for you?" The deep authoritarian voice demanded.

Momentarily frozen in memory, Renee suddenly turned to see Jack standing in the doorway wearing that magnificent headdress they had discovered together. He looked wonderful and ridiculous all at the same time in his black cowboy boots and a white sling that held up his left arm. What can be said about a crazy half-breed who wore nothing else other than the feathered bonnet?

"You're naked!" Renee laughed out her tearful words of joy and happiness of seeing him again.

"I am?" Jack answered her while looking down his wet body. The badge slipped through her fingers to the dirt under the awning before she rushed to him. Her arms encircled his body and as quickly her mouth found his. They locked in passionate embrace.

Renee pushed herself free of his lips and demanded he answer her questions of concern and enlightenment.

"You set this up, didn't you? You're wet and you've been in the pool without me! Why do you want to look so damn silly? Who in the hell do you think you're messing with anyway? I love you, you big silly clod. God! I love you with all my soul," she whispered.

Jack smiled without answering a single question and pulled her into his chest and hugged her tightly again.

"I thought you would want to meet here. It's kind of like our Sacred Place," he whispered back to her ear.

Looking up, Renee did not wish to say a word and pressed her lips against his. Breaking the blissfully long kiss was difficult for her. She tilted her head back and looked into his eyes for the answers to so many questions. Her eyes were tired and filled with concern when she asked with a distinct crackling to her voice "Did I kill Autie?"

The End

Epilogue

The Coyote secretly led the Maiden from her village and told her that there was an ancient Mushroom hidden in the Mother Earth. Once the Maiden had found its hiding place, she should sit upon it with the place of the child and drink from it the knowledge of the Wolf. Then, and only then, would she know the wisdom of the Eagle. But beware, the Coyote scolded, if you do not do this thing soon, or you do not do exactly as I have instructed you, you will not set the sly fox and his brood free.

The Coyote then ran up the trail ahead of the Maiden and buried himself so that only his penis stuck out from the dirt. In the distance, Watching Buffalo stood and waited patiently to fulfill his destiny.

Order Form for Additional Copies

Please send ___ copies of *Sacred Places* at US$14.95 each plus $3.50 for shipping and handling to:

Name:_____

Address: _____

City:_____State:___ Zip:_____

For information about multiple copies to one address or orders from outside the U.S., call 360 289-0309 or send email to rosen-little@mail.tss.net.

Mail this order form with your payment to:
John R. Little
229 State Route 115
Ocean Shores, WA 98569
Make your check or money order payable to John R. Little.
Washington residents, add 8% ($1.20) sales tax per book.

Order Form for Additional Copies

Please send ___ copies of *Sacred Places* at US$14.95 each plus $3.50 for shipping and handling to:

Name:_____

Address: _____

City:_____State:___ Zip:_____

For information about multiple copies to one address or orders from outside the U.S., call 360 289-0309 or send email to rosen-little@mail.tss.net.

Mail this order form with your payment to:
John R. Little
229 State Route 115
Ocean Shores, WA 98569
Make your check or money order payable to John R. Little.
Washington residents, add 8% ($1.20) sales tax per book.